1913

FLORIAN ILLIES

1913

THE YEAR BEFORE THE STORM

Translated by Shaun Whiteside
and Jamie Lee Searle

THE CLERKENWELL PRESS

The translation of this work was supported by a grant from the Goethe-
Institut, which is funded by the German Ministry of Foreign Affairs.

First published in Great Britain in 2013 by
THE CLERKENWELL PRESS
an imprint of Profile Books Ltd
3A Exmouth House
Pine Street
London EC1R 0JH
www.profilebooks.com

First published in Germany entitled *1913: Der Sommer des Jahrhunderts*
in 2012 by S. Fischer Verlag

10 9 8 7 6 5 4 3 2

Printed and bound in Great Britain by
Clays, Bungay, Suffolk

The moral right of the author has been asserted.

A CIP catalogue record for this book is available from the British Library.

ISBN 978 1 84668 951 2
Export ISBN 978 1 84668 964 2
eISBN 978 1 84765 981 1

The paper this book is printed on is certified by the © 1996 Forest Stewardship Council
A.C. (FSC). It is ancient-forest friendly. The printer holds FSC chain of custody SGS-
COC-2061

JANUARY

This is the month when Hitler and Stalin meet while strolling in the Castle Park at Schönbrunn, Thomas Mann nearly gets outed and Franz Kafka nearly goes mad with love. A cat creeps onto Sigmund Freud's couch. It's extremely cold, snow crunches under the feet. Else Lasker-Schüler is impoverished and in love with Gottfried Benn, gets a horse postcard from Franz Marc but says Gabriele Münter is a non-entity. Ernst Ludwig Kirchner draws the ladies of pleasure on Potsdamer Platz. The first loop-the-loop is flown. But it's no good. Oswald Spengler is already at work on The Decline of the West.

The first second of 1913. A gunshot rings out through the dark night. There's a brief click, fingers tense on the trigger, then comes a second, dull report. The alarm is raised, the police dash to the scene and arrest the gunman straight away. His name is Louis Armstrong.

The twelve-year-old had wanted to see in the New Year in New Orleans with a stolen revolver. The police put him in a cell, and early on the morning of 1 January they send him to a house of correction, the Colored Waifs' Home for Boys. Once there, his behaviour is so unruly that the only solution the institution's director, Peter Davis, can come up with is to hand him a trumpet. (What he really wants to do is slap him.) All at once Louis Armstrong falls silent, picks up the instrument almost tenderly, and his fingers, which had been playing with the trigger of the revolver only the previous night, feel the cold metal once again, except that now, still in the director's office, rather than a gunshot, he produces his first warm, wild notes from the trumpet.

'The gunshot at midnight. Cries in the alley and on the bridge. Ringing bells and clock chimes.' A report from Prague: Dr Franz Kafka, a clerk with the Workers' Accident Insurance Company for the Kingdom of Bohemia. His audience in faraway Berlin, in the apartment at 29 Immanuelkirchstrasse, is a lone individual, but to him she is the whole world: Felice Bauer, twenty-five, a bit blonde, a bit bony, a bit gangling. A shorthand typist with Carl Lindström Ltd. They had met briefly in August, the rain pelting down, she had had wet feet, and he'd quickly got cold ones. But since then they've been writing to each other at night while their families are asleep: hot-headed, enchanting, strange, unsettling letters. And usually another one the next afternoon. Once, when there hadn't been a word from Felice for a few days, after waking from unsettled dreams, in desperation he desperately started work on *Metamorphosis*. He told her about this story, which he had finished just before Christmas. (It now lay in his desk, warmed by the two photographs of herself that Felice had sent him.) But just how quickly her distant and beloved Franz could turn into a terrible mystery she would learn only from his New Year's letter. He asks her out of nowhere, by way of introduction, whether, if they had arranged to go to the theatre in Frankfurt am Main, and if he had instead just stayed in bed, she would have beaten him violently with an umbrella. And then, apparently innocuously, he evokes their mutual love, dreams that his hand and Felice's will be forever bound together. Before going on: it is, 'however, always possible that a couple might once have been led to the scaffold bound together in such a way'. What a charming thought for a prenuptial letter. They haven't even kissed, and here he is already fantasising about their walking hand in hand to the scaffold. Kafka himself seems momentarily startled by the thoughts spilling from him: 'But what sort of things are these, pouring out of my head?' he writes. The explanation is simple: 'It's the number 13 in the year.' And that is how 1913 begins in world literature: with a fantasy of violence.

Missing person notice. Lost: Leonardo's *Mona Lisa*. She was stolen from the Louvre in 1911; still no clues. Pablo Picasso is questioned by the Paris police, but he has an alibi and they let him go home. In the Louvre, French mourners lay bouquets against the bare wall.

In the first days of January, we don't know exactly when, a slightly scruffy 34-year-old Russian arrives at Vienna's Northern Station from Kraków. A flurry of snow outside. He is limping. His hair hasn't been washed this year, and his bushy moustache, which spreads like rampant undergrowth beneath his nose, can't conceal the pock-marks on his face. He is wearing Russian peasant shoes, and his suitcase is full to bursting. As soon as he arrives, he boards a tram for Hietzing. His passport bears the name Stavros Papadopoulos, which is supposed to sound like a mixture of Greek and Georgian, and in view of his scruffy appearance and the piercing cold, every border guard has let him through. In Kraków, in his other exile, he had beaten Lenin at chess one last time the previous evening, making that the seventh time in a row. He was plainly better at chess than he was at cycling. Lenin had desperately tried to teach him. Revolutionaries have to be quick, he had drummed that into him time and again. But the man, whose name was actually Josef Vissiaronovich Djugashvili and who now called himself Stavros Papadopoulos, couldn't learn how to ride a bike. Just before Christmas he had a bad fall on the icy cobbled streets of Kraków. His leg was still covered with grazes, his knee was sprained, and he had only been able to stand on it again for a few days. My 'magnificent George', Lenin had called him with a smile as he limped towards him to accept his forged passport for the journey to Vienna. And now *bon voyage*, Comrade.

He crossed borders unmolested, sat feverishly in the train, hunched over his manuscripts and books, which he frantically stuffed back into his suitcase every time he had to change trains.

Now, having arrived in Vienna, he had discarded his Georgian alias. From January 1913 onwards he said: My name is Stalin, Josef Stalin. When he had got out of the tram, on his right he saw the Schönbrunn Palace, brightly lit against the dull winter grey, and the park behind it. He enters the house at 30 Schönbrunner Schlossstrasse, which is what it says on the little slip of paper that Lenin had given him. And: 'Ring the bell marked Trojanow'. So he shakes the snow off his shoes, blows his nose in his handkerchief and slightly nervously presses the button. When the maid appears, he says the agreed code word.

A cat creeps into 19 Berggasse, Vienna, and into the study of Sigmund Freud, where the Wednesday club has just assembled. The cat is the second surprise visitor in a very short time: in the late autumn Lou Andreas-Salomé had joined the menfolk. At first she had been eyed suspiciously, but now she was fervently worshipped. On her garter belt Lou Andreas-Salomé wore the many scalps of the great minds she had bagged: she had been in a confessional in St Peter's with Nietzsche, in bed with Rilke and in Russia with Tolstoy, Frank Wedekind named his *Lulu* after her and Richard Strauss his *Salomé*. Now her latest victim, intellectually at least, was Freud – that winter she was even allowed to stay on the same floor as his study, discussed his new book about *Totem and Taboo*, on which he was currently working, and listened to his complaints about C. G. Jung and the renegade school of Zurich psychologists. Above all, however, Lou Andreas-Salomé, now fifty-two, the author of several books about eroticism and the mind, was receiving psychoanalytic training from the master himself – in March she would set up her own practice in Göttingen. So there she sits at the solemn Wednesday lecture. Beside her the master's learned colleagues, on her right the already legendary couch and everywhere the little sculptures that the antique-obsessed Freud collected to console himself about the present day. And into this devout room, as Lou stepped through the door, there slipped a cat. At first Freud was irritated, but when he saw the curiosity with which the cat was studying his Greek vases and Roman miniatures, he brought it some milk. But Lou Andreas-Salomé reports: 'As he did so, in spite of his mounting love and admiration, she paid him no attention, coldly turned the slanting pupils of her green eyes on him as if on a random object, and if for a moment he wanted something more than the cat's egoist-narcissist purring, he had to take his foot off the comfortable couch, and try to win her attention with enticing wiggles of the toe of his boot.' From then on, week after week, the cat was allowed to attend Freud's lectures, and if she wheedled she was allowed to lie on his couch, on gauze compresses. She clearly proved susceptible to therapy.

Speaking of sickly: where is Rilke, by the way?

Contemporaries are worried that 1913 may prove to be an unlucky year. Gabriele D'Annunzio gives a friend a copy of his *Martyrdom of St Sebastian* and in the dedication prefers to date it '1912 + 1'. And Arnold Schönberg refuses to mention the unlucky number. Not for nothing had he invented twelve-tone music – a fundamental principle of modern music, born in part of its creator's fear of what might come next. The birth of the rational out of the spirit of superstition. In Schönberg's music the number '13' does not occur, not even as a rhythm. Not even as a page number. When he realised with horror that the title of his opera about Moses and Aaron would have thirteen letters, he crossed out the second A from Aaron, and henceforth it was called *Moses and Aron*. And now a whole year fell under the shadow of that unlucky number. Schönberg was born on 13 September – and he was terrified at the idea of dying on Friday the 13th. It was no good. Arnold Schönberg did in fact die on Friday the 13th (although in 1913 + 38, or 1951). But 1913 also had a fine surprise in store for him. He would receive a slap in the face. But one thing at a time.

And now enter Thomas Mann. Early on 3 January, Mann takes his seat on the train in Munich. First of all, he reads some newspapers and letters, looks out at the snow-covered hills of the Thuringian Forest, and then, in the overheated compartment, he repeatedly nods off while worrying about his Katia, who has gone off once more for a spa treatment in the mountains. The previous summer he had visited her in Davos, and in the waiting room he had suddenly had an idea for a great short story, but now it strikes him as pointless, too remote from the world, this sanatorium-based tale. In any case, his *Death in Venice* would be published in only a few weeks.

Thomas Mann sits in the train and frets over his wardrobe: so annoying that long train journeys always leave those creases in one's clothes, he would have to have his coat ironed again in the hotel. He gets up, slides the carriage door open and decides to walk up and down the corridor. So stiffly that the other guests keep mistaking him for the conductor. Outside the castles of Dornburg fly past, Bad Kösen, the vineyards of the Saale, covered with snow, the rows of vines running across the slopes like zebra stripes. Pretty, in fact, but Thomas Mann senses anxiety mounting within him the closer he gets to Berlin.

When he has stepped out of the train, he immediately takes a cab to the Hotel Unter den Linden, and he looks around the lobby to see whether the other guests recognise him as they push their way to the lifts. Then he steps into his usual room to change into expensive new clothes and comb his moustache.

At the same time, in the Grunewald deep in the west of the city, Alfred Kerr is tying his bow tie in the dressing room of his villa at 6 Höhmannstrasse and combatively twirling the tips of his moustache.

Their duel is scheduled for eight o'clock that evening. At a quarter past seven they climb aboard their respective droschkes. They drive to the Kammerspiele of the Deutsches Theater, arriving at the same time. And they ignore one another. It is cold, they both hurry inside. Once (in Bansin, on the Baltic), strictly between ourselves, he, Alfred Kerr, Germany's greatest critic and vainest popinjay, had wooed Katia Pringsheim, the wealthy, cat-eyed Jewess. But she had turned him down, the proud and reckless man from Breslau, and thrown herself instead at Thomas Mann, the stiff northerner. Incomprehensible. But perhaps he can get his own back this evening.

Thomas Mann takes his seat in the front row and tries to emanate calm gravitas. This evening sees the première of his *Fiorenza*, the play he was writing when he met and fell in love with Katia. But he senses that tonight there may be a débâcle of sorts: the piece has long been his problem child. They shouldn't have made such a drama about keeping a drama off the stage, he thinks. 'I've tried to save some things, but no one listens to me', he wrote to Maximilian Harden before he left 13 Mauerkirchstrasse in Munich.

He hated walking eyes open into a disaster. It wasn't worthy of someone like Thomas Mann. What he had seen at the rehearsals in December didn't bode well. Tormented, he watches the play that is supposed to bring the Florentine High Renaissance to life, but it just refuses to get going.

Eventually Mann glances furtively over his left shoulder. There, in the third row, he spots Alfred Kerr, whose pencil is scurrying over his pad. The auditorium is pitch dark, but he thinks he can discern a smile on Kerr's face. It is the smile of the sadist, delighted that the production is providing ample material for torture. And when he catches Thomas Mann's anxious expression, an even more agreeable shiver runs through him. He is delighted to have Thomas Mann and his unfortunate *Fiorenza* in the palm of his hand. For he knows he is going to grip it very hard, and when he lets go, it will slump lifeless to the floor. The curtain falls and there is a ripple of friendly applause – so friendly, in fact, that the director, in his only successful production, manages to invite Mann on stage twice. In countless letters over the next few weeks he will not fail to mention the fact. Twice! So he tries to bow with great dignity, twice! And ends up looking rather awkward. Alfred Kerr sits in the third row, not clapping. That night, when he arrives at his elegant villa in Grunewald, he asks for some tea and begins to write. He sits down solemnly at his typewriter and sets a roman 'I' down on the paper. Kerr numbers his paragraphs individually, like volumes in a collected edition. First he whets his sabre: 'The author is a delicate, rather thin little soul, whose dwelling-place has its quiet roots in stasis.' Then he lets rip: the lady Fiorenza, who is presumably supposed to be a symbol of Florence, is completely bloodless, the whole thing was cobbled together in libraries, stiff, dry, feeble, kitschy, superfluous. Those are more or less his words.

When Kerr has numbered and concluded his tenth paragraph, he contentedly pulls the last sheet of paper from the typewriter. An annihilation.

The next morning, as Thomas Mann boards the train for Munich, Kerr has dispatched his piece to the editors of the newspaper *Der Tag*. It appears on 5 January. When Mann reads it, he breaks down. He is 'unmanly', Kerr writes – that will hit Mann the hardest. Whether Kerr was alluding to Thomas Mann's concealed homosexuality, or whether Mann only understood it as an allusion, is irrelevant. Kerr alone, apart from Karl Kraus, saw where his words could inflict the deepest wounds. At any rate, Thomas Mann was deeply hurt, 'to the marrow', he wrote. Throughout the whole spring of 1913 he would not recover from that criticism. Not one letter omits a reference, not a day passes without fury directed at this fellow Kerr. Mann writes to Hugo von Hofmannsthal: 'I had known more or less what to expect, but it exceeded anything I could have foreseen. A toxic affront, in which the personal bloodlust must surely be apparent even to the most unsuspecting!'

'He wrote that only because he didn't get me, my dear Tommy,' Katia says by way of consolation, and strokes his forehead maternally when she returns from her spa cure.

Two national myths are founded: in New York, the first edition of *Vanity Fair* is published. In Essen, Karl and Theo Albrecht's mother opens the prototype of the first Aldi supermarket.

And how is Ernst Jünger? 'Fair.' At least, that's what it says in the report the seventeen-year-old Jünger has been given in the reform school in Hameln for his essay on Goethe's 'Hermann and Dorothea'. He wrote: 'The epic takes us back to the time of the French Revolution, whose blaze disturbs even the peaceful residents of the quiet Rhine valley from the contented half-sleep of their everyday lives.' But that wasn't enough for his teacher, who wrote in the margin, in red ink: 'Expression too sober this time.' We learn: this means that

Ernst Jünger was already sober, when everyone else thought he was drunk.

Every afternoon Ernst Ludwig Kirchner boards the newly built underground train to Potsdamer Platz. The other painters of Die Brücke – Erich Heckel, Otto Mueller, Karl Schmidt-Rottluff – had moved to Berlin with Kirchner from Dresden, that wonderfully forgotten Baroque city where the group was founded. They were a community in every respect, sharing paints and women, their paintings indistinguishable from one another – but Berlin, that pounding mental overload of a capital city, turns them into individuals and cuts away the bridges connecting them. In Dresden all the others were able to celebrate pure colour, nature and human nakedness. In Berlin they threaten to founder.

In Berlin, in his early thirties, Ernst Ludwig Kirchner comes into his own. His art is urban, raw, his figures are overstretched and his drawing style as frantic and aggressive as the city itself; his paintings 'bear the rust of the metropolis like varnish on the brow'. Even in the underground carriages his eyes greedily absorb people. He makes his first, quick studies in his lap: two, three strokes of the pencil, a man, a hat, an umbrella. Then he goes outside, pushes his way through the crowds, sketchpads and brushes in hand. He is drawn to Aschinger's restaurant, where you can spend all day if you've bought a bowl of soup. So Kirchner sits there and looks and draws and looks. The winter day is already drawing to a close, the noise in the square is deafening, it's the busiest square in Europe, and passing in front of him are the city's main arteries, but also the lines of tradition and the modern age: come up out of the U-Bahn into the slushy streets of the day and you will see horse-drawn carts delivering barrels, side by side with the first high-class automobiles and the droschkes trying to dodge the piles of horse droppings. Several tram lines traverse the big square, the huge space rings with a mighty metallic scrape each time a tram leans into the curve. And in among them: people, people, people, all

running as if their lives depended on it, above them billboards singing the praises of sausages, eau de cologne and beer. And beneath the
arcades, the elegantly dressed ladies of the night, the only ones barely
moving in the square, like spiders on the edge of a web. They wear
black veils over their faces to escape the attention of the police, but
the striking aspect is their huge hats, bizarre towering constructions
with feathers, under the streetlights, whose green gaslight is lit when
early winter evening falls.

That pale green glow on the faces of the prostitutes in Potsdamer
Platz, and the raging noise of the city behind them, are what Ernst
Ludwig Kirchner wants to turn into art. Into paintings. But he doesn't
yet know how. So for the time being he goes on drawing – 'I'm on
familiar terms with my drawings,' he says, 'I'm more formal with my
paintings.' So he grabs his intimate friends, stacks of sketches that he's
done from his table over the past few hours, and hurries home, to his
studio. In Wilmersdorf, 14 Durlacher Strasse, second floor, Kirchner
has made a burrow for himself: nearly every inch hung with oriental
carpets, stuffed with figures and masks from Africa and Oceania and
Japanese parasols, as well as his own sculptures, his own furniture, his
own paintings. Photographs of Kirchner from those days show him
either naked or wearing a black suit and tie, his high-collared shirt
snow-white, his cigarette held as limply in his hand as if he were Oscar
Wilde. Always by his side, Erna Schilling, his beloved, the successor to
soft, scatty Dodo in Dresden, a 'new' woman with a free spirit beneath
a page-boy haircut, the spitting image of Kafka's Felice Bauer. She decorated the flat with embroideries based on her designs and Kirchner's.

Kirchner had met Erna and her sister Gerda Schilling a year
before at a Berlin dance hall, where Heckel's girlfriend, Sidi, was
also on stage. He lured the two pretty, sad-eyed dancers to his studio
that first evening, because he knew straight away: their architectur-
ally constructed bodies would 'train my sense of beauty in the creation
of the physically beautiful women of our time'. Kirchner first stepped
out with nineteen-year-old Gerda, later with 28-year-old Erna, and
in between with both. Flirt, muse, model, sister, saint, whore, lover
– it's hard to tell exactly which, where Kirchner is concerned. From

hundreds of drawings we know every detail of these two women: Gerda sensually provocative, Erna with small, high breasts and a wide bottom, calm, at melancholy peace. There is a glorious painting from these days: on the left, three naked women, soliciting; on the right, the artist in his studio, cigarette in his mouth, checking the women out like a connoisseur. That's how he likes to see himself. 'Judgement of Paris', he writes in black paint on the back of the canvas, '1913, Ernst Ludwig Kirchner'.

But when Paris Kirchner comes home from Potsdamer Platz that evening, the lights are out, Paris comes home too late for his judgement, and Erna and Gerda have gone to sleep, buried in the enormous cushions in the sitting room that this *trio infernal* will turn into the most famous Berlin room in the world.

Prussian Crown Princess Victoria Louise and Ernst August of Hanover kiss for the first time in January.

The New Year edition of *Die Fackel*, Karl Kraus's legendary one-man Viennese magazine, contains a cry for help: 'Else Lasker-Schüler seeks 1,000 Mk towards the education of her son.' It is signed by, among others, Selma Lagerlöf, Karl Kraus and Arnold Schönberg. After her divorce from Herwarth Walden, the poet could no longer pay the fees of the Odenwaldschule in which she had placed her son Paul. Kraus had wrestled with himself for six months about whether to publish the appeal. In the meantime Paul had been sent to a boarding school in Dresden, but at Christmas even Kraus, the cool executioner who could strictly separate emotion and rationality, was overwhelmed by generosity. He places the small ad in the last free space in *Die Fackel*. Before it, Kraus writes: 'I see an apocalyptic Galopin preparing for the end of the world, the herald of ruin, overheating the limbo of temporality.'

The tiny attic room at 13 Humboldtstrasse in Berlin-Grunewald is ice-cold. Else Lasker-Schüler has just wrapped herself up in lots of blankets when she hears the shrill doorbell dragging her from her daydreams. Lasker-Schüler – wild, black eyes, dark mane, lovesick, unfit for life – envelopes herself in her oriental dressing gown and opens the door to the postman, who holds out her mail: her severe and distant friend Kraus's bright red *Die Fackel* from Vienna and then, just below, a little blue miracle – a postcard from Franz Marc, the Blaue Reiter artist. Lasker-Schüler, with her gaudy garments, her jangling rings and bracelets, her wild, fairy-tale imagination: in those days she was the embodiment of a society dashing into the modern age, a dream figure, the object of desire of such diverse men as Kraus, Wassily Kandinsky, Oskar Kokoschka, Rudolf Steiner and Alfred Kerr. But you can't live on deification. Else Lasker-Schüler is in a bad way now that her marriage to Herwarth Walden, the great gallery owner and publisher of *Sturm* magazine, is at an end, and he's with the appalling Nell, his new wife, sitting around in cafés from which Else has been banned, precisely because it means she won't be there. But it was in just such an artists' café, in December, that she met Franz and Maria Marc, who would become her guardian angels.

So Else Lasker-Schüler picks up her copy of *Die Fackel*, oblivious to the touching advertisement by Karl Kraus, and then she turns over the postcard that Franz Marc has sent her. She freezes in silent jubilation. On the tiny space her far-off friend has painted her a *Tower of Blue Horses*, powerful creatures towering up to the sky, outside of time and yet firmly within it. She senses that she's been granted a unique gift: the first blue horses of the Blue Rider. Perhaps this special woman, who always senses everything, and more – senses that in the weeks that followed, the idea of his postcard will produce an even bigger 'tower of blue horses' in faraway Sindelsdorf, a painting as a programme, an artistic landmark. The larger painting will later be burned, and all that remains of it will be that postcard, which bears the fingerprints of both Marc and Lasker-Schüler, and which will always tell the tale of the moment when the Blue Rider began its gallop.

Touched, the poet notes how the great painter has included her emblems, the half-moon and the golden stars, into his little painting of horses. A dialogue begins; associations, words and postcards fly back and forth. She appoints him the imaginary 'Prince of Cana'; she is 'Prince Yussuf of Thebes'. On 3 January, Else writes back and thanks him for her blue miracle: 'How beautiful this card is – I've always wished my own white horses could be joined by horses in my favourite colour. How can I thank you!!'

When Marc then invites her by postcard to come to Sindelsdorf, completely exhausted by the divorce and by Berlin, she boards the train with the Marcs. She is far too thinly dressed, so Maria Marc wraps her in a blanket she has brought along. It's entirely possible she's sitting in the same train in which Thomas Mann is hurrying back to his family fortress after his bungled *Fiorenza* première. It's a lovely idea: the north and south poles of German culture in 1913, together in a single train.

When the enfeebled poet arrives in Sindelsdorf in the alpine uplands, she lives at first with Franz Marc and his wife, Maria, a strapping matron under whose wings Marc snuggled when the winds blew too chill. 'Painter Marc and his lioness', as Else called them. She manages only a few days in the childless couple's guest room, before moving on to the Sindelsdorf inn, with its terrific view across the moor to the mountains. But even here she can't find peace. The worried landlady advises her to take a Kneipp cure and lends her the requisite books. Nothing does any good. Else Lasker-Schüler hurries from Sindelsdorf to Munich and finds a room in a pension on Theresienstrasse.

The Marcs come after her and find her in the breakfast room, with whole armies of tin soldiers that she's probably bought for her son Paul, 'fighting out violent battles' on the blue and white table-cloth, 'instead of the battles that life constantly threw her way'. She is in a fighting mood, furious, quivering, not entirely in her right mind. At the end of January, in the Galerie Thannhauser, at the opening of the big Franz Marc exhibition, she meets Kandinsky, then gets into a squabble with the painter Gabriele Münter. She had made a remark that Lasker-Schüler had taken as an insult to Marc, whereupon she screeched through the gallery: 'I'm an artist and I'm not going to stand for that from some nonentity.'

Maria Marc stands between the bickering women, entirely at a loss, shouting, 'Children, children'. Later she will claim that Else Lasker-Schüler already had 'much of the pose of the world-weary writer about her', but still, 'she'd really experienced a great deal compared to the young Weltschmerz gang in Berlin.' So that's what the world of 1913 looks like from the vantage point of Sindelsdorf.

On 20 January, in Tell el-Amarna, in central Egypt, the spoils of the latest digs by the German Oriental Society, financed by the Berliner James Simon, are being divided: half are promised to the Cairo Museum, the other half to the German museums, including the 'painted plaster bust of a royal princess'. The director of the French antiquities commission in Cairo authorises the division, suggested by the German archaeologist Ludwig Borchardt. Borchardt alone sensed straight away that what he was holding was the kind of discovery that comes along once in a thousand years, when an excited Egyptian assistant pressed the little statue into his hand. A few days later the plaster bust sets off on its journey to Berlin. It does not yet bear the name Nefertiti. It isn't yet the most famous bust of a woman in the world.

The world bubbles over with excitement. Small wonder, then, that in 1913 the Russian pilot Piotr Nikoayevich Nesterov flew the first loop-the-loop in human history in his fighter plane. And that the Austrian figure-skater Alois Lutz spun so skilfully in the air on a deep-frozen lake in that bitter cold January that the jump bears the name Lutz to this day. To perform it, you have to take a backwards run-up, then

jump from the left back outside edge. You achieve the spin by suddenly drawing your arms into your torso. Logically enough, for the
double-Lutz you do the same thing twice.

Stalin will stay in Vienna for four weeks. Never again will he leave
Russia for such a long time; his next foreign trip of any length will
be thirty years later, to Tehran, where he will take part in discussions
with Churchill and Roosevelt (in 1913 the former was First Lord of
the British Admiralty, the latter a senator in Washington, campaign-
ing against the stripping of the American forests). Stalin rarely leaves
his secret hideaway at 30 Schönbrunner Schlossstrase, the home of the
Troyanovskys; he is completely preoccupied with writing his essay
'Marxism and the National Question', commissioned by Lenin. Only
very occasionally, early in the afternoon, does he stretch his legs in
the nearby park at Schönbrunn Palace, which lies cold and neat in
the January snow. Once a day there's a moment of excitement when
Kaiser Franz Joseph leaves the palace and sets off in his coach to do a
spot of governing. Franz Joseph has now been in power for an incredible sixty-five years, since 1848. He has never got over the death of
his beloved Sissi, the Empress Elisabeth, and even now her life-size
portrait hangs above his desk.

The grizzled monarch hobbles the few steps to his dark green
coach, his breath leaving a little cloud in the cold air, then a liveried
footman shuts the door of the coach and the horses trot off through
the snow. Then silence again.

Stalin walks through the park, thinking. It's already getting dark.
Then another walker comes towards him, twenty-three years old,
a failed painter who's been turned down by the Academy and who
is now killing time in the men's hostel on Meldemannstrasse. He is
waiting, like Stalin, for his big break. His name is Adolf Hitler. The
two men, whose friends at the time say they liked to walk in the park
at Schönbrunn, may have greeted one another politely and tipped
their hats as they made their way through the boundless park.

The age of extremes, the terrible short twentieth century, begins on a January afternoon in 1913 in Vienna. The rest is silence. Even when Hitler and Stalin sealed their fatal 'pact' in 1939, they never met. So they were never closer than they were on one of those bitterly cold January afternoons in the park of Schönbrunn Palace.

The drug 'ecstasy' has been synthesised for the first time; the patent application drags on through 1913. Then it's completely forgotten about for several decades.

Here's Rainer Maria Rilke, at last! Rilke is on the run from winter and his writer's block, and has ended up in Ronda, in southern Spain. A female acquaintance had recommended during a séance that he should travel to Spain, and since Rilke always relied throughout his life on the advice of mature ladies, he clearly had to turn to the inhabitants of the beyond for orders. Now he's staying in Ronda, at the elegant Hotel Reina Victoria, a British hotel of the very latest kind, but now, out of season, almost empty. From up here he writes to his 'dear, good Mama' every week like a good boy. And to the other faraway ladies that he pines after so beautifully: to Marie von Thurn und Taxis, to Eva Cassirer, to Sidonie Nádherný, to Lou Andreas-Salomé. We will be hearing more about these ladies this year, don't you worry.

Right now it is Lou, the woman who took his virginity and persuaded him to change his first name from René to Rainer, whose star is suddenly in the ascendant: 'Merely to see one another, dear Lou [the word 'dear' is underlined three times], that's my greatest hope.' And he goes on to scribble in the margin, 'my support, my everything, as ever'. Then off to the mail train, which takes three hours to get to Gibraltar. And from there it travels on to 19 Berggasse, Lou Andreas-Salomé, c/o Prof. Dr Sigmund Freud. And Lou writes to her 'dear, dear boy' that she thinks she can be tougher with him than before.

And 'I think you will always have to suffer, and always will.' Is it sado-masochism, or is it love?

The days go by, filled with suffering and letter-writing. Sometimes Rilke goes on working on his *Duino Elegies*. He manages the first thirty-one lines of the sixth Elegy, but he simply can't finish it; he'd rather go walking in his white suit and his pale hat, or read the Koran (before going on to write ecstatic poems about angels and the Assumption of Mary). You could feel good here, far away from the dark winter, and at first Rilke too enjoys the fact that the sun doesn't sink behind the mountains before half-past five, even in January, that before it does so it bathes the city, perched on its rocky plateau, in a warm glow one last time – 'an unforgettable spectacle', as he writes to his dear Mama. The almond trees are already in blossom; so too the violets in the hotel garden, even the pale blue iris. Rilke pulls out his little black notebook, orders a coffee on the terrace, wraps his blanket around his hips, blinks into the sun one last time and then notes: 'Ah, if only one knew how to blossom: one's heart would be/ Consoled for both the slighter dangers and the greater.'

Indeed, if only one knew how to blossom. In Munich, Oswald Spengler, the 33-year-old misanthrope, sociopath and unemployed maths teacher, is working on the first chapter of his monumental work *The Decline of the West*. He himself has already set an example with regard to this decline. 'I am', he writes in 1913, in the notes for his autobiography, 'the last of my kind.' Everything, he writes, comes to an end; the suffering of the West is visible within him and on his body. Negative megalomania. Fading blossoms. Spengler's primal emotion: fear. Fear of setting foot inside a shop. Fear of relatives, fear of others speaking dialect. And of course: 'Fear of women, when they take their clothes off.' He knows fearlessness only in his mind. When the *Titanic* sank in 1912, he discerned in it a profound symbolism. In the notes he made at the time, he suffers, laments, complains about his unfortunate childhood and an even more unfortunate present. Every day he records it anew: a great era is coming to an end, hasn't anybody noticed? 'Culture – one last deep breath before extinction.' In *The Decline of the West* he puts it like this: 'Every culture has its new expressive possibilities, which appear, ripen, fade and never return.' But such a culture sinks more slowly than an ocean liner, of that you may be sure.

Since the beginning of the year the Carl Simon Verlag in Düsseldorf had been selling a new series of original transparencies featuring seventy-two original colour glass plates in cardboard boxes inside a wooden case, along with a thirty-five-page accompanying brochure. Subject: 'The Sinking of the *Titanic*'. All over the country slide shows were held. First you see the captain, the ship, the cabins, then the approaching iceberg. The disaster, lifeboats. The sinking ship. It's true: an ocean liner goes down more quickly than the West. Leonardo DiCaprio has not yet been born.

Franz Kafka, a man who is terrified when women take off their clothes, has a quite different concern. A white-hot idea has come to him. In the night of 22–3 January he writes roughly his 200th letter to Felice Bauer, and asks, 'Can you actually read my handwriting?'

Can you read the world? That's what Pablo Picasso and Georges Braque wonder, and keep coming up with new codes that viewers are supposed to decipher. They've just taught the world that you can paint shifting perspectives – it's known as Cubism – and now, in January 1913, they're taking it one step further. Later it will be called Synthetic Cubism, when they stick bits of wood fibre and all kinds of other things onto their paintings; the canvas now becomes an adventure playground. Braque had just moved into a new studio in Paris, right at the top of the Hotel Roma in Rue Caulaincourt, when he suddenly picked up a comb and ran it through his painting *Fruit-Dish, Ace of Clubs* and the lines looked like wood-grain. Picasso discovered the same thing the same day. And, as always, he was soon better at it than the inventor himself. So the artistic revolutionaries dashed ever onwards, impelled by their horror of being fully understood by the bourgeois public. Picasso might have been reassured had he known that Arthur Schnitzler wrote in his diary on 8 February: 'Picasso: the early paintings outstanding; violent resistance to his current Cubism.'

He only just managed to survive. And now Lovis Corinth must pay dearly for his life's work. On 19 January a spectacular exhibition of 228 paintings, entitled 'Life's Work', is due to open in the Secession building at 208 Kurfürstendamm. Today, on the first day of the year, lying hungover and exhausted on a sofa at 49 Klopstockstrasse, he is rather dreading it. It's barely four o'clock and already it's dark again, and sleet is falling from the sky.

So now Weber's, the framers, from 28 Derfflingerstrasse, want their money for the framing of the 'Life's Work' – a hefty 1,632.50 Marks. And for the reception that he's giving for the opening, the caterer, Adolf Kraft Nachfolger, 116 Kurfürstendamm, wants 200 Marks up front. For this he will deliver: '1 dish tongue. 1 dish Coburg ham with Cumberland sauce. 1 dish saddle of venison with Cumberland sauce. 1 dish roast beef with remoulade.' Even reading about it makes Lovis Corinth feel ill. Life's Work with Cumberland sauce. Last night's Polish carp still lies heavy on his stomach. When his beloved Charlotte is away, he invariably eats too much: it's yearning, he knows that. And so he writes a New Year's letter to his wife, Charlotte, who is hiking through the snow, far away in the mountains: 'Who knows how this New Year will go; the last one was awful. Forget it!' Indeed. Corinth, a painter always bursting with vigour, who swept out of the High Baroque into the Berlin of the early twentieth century, had been felled by a stroke, and his wife had looked after him at great personal sacrifice. When the 'Life's Work' exhibition was being planned, everyone was afraid that Corinth's was in fact over. But he had fought his way back to life. And back to the easel. Now the posters for his big exhibition were hanging all over the city, 9 to 4 every day, admission 1 Mark, with a picture of Corinth, amazed at himself, while Charlotte recovered from him off in the Tyrol. She's back in time for the reception. 'You're looking well, Madame', Max Liebermann says to her at the reception on 19 January at the Secession, his saddle of venison with Cumberland sauce in his right hand. My life's work is looking good, Lovis Corinth thinks to himself as he stomps and grumbles his way through the exhibition halls. So it goes on. But – please – no more of that awful Cubism.

Back to Freud's, at 19 Berggasse. He's spending these January days in his study, finishing off his book on *Totem and Taboo*. And it's quite natural that the unconscious should be forcing its way powerfully into this book about taboo-breaking and fetishisation. But there's one thing he doesn't seem to be aware of: at that moment, at any rate, when his pupils, above all the Zurich psychologist C. G. Jung (b. 1875), are challenging him and hurling violent accusations at him, Freud (b. 1856) is developing his theory of parricide. So in December 1912 Jung had written to Freud: 'I would like to make you aware that your technique of treating your pupils as patients is a mistake.' By so doing Freud is creating 'impudent rogues' and 'slavish sons', he writes. And he continues: 'Meanwhile you always remain comfortably on top as the father. Out of pure subservience, no one dares to tug the prophet's beard.'

Seldom in his life has anything hit Freud as hard as this act of parricide. During those few months, when his beard must have sprouted new grey hairs, he drafts a first reply which he doesn't send, and which will only be found in his desk after his death. But on 3 January 1913 he summons all his strength and writes to Jung in Küsnacht: 'Your assumptions that I am treating my pupils as patients are demonstrably inaccurate.' And then:

> Besides, your letter is unanswerable. It creates a situation that would cause difficulties in spoken communication, and is entirely insoluble through written channels. But anyone encountering abnormal behaviour who shouts that it is normal arouses suspicions that he lacks an understanding of illness. I therefore propose that we abandon our private relationship entirely. I will lose nothing, because I have long been joined to you only by the thin thread of the further development of past disappointments.

What a letter! A father, challenged by his son, stabs furiously back. Never has Freud lost his temper so badly as during these January days. Never has she seen him so depressed as in 1913, his beloved daughter Anna will later say.

Jung replies on 6 January: 'I will comply with your wish to abandon the personal relationship. Besides, you will probably know better than anyone what this moment means for you.' He writes that in ink. Then he adds by typewriter, and it looks like a tombstone for one of the great intellectual friendships of the twentieth century: 'The rest is silence.' It's a fine irony that one of the most interpreted and most discussed break-ups of 1913 should begin with a vow of silence. From this moment on Jung will chafe at Freud's methods, and Freud, conversely, at Jung's. Before that he gives a precise definition of parricide among primitive people: they put on masks of the murdered father – then pray to their victim. You might almost call it the Dialectic of Enlightenment.

And speaking of Enlightenment, the ten-year-old Theodor W. Adorno, nicknamed 'Teddie', who will later come up with that phrase, is living at 12 Schöne Aussicht, Frankfurt am Main. The key person in his life, apart from his mother, is the chimpanzee Basso in Frankfurt Zoo. At the same time Frank Wedekind, author of *Spring Awakening* and *Lulu*, is friends with Missie, a chimpanzee from the Zoological Garden in Berlin.

Marcel Proust sits in his study at 102 Boulevard Haussmann in Paris, building his own cage. Neither sunlight nor dust nor noise must bother him while he's working. It's a special form of work/life balance. He has hung his study with three layers of curtains and papered his walls with cork panels. In this soundproofed room Proust sits by electric light, sending excessively polite New Year letters, as he does every year, with the urgent request that they henceforth spare him presents. He was constantly receiving invitations, but anyone who sent them knew how exhausting it was for him, because he sent letters and notes in advance about whether he was coming or not, and how he probably wouldn't etc. – a great procrastinator, actually matched in this respect only by Kafka.

Here sits Marcel Proust, in this soundproofed room of the mind, trying his hand at his novel about memory and the search for lost time. The first part would be called 'A Love of Swann's', and in fine ink he writes the final sentence down on paper: 'The reality I once knew no longer exists. The memory of a particular image is the melancholy remembering of a particular moment; and houses, streets, avenues are fleeting, oh! the years.'

Must memory be melancholy remembering? Gertrude Stein, the great Parisian salon hostess and friend of the avant-garde, is shivering a few streets away from Proust. She is engaged in a terrible fight with her brother Leo; their decades-long flat-share is threatening to come apart at the seams. Is everything ephemeral? She dreams of the spring. She draws warmth from a thought. She looks at the Picassos and Cézannes on her wall. But does one thought make a spring? She writes a short poem including the phrase 'A rose is a rose is a rose'. Just like Proust, she is trying to capture something that wants to be forgotten. So this is the world of poetry, the world of the imagination, in January 1913.

Max Beckmann finishes his painting *The Sinking of the Titanic*.

FEBRUARY

Things are livening up now. In New York the Armory Show is modern art's Big Bang, with Marcel Duchamp showing his Nude Descending a Staircase. *After that, his star is firmly in the ascendant. Nudes are everywhere, especially in Vienna: a naked Alma Mahler (by Oskar Kokoschka) and lots of other Viennese socialites in works by Gustav Klimt and Egon Schiele. Others bare their souls to Sigmund Freud for 100 Kronen an hour. Meanwhile, Adolf Hitler is painting quaint watercolours of St Stephen's Cathedral in the common room of Vienna's boarding-house for men. In Munich, Heinrich Mann is working on* Man of Straw *and celebrating his forty-second birthday at his brother's house. The snow still lies thick on the ground. Thomas Mann buys a plot of land and builds himself a house. Rilke continues to suffer, and Kafka continues to hesitate. A small hat shop belonging to Coco Chanel expands. Archduke Franz Ferdinand, heir to the Austrian throne, races around Vienna in his golden-wheeled car, plays with his model railway and worries about assassination attempts in Serbia. Stalin meets Trotsky for the first time — and in the very same month, in Barcelona, a man is born who will later murder Trotsky on Stalin's orders. Is 1913 perhaps an unlucky year after all?*

When will his time finally come? All the waiting around is driving Franz Ferdinand mad. The 83-year-old Emperor Franz Joseph has been on the throne for an incredible sixty-five years and has no intention of giving it up for his nephew, who is now next in line following the deaths of Sissi, Franz Joseph's beloved wife, and Rudolf, his beloved son. The young heir's only consolation is that his car has wheels with golden spokes, just like the ones on the Emperor's carriage. But when it comes to the majestic title, well, the only man to have held that since 1848 is Emperor Franz Joseph. Or, to be more precise:

> His Imperial and Royal Apostolic Majesty, by God's Grace Emperor of Austria, King of Hungary and Bohemia, of Dalmatia, Croatia, Slovenia, Galicia, Lodomeria and Illyria; King of Jerusalem etc.; Archduke of Austria; Grand Duke of Tuscany and Kraków; Duke of Lorraine, Salzburg, Styria, Carinthia, Carniola and Bukowina; Grand Prince of Transylvania, Margrave of Moravia; Duke of Upper and Lower Silesia, of Modena, Parma, Piacenza and Guastalla, of Auschwitz and Zator, of Teschen, Friaul, Dubrovnik and Zadar; Princely Count of Habsburg and Tyrol, of Kyburg, Gorizia and Gradisca; Prince of Trento and Brixen; Margrave of Upper and Lower Lusatia and Istria: Count of Hohenems, Feldkirch, Bregenz, Sonnenburg etc.; Lord of Hohenems, Kotor and the Windic March; Grand Voivod of the Voivodship of Serbia etc., etc.

The schoolchildren who had to learn this by heart always laughed hardest at the 'etc., etc.', for it sounded like the whole world belonged to him, and as if only a small portion of it had been mentioned. But for Franz Ferdinand, heir to the throne, it's the three words right before the 'etc., etc.' that really make him seethe: the 'Voivodship of Serbia'. A battle is raging down in the Balkans, and he's deeply unsettled by it. So he requests a meeting in Schönbrunn Palace with the 'Grand Voivod of the Vovoidship of Serbia' – the Emperor, whose white side-whiskers are as long as his title.

Arriving at Schönbrunn, Franz Ferdinand alights from – or rather, springs out of – his Gräf & Stift automobile in his general's uniform, and bolts up the steps towards Franz Joseph's study. He announces that urgent action needs to be taken in order to stop the Serbs. The Kingdom of Serbia is becoming too rebellious at the southeastern flank of the Empire, he says, destabilising things, playing with fire. But they will have to act with good judgement. Under no circumstances should they wage a pre-emptive war, such as the one the General Chief of Staff called for in his memorandum of 20 January, because that would be sure to alert Russia to the plan. The Emperor listens impassively to his blustering, clamouring, trembling nephew: 'I'll give it some thought.' Then he utters a cool farewell. The rest is silence. Agitated, Franz Ferdinand rushes off to his enormous automobile. The liveried chauffeur turns on the engine and, spurred on by the heir, roars off down Schönbrunner Schlossstrasse at breakneck speed. If Franz Ferdinand must resign himself to spending his whole life waiting, then at least he shouldn't do so stuck in traffic.

Standing by an upstairs window in the Troyanovsky household, Stalin is taking one of his short breaks from his work. He pulls the curtain aside and peers curiously but distractedly down at the heir's automobile, which is racing along at great speed beneath his gaze. Lenin too had once stood in that very spot, always staying with the Troyanovskys when he was in Vienna. Elsewhere in the city in that February of 1913, a young Croat casts an expert eye over the car with the golden wheels as it races past. As a car mechanic and, as of recently, a test driver for Mercedes in Wiener Neustadt, he's intimately acquainted with the qualities of the heir's automobile. His name is Josip Broz, a

21-year-old daredevil and lady's man who is currently being 'kept' as a lover by the upper-class Liza Spuner, an arrangement that includes having his fencing lessons paid for. (He also uses her financial aid to send child support back to his homeland for his newborn son Leopard, whose mother he has recently left.) Liza has him drive her all over Austria in his test car on trips to buy her new clothes. When she falls pregnant, he leaves her too. And so it goes on. At some point he will return to his homeland, which will by then be called Yugoslavia, and assume control of it. Josip Broz will then call himself Tito.

So, in the first months of the year 1913, Stalin, Hitler and Tito, two of the twentieth century's greatest tyrants and one of its most evil dictators, were, for a brief moment, all in Vienna at the same time. One was studying the question of nationality in a guest room, the second was painting watercolours in a men's boarding house, and the third was circling aimlessly around the Ringstrasse to test how well various automobiles handled the corners. Three extras, or non-speaking parts, one might think, in the great play that was 'Vienna in 1913'.

It was icy cold that February, but the sun was shining, which was and is rare for the Viennese winter, but it made the new Ringstrasse gleam all the more in its snow-white splendour. Vienna was bubbling over with vitality; it had become a world city, and this could be seen and felt all over the world – everywhere except in Vienna itself, where, through sheer joy in self-destruction, people hadn't realised that they had unexpectedly moved to the apex of the movement which called itself Modernism. Because self-doubt and self-destruction had become a central component of the new way of thinking, and what Kafka called the 'Nervous Era' had dawned. And in Vienna nerves – virtually, metaphorically, artistically and psychologically – were laid bare like nowhere else.

Berlin, Paris, Munich, Vienna. These were the four capitals of Modernism in 1913. Chicago was flexing its muscles, New York was blossoming gradually but didn't definitively take the baton from Paris until 1948. And yet 1913 saw the completion of the Woolworth Building, the first one in the world to rise above the Eiffel Tower, and of Grand Central Station, making it the biggest railway station in the world, and the Armory Show made sure that the sparks of the avant-garde ignited in America too. But Paris was still in a league of its own that year, and the French press saw neither the Woolworth Building nor the Armory Show as cause for excitement. Why should they be? After all, the French had Rodin, Matisse, Picasso, Stravinsky, Proust, Chagall 'etc., etc.' – all of whom were working on their next great masterpieces. And the city itself, at the peak of its affectation and decadence, embodied in the dance experiments of the Ballets Russes and Sergei Diaghilev, had a magnetic attraction for every cultivated European, in particular four *über*-cultivated individuals in white suits: Hugo von Hofmannsthal, Julius Meier-Graefe, Rainer Maria Rilke and Harry Graf Kessler. In the Paris of 1913 only Proust wanted to reminisce; everyone else wanted to keep moving forwards, but, unlike in Berlin at the time, preferably with a glass of champagne.

Over in the German-speaking world, Berlin's population was exploding, but culturally speaking its golden age was still to come. It forged ahead rather impetuously – but word that 'Berlin's nightlife was its speciality' had already reached Paris and the artistic circle surrounding Marcel Duchamp. Munich, by contrast, was stylish and yet had taken a kind of well-earned rest – most evidently in the fact that self-glorification was becoming all the rage there (and no one in Berlin had any time for that). One other indicator is, of course, that the bohemians are becoming completely bourgeois: Thomas Mann is seeking – for the sake of his children – a house in the suburbs, in a peaceful location with a large garden. On 25 February 1913 he buys a plot of land at 1 Poschingstrasse and has a magnificent villa built there. His brother Heinrich has sought out Munich as an excellent location from which to write about Berlin, the city hurling itself into the future that is the setting for *Man of Straw*, the epic novel that he is completing. If one were to read Munich's satirical magazine *Simplicissimus*, one would find him mocking the fact that the policemen worry about falling asleep out of boredom after eight o'clock in the evening; the great magazine of the *fin de siècle* can't even provoke its own city any more and seems, in the most pleasant of ways, to be fatigued, as if it were stretched out on a chaise longue with a cigarette in its left hand. The magazine's counterparts in other cities are *Die Fackel* in Vienna, and *Der Sturm*, *Die Tat* and *Die Aktion* in Berlin, their breathless names alone revealing that the true battles of the modern era are being fought there.

And of course, Munich's quiet, gentle abdication as the capital of Art Nouveau and the *fin de siècle* can also be witnessed in the name of the guest house in Theresienstrasse where Else Lasker-Schüler is living in February 1913: the Pension Modern (not to be confused with La Maison Moderne, the legendary Parisian gallery of Art Nouveau set up by the German art propagandist and writer Julius Meier-Grafe, which closed in 1904). So if the guest houses proudly carry their modernity in their names, then it has clearly long since moved on – to the Café Grössenwahn in Berlin (whose name means 'megalomania') and to the Café Central at 14 Herrengasse in Vienna, to be precise. Names can be so revealing.

And so the capital of the modern age *anno* 1913 is Vienna. Its star players are Sigmund Freud, Arthur Schnitzler, Egon Schiele, Gustav Klimt, Adolf Loos, Karl Kraus, Otto Wagner, Hugo von Hoffmannsthal, Ludwig Wittgenstein, Georg Trakl, Arnold Schönberg and Oskar Kokoschka, to name but a few. Here the battles raged: about the unconscious, about dreams, the new music, the new way of seeing, the new architecture, the new logic, the new morality.

❧

'Fear of women – the minute they take their clothes off.' There are two places in Europe in 1913 where this fear of Spengler's is not an issue. One is Monte Verità in Ascona, near Lake Maggiore, where a wonderfully eccentric group of free-thinkers, free spirits and nudists are doing their exercises, a specific blend of eurhythmics, yoga and physiotherapy. The others are Gustav Klimt and Egon Schiele's studios in Vienna. Their drawings, whose lines teetered so sensually between pornography and the so-called New Objectivity, delineated the curves of the 'most erotic city in the world', as Lou Andreas-Salomé declared Vienna to be back then. Although the women in Klimt's paintings were always swathed in golden ornament, he encircled the bodies in his sketches with an inimitable line that swept across the page, softly undulating like curls falling loose over a shoulder. Egon Schiele went even further in his explorations of the human body – the forms he depicted were tormented, strained with nerves and martyred, distorted, more sexual than erotic. Where Klimt's work reveals soft skin, Schiele shows nerves and sinews; where Klimt's bodies flow, Schiele's splay, entangle and contort. Klimt's women lure, while Schiele's shock.

'I'm not interested in my own person', said Klimt, 'but rather in other people, especially women.'

If these drawings, which made a voyeur of everyone exposed to them, were well known, they were soon subjected to censorship, thereby increasing the notoriety of their creators. When Schiele wanted to exhibit his work *Friendship* in Munich, he received an interesting rejection letter. The director of the gallery wrote to inform him that his work could not be shown under any circumstances because of its extreme nature, and that it would offend common decency. Full stop. New paragraph. He, however, would be very interested in purchasing the work. There, neatly encapsulated, is the chasm between public and private morality in 1913.

Berlin is becoming too bright. The gas lanterns, neon signs and city lights are threatening to outshine the stars in the night sky. In 1913 the demolition vehicles roll in to tear down the New Berlin Observatory, near Hallesches Tor. Located between Lindenstrasse and Friedrichstrasse, the new Prussian observatory was completed by Karl Friedrich Schinkel in 1835. Like everything else from this most beautiful decade of German history, it was barely surpassed in either practical or aesthetic terms. A wonderfully simple building, over which the dome sits enthroned like a church tower – a church of the world, but with a view straight up to the heavens. A few comets were discovered here, and a few asteroids too. But the most significant discovery was the planet Neptune. In 1913, however, no one was interested in that. It only took a few weeks before there were only fields where one of Schinkel's boldest structures had once stood. The observatory was relocated to Babelsberg, where the sky was darker and where Neptune could be seen more easily. And because they were good with figures in Prussia, the land between Lindenstrasse and Friedrichstrasse was sold: 1.1 million Goldmarks from the sale were used for the construction of the new observatory, and 450,000 for the purchase of new instruments. The land itself funded the Royal House – in the grounds of the Babelsberg Palace Park. And so it was that by 1913, perfectly timed after the foundation of the film studio the year before, everything in Berlin to do with stars and starlets ended up in Babelsberg.

On 6 February, according to the Chinese calendar, the year of the buffalo begins. The buffalo, according to an ancient Chinese saying, prefers fresh grass to a golden trough.

In Sindelsdorf, Franz Marc is back to work on his masterpiece, and Else Lasker-Schüler has returned to Berlin. He has set up his studio in the unheated attic of the old farmhouse in Sindelsdorf, from where he can barely hear Maria Marc playing the piano downstairs. It's so cold that even Hanni, their beloved cat, retreats to the stove. Kandinsky comes to visit from Munich and reports:

> Outside, everything is white – snow covers the fields, the
> mountains, the forests – the frost nips at your nose. Upstairs
> in the humble attic (where you constantly bang your head
> against the rafters), *The Tower of Blue Horses* is perched on

the easel, and Franz Marc stands there in his fur coat, a big
fur hat and straw shoes that he made himself. Now, tell me
in all honesty what you make of this picture!

What a question.

On 13 February there is still no sign of Leonardo's *Mona Lisa*. The
Louvre's new catalogue is published, no longer listing the painting.
In Berlin, on 13 February, Rudolf Steiner holds one of his great lectures – 'Leonardo's Spiritual and Intellectual Greatness at the Turning Point of the New Age'. Steiner speaks for a long time, almost two
hours. The audience hang on his every word. He, just like Oswald
Spengler, talks a lot about things falling into ruin, about the decline
of an era. But he regards this as necessary to make room for the new:

> For in those dying forces we finally sense, even see, the forces
> preparing themselves for the future, and in the sunset, the
> promise and hope of a new dawn moves closer to us. Our
> souls must always respond to human evolution in such a way
> that we tell ourselves: All progress is so. When what we have
> created turns to ruin, we know that out of those ruins, new
> life will always blossom forth.

On 17 February the Armory Show, one of the most important art
exhibitions of the century, opens in a former arsenal in New York.
Which century, I hear you ask? Well, you could say that the art of the
nineteenth century only came to an end when the first Armory Show
began. And it led to the supremacy of modern art not only in Europe
but globally too.

  Towards the end of 1912 three Americans with highly inquisi-
tive natures and the necessary expertise – the painters Walter Pach,
Arthur Davies and Walt Kuhn – travelled to Europe to identify the

most interesting artists and bring their key works back to New York. Great painters and photographers such as Claude Monet, Odilon Redon and Alfred Stieglitz sat on the selection committee – and the American public quickly realised that it was about pitting the Cubists and Futurists and Impressionists of Old Europe against the affluent American *fin-de-siècle* art scene. This was war. And for the first time the war was being waged on American soil – now that Europe's battles had been fought. In total there were 1,300 paintings on display, only a third of them from Europe. But it was this third that made the American pictures look ancient – particularly the eight Picassos and twelve Matisses. The Brancusi sculptures and paintings by Francis Picabia and Marcel Duchamp provoked particularly outraged debate. *Camera Work*, Stieglitz's legendary magazine, reported: 'The exhibition of new work from Europe dropped on us like a bomb.' And the force of the detonation was just as intense – rage, incomprehension and laughter were among the reactions, but people flocked to the exhibition in order to see it for themselves. The newspapers printed caricatures almost every day, and during the exhibition's second residency, in Chicago, there was even a protest staged by students of The Art Institute of Chicago – who reportedly burned copies of three Matisse paintings. In the eyes of the American public Matisse was the most 'primitive' of all the artists. That has always been the supreme guarantee of quality.

The greatest sensation was caused by the three brothers Raymond Duchamp-Villon, Jacques Villon and Marcel Duchamp. Seventeen of their works were exhibited, and all but one were sold. Marcel Duchamp's *Nude Descending a Staircase* became the focal point of the Armory Show, the most discussed and most caricatured art work on show. One critic called it *Explosion in a Shingle Factory,* a comment that, although intended to ridicule the work, instead demonstrated how strong the shock waves caused by the piece really were. A woman striding through space and time – a genial combination of Cubism, Futurism and relativity theory. The room housing the picture was flooded with visitors every single day; people queued for over forty minutes just to catch a glimpse of the scandalous painting. Evidently, for the traditionally minded Americans, this work was the embodiment of a strange, irrational Europe. An antique dealer from San Francisco bought it – somewhere along his endless train journey back from New York, at a provincial station in New Mexico, he got off and sent a telegram to New York: 'I will buy Duchamp nude woman descending stairway please reserve.'

The Duchamps went on working away in their studio in Neuilly, oblivious to their new-found American fame – until the cheques suddenly started coming in the post. Marcel Duchamp received $972 for his four sales – not a high price, even in 1913. Cézanne's *La Colline des Pauvres*, for example, was sold from the exhibition to the Metropolitan Museum for $6,700. Duchamp was pleased nonetheless.

At the moment when America and Paris too had started to pay attention to his work, Marcel Duchamp had turned his back on Cubism and the theme of motion – or, as he so eloquently put it, 'motion mixed with oil paint'. At the very moment when he should have become one of the greatest artists of his generation Duchamp declared that he was bored with painting. He was looking for something different, something new.

❧

In Prague, Franz Kafka is suffering. He's suffering because Felice, for whom he has been pining from afar in letters, hasn't said a word about the book *Contemplations*, which he sent her in December. And because his sister Valli is getting married, and because it's always too noisy in the apartment (the doors are always banging, and his parents and sister have the impertinence to talk to one another), and because he's working for an insurance company by day and writing by night. He also has to contend with work trips, interruptions and colds. But above all he's suffering from the fear that his creativity has withered away. And as dreadful as the idea of living as a bachelor is – perhaps it was the only way of being a writer. In moments of panic he is overwhelmed by the question 'What will become of me if I get married?' How would he deal with what he called 'A Wife's Rights'? For him there were two equally horrific scenarios: the physical demands of the wife and, above all, the demands on his time. He implored Felice never again to write that she wanted to sit by him while he was working on his books – for if she or anyone else were to sit behind him, the secret of writing would be destroyed. And then he also wrote: 'I would never expose myself to the risk of becoming a father.' Is it possible to warn someone off more than Kafka did in these letters? But Felice responds, although torn between office and home, letter-writing and worries about her family, as if it were her true calling to be his addressee, a reader both for Kafka and for world literature. She assumes the role calmly and in complete earnest.

In 1913 art everywhere is driving towards abstraction. Kandinsky in Munich, Robert Delaunay and František Kupka in Paris, Kasimir Malevich in Russia and Piet Mondrian in the Netherlands – each in their own way they are trying to free themselves from all reference to reality. And then there's that young, well-brought-up, reserved young man in Paris: Marcel Duchamp, a painter who has suddenly decided he doesn't want to paint any more.

In Munich a benefit auction held for Else Lasker-Schüler turns into a complete disaster. In a touching gesture Franz Marc asked artist friends to donate paintings to raise more money for the relief effort initiated by Karl Kraus in *Die Fackel*. His call doesn't go unanswered, with oil paintings arriving from Ernst Ludwig Kirchner, Emil Nolde, Erich Heckel, Karl Schmidt-Rottluff, Oskar Kokoschka, Paul Klee, August Macke, Alexej von Jawlensky, Wassily Kandinsky and Franz Marc himself for the auction on 17 February. Only Ludwig Meidner from Berlin declines (saying he himself has no money and is starving). An auction is held in the Neuer Kunstsalon, but no one shows any interest. So, to avoid total embarrassment, the artists all bid for each others' work, and raise 1,600 Marks.

The total value of the works unauctioned on 17 February 1913 would amount to around 100 million Euros today. Oh, what the heck – probably closer to 200 million.

Sigmund Freud continues to work on his theory of parricide. At the same time, in the newly founded film studios in Potsdam-Babelsberg, filming begins on *The Sins of the Fathers*, starring Asta Nielsen. In keeping with the title, Nielsen later feels partly to blame for the 'kitsch in that early dawn of film'. The film poster shows her wearing a tight skirt and a plunging blouse. She was slim, unusual at the time, and a source of great joy for cartoonists, who immediately saw a stick figure in the making. Most men too were quite happy with how she looked. In 1913 Asta Nielsen was the ultimate sex symbol, and a big contract led to her making eight films between 1912 and 1914, which were filmed and released back to back. The new magazine *Bild und Film* put it like this: 'People are queuing up to see the film as if they're at a bakery during a famine, almost breaking their necks to get a ticket. Many people watch the film two or three times in quick succession and are enchanted by it again and again.' Samuel Fischer, the most renowned publisher of his time, watched with increasing amazement as Nielsen captivated the masses. Believing film to be the medium of the future, he tried to convince his most famous authors to write screenplays as well.

It's 1913, but disaster has yet to strike for Arnold Schönberg. On Sunday 23 February, at around half-past seven in the evening, his *Gurrelieder* are premiered at the Great Music Hall in Vienna – and the public are expecting a new scandal. His recent appearances and compositions have already unsettled Vienna, causing great commotion, and the former Romantic has emphatically transformed himself into a *Neutöner*, an exponent of the new music. The previous year he caused uproar with his *Pierrot Lunaire* (*opus* 21). But now this. All of a sudden, they're no longer hearing modern radicalism from Schönberg, but pure late Romanticism. Five vocalists, three four-part male choirs and a huge orchestra with every kind of flute and drum and stringed instrument. Eighty strings were used in the first performance alone: the gigantism of the new century is forging ahead. Schönberg declares that the oratorio cannot be performed without a 150-piece orchestra. The piece itself is a great, bombastic, murmuring and pulsating spectacle of nature, about storms and the summer winds. Vast choirs sing about the beauty of the sun – a spectacular wonder of nature, just as Schönberg once experienced it after a night of drinking led him to the Anninger, one of Vienna's city mountains.

'*Schadenfreude* lurks already in a hundred pairs of eyes: today will show once again whether he can really afford to compose as he chooses rather than how others before him have composed', writes Richard Specht for his review in the Berlin journal *März*. But the scandal never comes: instead, it's a triumph.

> The resounding cheers that broke out even after the first section rose to a commotion after the third [...] And when the choir's powerfully surging dawn greeting was over, [...] the cheering knew no bounds; with tear-stained faces, the audience called out their gratitude to the composer, sounding more warm and insistent than is usually the case with such a 'success': instead, it sounded like an apology. A few young people, unknown to me, came over, their cheeks aglow with shame, and admitted they had brought their house keys with them to add their – in their view appropriate – music to Schönberg's, but now he had won them over so completely that nothing could turn them against him.

The *Gurrelieder*, with their hymnal, magnificent melodic arcs, were the greatest success that Schönberg would ever experience. But never again did he come as close to his audience as here – and this was clearly to do with his terror about the disaster looming over the year 1913. The *Gurrelieder* is a sumptuous and lavish piece of late

Romanticism, melodic even though its composer had long since crossed the border of tonality. Bewitching beauty, bordering on kitsch. It had taken ten years for Schönberg to find the right orchestration, but the composition itself originated at the turn of the century – and thirteen years later was perfectly in tune with the taste of the Viennese public. The house keys with which they had planned to drown out Schönberg's music stayed in their pockets.

But not for long.

It's just one thing after another in Vienna in 1913.

On that very same evening the performance ban on Arthur Schnitzler's new play *Professor Bernhardi* is breached in the form of a 'reading' of the play in the Koflerpark club house, right by the stop for the number 8 tram, 'at precisely seven in the evening'. This contravened the ruling of the Viennese police department that

> Even if such reservations as exist regarding the performance of the work – from the perspective of safeguarding the religious sentiments of the people – could be overcome by editing or altering certain sections of the text, the entire construction of the play, through its combination of episodes relating to Austrian state establishments and exploring public life, grossly distorts conditions here in such a disparaging way that its performance on a domestic stage cannot be permitted with a view to the necessity of safeguarding public interest.

After the *Gurrelieder* evening an illustrious circle meets in Arthur Schnitzler's drawing room at a quarter to six on Monday. Hugo von Hofmannsthal had accepted the invitation on 21 February: 'Because I consider the opportunity to hear you read one of your new works to be one of the greatest and purest pleasures – and also because I am continually saddened by the fact that I so seldom see you. Heartfelt wishes, your Hugo.' Schnitzler himself struggles through the reading, coughing and sweating; he has a bad fever, which kept him from attending the *Gurrelieder*. It is well known that doctors rarely make good patients, so on Monday evening he bravely reads from *Frau Beate and her Son*, his latest novella, an Oedipus story which Freud very much enjoyed. It's a long text, but Schnitzler manages to read it to the end. A woman sleeps with the friend of her teenage son. The friend boasts about it to others, the son is mortified with shame, the mother is mortified with shame, mother and son row out onto a lake, make love and then their shame really does become mortal when they drown themselves. Schnitzler was regarded by everyone, even his critics, as knowledgeable in matters of sensuality. Even more so today, now that his diaries have been discovered.

While his wife, Olga, with whom he spends 1913 immersed in subversive positional warfare, eats and drinks with the guests, he retreats to his room and writes in his diary: 'Reading aloud from *Beate* while struck down with the flu from six to almost nine in the evening. Richard, Hugo, Arthur Kaufmann, Leo, Salten, Wasserman, Gustav, Olga.' Salten, by the way, was Felix Salten, the wonderfully enigmatic Viennese double talent of the early twentieth century, who published the story 'Bambi' and – under his pseudonym – *The Memoirs of Josefine Mutzenbacher*, a pornographic work in Viennese dialect that was challenging even for Vienna, advanced as the city was in sexual matters. From porn to Bambi – this was precisely the Janus-faced character that made up the particular enchantment and the particularly subversive force of Vienna at that time. Adolf Loos came up with a unique description for all the figures from Sigmund Freud's analysis, Arthur Schnitzler's stories and Gustav Klimt's pictures: *Ornament and Crime*.

The day after the reading at the Schnitzler residence, on Tuesday 25 February, Thomas Mann buys a plot of land at 1 Poschingerstrasse in

Munich. That very same day he commissions the architects Gustav and Alois Ludwig to build a villa worthy of him: tranquil, supercilious, somewhat stiff. Together with the architect, he waits right next to the plot of land for the number 30 tram into the city centre. His red-handled walking-stick hangs, as ever, from his left arm. Noticing a speck of dust on his overcoat, he brushes it away. Then he hears the tram coming down from the Bogenhausener Höhe.

Picasso owns three Siamese cats, Marcel Duchamp only two. And that remains the score, even today, between the two great revolutionaries: 3–2.

Franz Kafka's letters to Felice are the most important work he will produce in 1913.

It is a work full of earnestness, full of despair, full of comedy. On 1 February he writes: 'My stomach, like my whole being, has been out of sorts for days, and I am trying to deal with it by fasting.' Then he tells her, in the most wonderful words, about a reading by Franz Werfel the previous day: 'How a poem like that rises up – its inherent ending within its beginning – with an uninterrupted, inner, flowing development – how I widened my eyes, perched there on the couch!' He has even asked Werfel to dedicate a copy of his new volume of poetry 'to an unknown woman'; but 'oh dear': 'I will send you the book soon … if only the necessity of preparing the package and the task etc. didn't vex me so.' So Franz Kafka sits there in his room in Prague, despairing over how to pack a book. Luckily for him, the proofs of *The Judgement* turn up at that very moment.

But what must be going through the mind of Felice, that sociable, modern, tango-dancing young working woman in her prime, when she reads lines like these from her Franz: 'My dearest, tell me why, of all people, you choose to love such an unhappy boy, one whose unhappiness is so contagious. I'm always compelled to carry an atmosphere of unhappiness around with me. But don't be afraid, my dearest, stay by my side! Close by my side!'

After that, he complains of discomfort in his shoulder, of constant colds and digestive problems. Then, on 17 February, come perhaps the most sincere and certainly the most beautiful words that he wrote to his beloved enchantress in faraway Berlin: 'Sometimes I wonder, Felice, given that you have such an intense power over me, why you don't just turn me into someone who's capable of ordinary, everyday things.'

In this she will not succeed.

On 16 February 1913 Josef Stalin boards a train at Vienna's Nordbahnhof and travels back to Russia.

His daily ration is one corpse. In total, between 25 October 1912 and 9 November 1913, Dr Gottfried Benn dissects 297 bodies – draymen, prostitutes, anonymous drowned corpses. Day after day throughout that cold, wretched February he climbs down into the cellar of the clinic in Berlin-Charlottenburg wearing his white coat and brandishing his scalpel. He rummages through the bodies, finding cause of death, but no souls. It's hell on earth for the sensitive priest's son from Neumark, just twenty-six years old: ceaselessly cutting open, filling up, sewing up, cutting open. Throughout those lonely months, underground and surrounded by death, Benn's eyelids begin to draw shut a little from above and below, as the photographs show. Never again will he fully open them. 'He saw only sparsely through his eyelids', writes Benn, barely out of the autopsy cellar, as he tries to scrape the suffering away from his soul in the character of 'Rönne'. Peering sparsely through his own eyelids, Benn foresees, blinking uncontrollably, the model for the twentieth century in his gloomy cellar of corpses: eyes wide shut. In the evenings, after his second or third beer, he writes poems about it on scraps of paper: 'The crown of creation: the pig, man.' He knows that, come dawn the next day, the next corpse will be waiting downstairs in the cellar. Perhaps it's even still alive and roaming around. By the next spring he is distraught, pleading to be dismissed. Professor Dr Keller lies in his final report: 'During his time in office Herr Dr Benn showed himself to be up to the task in every way.' Benn's début collection, *Morgue*, published in mid-1912, begs to differ: merciless, cold yet daring late Romantic poems about the body, cancer and blood, they reveal a great existential trauma, and to this day cannot be read on an empty stomach.

But their rage and force turn their author – an unremarkable pathologist, barely 5 foot 5 inches tall, with a receding hairline and the beginnings of a paunch, into a highly mysterious figure of the Berlin avant-garde. The *enfant terrible* in a three-piece suit. 'As soon as my first collection of poetry was published, I gained a reputation as a brittle *roué*,' Benn later recalled, 'an infernal snob and one of the typical coffee house literati, while in reality I was marching along on military exercises in the potato fields of the Uckermark and setting off at an English trot over the pine-covered hills with the division commando in Döberitz.' We don't know whether it was the military doctor Benn who went over to Else Lasker-Schüler's table one evening at the Café des Westens on the Ku'damm (corner of Joachimstalerstrasse) or the other way around. But there was no better place for these two outsiders, trembling with lyrical emotion, to find one another. The artists' haunt was run down, but nobly so, and there was mediocre Viennese cuisine on offer, of the sort that you might find in any Berlin artists' haunt today. The air was dense with cigarette smoke, the deafening noise from the street forced its way inside, the newspapers were stamped 'Stolen from Café des Westens', and there the bohemians sat running up a tab. A cup of coffee or a glass of beer cost 25 Pfennigs, and you could sit in front of it until five o' clock in the morning.

Benn and Lasker-Schüler came here all the time. They eyed each other like two predators at first, prowling around one another, satiating their hunger by reciting each other's poems aloud for weeks on end as they headed home at night through the newly built streets of the west. At the time she wrote the following about Benn: 'Every one of his verses a leopard's bite, the pounce of a wild animal.' Else Lasker-Schüler, a poet seventeen years his senior, recently separated from her second husband, tangled up in love affairs with all the prominent figures of the Berlin bohemian scene, abundantly draped with jewellery, ankle bells and oriental garments, immediately falls under the spell of the stiff doctor with the sleepy gaze and the shy, almost uninterested, tone of voice, with which, as in his poetry, he could say devastating things about death, corpses and the female body as casually as if he were ordering a coffee. And Gottfried Benn, still somewhat pompous and insecure, falls under the spell of the sensuous, mature woman with eyes that sparkle like black diamonds.

The two people who meet and become close during this cold Berlin winter are both failures: she forty-four years old and he almost twenty-six. Else Lasker-Schüler, once a cosseted banker's daughter from Elberfeld, is now a pauper, surviving for weeks on end on just nuts and fruit. Wracked with fever, she roams through the night with her son, sheltering under bridges and in hostels, scrounging every cup of coffee. In her worn-out, oriental robes she looks like a tramp from the *Arabian Nights*. She writes on telegram slips from the Central Post Office. Benn, the lost, cosseted preacher's son from the countryside, is searching desperately for his vocation in life and has just failed for the second time: first as a doctor in the Charité psychiatry department, then as an army doctor, where he has been laid off temporarily. Reports state that he has problems interacting with people. They recommend that he interact with corpses instead. Shortly after he moves into the pathology field his beloved mother dies. Benn, by now well versed in sewing people up, writes: 'I carry you around on my brow like a wound that will never heal.' Biographically, this is the moment when Benn and Lasker-Schüler first see each other and cling onto each other like drowning souls. 'Oh, Your Hands' is the name of Lasker-Schüler's poem from October 1912 – revealing for the first time the handwriting of Gottfried Benn on her heart. She can even, such is their luck, write to him in Hebrew, for the priest's son knows the Old Testament in theory from his Bible study days. Now the time has come to put it into practice.

Will things work out?

19 Berggasse is the residence of Dr Sigmund Freud, and the most famous address in Vienna even during his lifetime. His analyses have made him a rich man, he can get through up to eleven appointments a day, receiving 100 Kronen for each one: as much as his servants earn in a whole month. Alma Mahler will resent him for the rest of her days, ever since he wrote to the executor of Gustav Mahler's will trying to collect payment for a stroll he and the late composer had once taken together. By 1913 his reputation is legendary, his research into dreams and sexuality common knowledge; when Schnitzler and Kafka jot down their dreams, they are always accompanied by the question of what Dr Freud would make of them. The focus of his research was sexuality, repressed not only by others, but also, according to the state of his research that day in 1913, by himself. After his wife had borne him six children, he apparently chose to abstain from sex. There are no known affairs; the only cause for speculation was his unexplained relationship with Minna Bernays, the sister-in-law, who lived with the couple, but nothing is known for certain.

It was a cause of great amusement to Freud that the Viennese began to take his research into the suppressed and unconscious seriously at the very time when he was appointed Professor. 'Congratulatory messages and bouquets of flowers are raining down now, as if the role of sexuality had suddenly been given the official seal of approval by His Majesty, as though the meaning of dreams had been confirmed by the Council of Ministers.'

Dr Freud and Dr Schnitzler seemed like Siamese twins even to their contemporaries: *The Interpretation of Dreams* here, the *Dream Novella*

there; the Oedipus complex here, *Frau Beate and her Son* there. But precisely because there were so many similarities between them, they politely avoided each other's company. Once, Freud roused himself to write to Schnitzler about his timidity at the prospect of meeting him, a 'kind of *Doppelgänger* anxiety'. He had received the impression, from his reading of Schnitzler's stories and plays, that 'you know through intuition – although really as a result of your keen self-awareness – all that I have uncovered through painstaking work with other people.' But even this confession was not to change things. Like two similarly charged magnets, they couldn't get too close to one another. Both approached the issue with humour. When the son of an industrialist was brought into Dr Schnitzler's clinic in 1913, drenched in blood after having his penis bitten by a pony, the doctor ordered: 'Take the patient to the emergency clinic straight away – and the pony to Professor Freud.'

The big Berlin cigarette company Problem advertised all over Berlin, on its buses and cabs, promoting a brand of cigarettes bearing the name Moslem. So anyone walking across Potsdamer Platz or down the Ku-damm could see the words, spelt out in large letters: 'Moslem. Problem Cigarettes.'

Heinrich Mann is now living in Munich with Mimi Kanova, a woman whom he met – quite fittingly – during the Berlin rehearsals of his play *The Great Love* in 1912. She is a little on the fat side. He calls her 'Pummi'. She writes to him to say that if he can find her more work at the theatre she will 'care for him like a baby'. He clearly found that to be an attractive prospect. Everyone else turns up their noses at the vulgar woman and their low-class relationship (including, of course, his brother Thomas, who always purses his lips whenever Heinrich acts in too aggressively heterosexual a manner). Heinrich, whose pointy beard and softly drooping eyelids make him look like a Spanish aristocrat, contentedly spends his days with his Mimi at 49 Leopoldstrasse in Munich and writes.

When Heinrich's forty-second birthday approaches, Thomas invites his brother and his wife over for an intimate dinner. Other than that, he spends most of his time working on his big book *Man of Straw*. He is disciplined, filling page after page of his small, square notebooks with delicate handwriting. His merciless analysis of German society under Kaiser Wilhelm II is almost finished. Now and then he sketches nudes, mostly stout women in risqué poses, rather reminiscent of George Grosz's brothel sketches. Later, after his death, they will be found in the bottom drawer of his writing desk.

Heinrich Mann negotiates with different journals about an advance publication of *Man of Straw* and strikes a deal with the Munich magazine *Zeit im Bild*. Publication is set to begin on 1 November 1913. In exchange for a payment of 10,000 Reichmarks, Mann consents to 'undertake the deletion of sections of an overly erotic nature' where necessary. Fair enough, Mann may have thought to himself, in this case it's more a question of 'scenes of an overly socially critical nature'. The idea had come to him a few years before, in a café on Unter den Linden in Berlin, when he witnessed the sight of crowds of bourgeois pressing curiously up against the windowpanes to see the Kaiser pass by. 'The old inhumane Prussian military spirit has been joined here by the machine-like, massive scale of the metropolis,' wrote Mann, 'and the result is the lowering of human dignity below every known measure.' Mann quickly comes up with the idea for a paper factory which prints nothing but postcards glorifying the Kaiser; he engages in thorough research, travels to paper mills and printworks, makes fastidious notes, talks with the workers, acting like a reporter. Richard Wagner – particularly his vexingly narcotic effect on the spirit of protest – is such a puzzle to him that, for the first time, and in the interests of research, he goes to see *Lohengrin*. So while his brother is preoccupied with *Royal Highness* and the con-man Felix Krull, Heinrich Mann is in search of German subservience – and establishes with horror that it is, in fact, everywhere. He has a judge explain the legal implications of the crime of 'Offence against the Sovereign' to him in minute detail. But that is precisely what it will be, his book *Man of Straw*: an insult to His Majesty, to the German bourgeois spirit.

❧

Hermann Hesse is living very unhappily in Bern with his wife, Maria. He, together with Theodor Heuss (yes, the future President of the Federal Republic), becomes involved with the journal *März,* but the situation at home is taking its toll on both him and his writing. Not even the move from Lake Constance, where they were attempting to live a healthy, vegetarian life, to the peaceful capital of Switzerland, his wife's home, helps their relationship. They have three children: Martin, the youngest, has just turned two, but the bond between his parents has worn thin. And so Hesse reaches for the medicine that only writers can prescribe themselves for difficulties of the heart: fictionalisation. He squabbles with his wife in the parlour, then goes into his office, puts a new ribbon into his beloved typewriter and writes down the row as dialogue. And so *Rosshalde* comes into being in 1913, and is published that same year in *Velhagens & Klasings Monatshefte*. The main character, Johannes Veraguth, relives all of Hesse's suffering, all of his raptures, and of course it ends in disillusionment. The wife in the novel is named Adele, and she is as stubborn and embittered as Maria. He openly takes as his subject not only the failure of his marriage but also, fundamentally, the impossibility of retaining a sense of yourself as an artist within a marriage and within society. The law student Kurt Tucholsky, twenty-three years young, who has been working for the magazine *Schaubühne* (later *Weltbühne*) since January 1913, writes very shrewdly of *Rosshalde*: 'If the name Hesse did not appear on the title-page, there would be no way of knowing that he had written it. This is not the dear, good old Hesse we know: this is someone different.' Furthermore, Tucholsky immediately sees through the feeble boundaries between fiction and reality: 'Hesse is like Veraguth: he has abandoned the heaven of marriage – but where will he go now?' Good question.

Not everything goes according to plan in 1913, of course. Preparations have been under way for a touring exhibition, opening in Frankfurt, which is to unite the work of the Berlin Expressionist and Secessionist artists with that of the Blaue Reiter. But to their surprise, the Blaue Reiter in Upper Bavaria soon find their pictures sent back to them from Berlin. Aggrieved, Franz Marc writes a letter from Sindelsdorf, with the seal of the Blaue Reiter on the letterhead, to Georg Tappert, the Chairman of the New Secession in Berlin:

> While unpacking my crate of paintings, I was greatly frustrated to see that the *Deer* was among them, despite the fact that I had stipulated it be included in the tour (Frankfurt in April). Then Kandinsky writes to me today saying that, to his immense surprise, his Berlin paintings have been returned to him in Munich. How should we respond to this? Logic would imply that the tour has come to nothing. But how can you simply send the pictures back to us out of the blue, without even speaking to us about it first?

It isn't all over yet. In autumn the unique summit meeting of the two poles of German Expressionism will take place after all.

It's too hot for Rainer Maria Rilke, even in early February. He has flown south in search of the sun. But now, lying on a garden lounger at the Hotel Reina Victoria in Ronda, in his white summer suit, he longs for the cool North. If he didn't, he wouldn't be Rilke. His ability to understand women, to be at one with nature and connect with others is so strong that he even suffers along with the towns themselves when they are 'worn out from the relentless summer'. That's probably why only someone like Rilke would sense the destructive force to come in the year's first warm beams of sunlight. And so he complains in letters to his mother and faraway soulmates that spring doesn't suit him: 'The sun is too strong; at seven in the morning it's quite clearly February, but by eleven one could easily believe it to be August.' She would surely understand, he writes to Sidonie Nádherný, that it is simply 'unbearable' when the sun beats down like that. On 19 February he hurriedly departs. At the end of the month he moves into his new apartment in Paris, in the Rue Champagne-Première. After eighteen months on the run from himself across half of Europe, he arrives in the metropolis as it shimmers with early spring. He is afraid of arriving. But he wants to try one more time, here, in this Paris, in this place. But he can't remember how you do those things: sitting, working, staying calm. Living.

In the spring of 1913 Charles Fabry successfully concludes a series of experiments culminating in the discovery of the ozone layer. It is still fully intact.

Vienna is only a day's train ride away from the Austrian Crown land of Galicia, and that's why it has become the most popular political exile for refugee revolutionaries from Russia. In the Döblinger Rodlergasse, for example, the writer and journalist Leo Bronstein, better known as Leo Trotsky, is working in a humble yet bourgeois atmosphere with his wife, Natalia, and their children. At Christmas the Trotskys stretch to a tree, trying to act as if they belong and never want to leave. Trotsky earns very little from his journalism for various liberal and social-democratic pamphlets, and often spends entire days sitting in the Café Central playing chess. In 1913 'Herr Bronstein' is regarded as the best chess player in the Viennese café scene, and that is saying something. Whenever he needs money, his only option is to bring some of his books to the pawnshop. He has no choice.

By the beginning of February, Stalin is back to working on *Marxism*

and the National Question, which is to become his most famous work
– and the mix of peoples in the Austro-Hungarian Empire provides
him with a vivid learning exercise. In Vienna, Stalin develops the idea
of a central empire behind feigned national autonomy – which, in the
end, amounts to the aims and objectives of the Soviet Union. Stalin,
'Sosso' to his friends, talks about nothing else, even with the Troyanovskys' children. He makes a brief attempt to flirt with the nanny,
but nothing comes of it, so he flees back to his work. And quite rightly
so; he has little time to waste on the practical application of the evils of
capitalism. On one of his walks with the mother through Schönbrunn
Park, he bets her that Galina, the temperamental daughter, will run
to him if they both call out to her (based on the belief that she'll be
hoping he's bought sweets for her again). He turns out to be right.

Two men visit him during his stay in the Troyanovsky residence.
To Stalin's delight Nikolai Bukharin helps him with translations, but,
unlike Stalin, Bukharin proves to be successful with the nanny, for
which the former will never forgive him (and for which Bukharin
will one day have to pay with a bullet in the head). Even Trotsky
drops by once: 'I was sitting next to the samovar at the table in Sko-
below's apartment [...] in the old Habsburg capital,' writes Trotsky,
'when, after a brief knock, the door suddenly opened and a stranger
walked in. He was short [...] thin [...] pock marks covered his grey-
brownish skin [...] I couldn't see even the slightest trace of friendli-
ness in his eyes.' It was Stalin. He fetched himself a cup of tea from
the samovar and went out as quietly as he had come in. He didn't
recognise Trotsky – luckily, for in one of his articles he had already
labelled him a 'gimmicky athlete with fake muscles'.

In that same February of 1913, as Stalin and Trotsky see each other
for the first time, a man is born in faraway Barcelona who will later
murder Trotsky, on Stalin's orders. His name is Jaime Ramón Mer-
cader del Río Hernández.

On 23 February, Josef Stalin is arrested on the street in St Petersburg. Dressed in women's clothes and a wig, he is running for his life. His attire has nothing to do with carnival fancy dress or any special predilection for women's clothing. The revolutionary is in Russia illegally, and has stolen the clothes from the wardrobe of a musical benefit performance for *Pravda* which was raided by police. They apprehend the limping fugitive and rip the gaudy summer dress and wig from his person, revealing Stalin. He is recognised and exiled to Turukhansk in Siberia.

In turbulent Vienna there is an affair that stuns even the Viennese. Alma Mahler, the most beautiful girl in Vienna, with a legendary waist and a generous bosom, newly widowed after the death of the great composer and still dressed in mourning, falls for Oskar Kokoschka, the ugliest painter in Vienna, a brash provocateur who walks around with his trousers hanging low or his shirt unbuttoned, and whose most famous painting is entitled *Murderer, Hope of Womankind* – he means every word. But almost as soon as he captures the beautiful young widow's heart, he gets scared. Not of her – but of his potential love rivals: 'Almi, I don't like it when other people can see your bare breasts, whether in night-dress or frock. Cover up the secrets, my secrets, of your beloved body.' Hardly anything in the Vienna of 1913 was as unabashedly sexual as the letters and affair between Kokoschka and Alma Mahler – by day Alma was able to pursue her social life as the city's First Widow, holding receptions and salons in her apartment. But by night Kokoschka asserted his rights. He could only work if he could sleep with her every night, he told her, and she becomes obsessed with his obsession. The day when she is supposed to sit for him, in the house belonging to the Mools, her parents-in-law, she drags him into the neighbouring room and sings a heartbreaking rendition of Isolde's *Liebestod*. She throws herself into the affair with operatic totality. Kokoschka is no longer able to paint anything but her. Mostly naked, her hair cascading wantonly over her shoulders, blouse open, he paints her as wildly and violently as he loves her. Impatient that it's taking too long, he throws away his paintbrush and paints with his fingers instead, using the palm of his left hand as a palette and scratching lines into the mounts of colour with his fingernails. Life, love, art: all one great battle.

When Kokoschka isn't painting Alma alone, he is painting Alma and himself: for example, the *Double Portrait of Oskar Kokoschka and Alma*. He calls it the 'Engagement Picture'. He wants to marry her, hoping to capture her for ever. But Alma is cunning. She can only marry him, she explains, once he creates an absolute masterpiece. Kokoschka hopes that this engagement picture will be his masterpiece. By the end of February he is almost finished, and Alma is restless. He pleads with her: 'Please write me a long letter, my love, so I don't regress and lose time on the painting.' But Alma has just aborted their child, and is angered by the bump on her belly in Kokoschka's painting. The picture shows the two of them strangely entangled – Kokoschka's gaze is full of suffering, Alma's calm and composed. She travels with her mother to Semmering and looks for a plot of land on the estates Gustav Mahler once bought for the two of them. Now she is planning a love nest with his successor. Once the 'Engagement Picture' is ready, Kokoschka sends it to Berlin, to the Secession. It is, of course, what he hoped it would be: a public engagement notice. Upon seeing the picture in Berlin, Walter Gropius breaks down. The great architect, whose Fagus Factory was under construction at the time, had also hoped to marry Alma. The picture has achieved its desired impact. (But, between ourselves, it is he who will marry Alma in the end, not Kokoschka.)

Albert Schweitzer is in Strasbourg, working on his third doctorate. He has already been a D.Phil. for some time, ever since completing his philosophical dissertation 'The Religious Philosophy of Kant from the *Critique of Pure Reason* to *Religion within the Boundaries of Mere Reason*'. He's a doctor of theology too: 'The Problem of the Last Supper: A Study Based on the Scientific Research of the Nineteenth Century and the Historical Accounts'. After becoming a lecturer in theology in Strasbourg and even vicar of the Church of St Nikolai, he decided to become a doctor of medicine as well, receiving his licence to practice in 1912. But the Doctor and Vicar and Lecturer and D.Phil. and Lic.Theol. aren't enough. His doctoral thesis 'The Psychiatric Study of Jesus' has yet to be completed. With the burden of threefold roles tiring him out, the secondary literature threatens to defeat him. To make sure he doesn't fall asleep while reading, he develops the habit of putting a bucket of cold water under his desk. When he can't follow the explanations in the books any more, he takes off his socks, puts his feet in cold water, then goes on reading. He's almost finished now. And he has his next great goal in sight: Africa.

MARCH

In March, Kafka actually goes to Berlin to see Felice Bauer, and they try to go for a walk together, but it doesn't work. Robert Musil consults a neurologist and is allowed to go home, Camille Claudel goes into a clinic for nervous diseases and has to stay there for thirty years. And in Vienna, on 31 March, the great 'ear-boxing concert' takes place: Arnold Schönberg receives a public box on the ear for making excessively shrill noises. Albert Schweitzer and Ernst Jünger dream of Africa. In Cambridge, Ludwig Wittgenstein launches his coming-out process and his new logic. Virginia Woolf has finished her first book, and Rainer Maria Rilke has the sniffles. The big question on everybody's lips: 'Whither are we drifting?'

The parliament of the German Reich authorises Prussia to mint 12 million Marks as commemorative coins in 1913. They are to commemorate Prussia's revolt against the French occupation in 1813 as well as the twenty-five-year Jubilee of the German Kaiser Wilhelm II on 15 June.

❧

'A war between Austria and Russia', Lenin wrote to Maxim Gorky in 1913, 'would be very useful to the revolution in Western Europe. But it is hard to imagine Franz-Joseph and Nicholas doing us this favour.'

❧

Albert Einstein, the great theorist of relativity, reveals himself to have a keen practical sense. In 1913, living in Prague, he is becoming increasingly remote from his wife, Mileva. He stops telling her about his research, his discoveries, his concerns. And she says nothing and puts up with it. They are getting on just as badly as Hermann Hesse and his wife in Bern and Arthur Schnitzler and his wife in Vienna, to name but two other couples. Anyway, in the evening Einstein goes to coffee houses or bars all by himself and drinks a beer – Max Brod, Franz Werfel and Kafka might be sitting at the next table, but they don't know each other. And then, in March 1913 – just like Kafka – Albert Einstein writes long letters to Berlin. On a visit to the city he has fallen in love with his recently divorced cousin Elsa. He writes her terrible things about his marriage: he and Mileva no longer sleep in the same room, he avoids being alone with her under all circumstances, she is an 'unfriendly, humourless creature', and he treats her like an employee whom regrettably he is unable to fire. Then he puts the letter in an envelope and off he goes to the post office – and so Einstein and Kafka's epistolary laments travel, presumably in the same postbag from Prague to Berlin, to the far-off girls of their dreams, Felice and Elsa.

In New York the Federal Reserve, the 'Fed', is founded. The most important shareholders are the banking houses Rothschild, Lazard, Warburg, Lehmann, Rockefellers Chase Manhattan and Goldman Sachs. The introduction of the Fed ensures that American governments are no longer able to print new money. In 1913, on the other hand, income tax is introduced.

The industrialist Walther Rathenau far-sightedly recognises the economic challenge represented by the USA. And in 1913, the year of the arms race, he sketches the picture of a peaceful European union with close European ties: 'One last possibility remains: the emergence of a Central European Tariff Union. The task of creating the freedom of economic movement for the countries in our European zone is difficult but not insoluble.'

In the *Cambridge Review*, vol. 34, no. 853 (6 March 1913), p. 351, the first publication by the student Ludwig Wittgenstein appears: a critical review of Peter Coffey's *The Science of Logic*, but in fact the first manifesto of Wittgenstein's very own logic. He considers what Coffey says to be illogical. The Viennese industrialist's son, about to turn twenty-four, is also spiky with his teacher at Trinity College, Cambridge, the legendary Bertrand Russell. During the holidays he travels with his lover, the maths student David Pinsent, to Norway, where they have bought a little cabin in Skjolden, and works on the foundations of his theory which, when published as the *Tractatus Logico-Philosophicus* will be among the most important texts of the century. (It is, incidentally, so complex that Russell, when he receives a letter asking him to copy-edit the book, asks to have his own questions sent back to him so that he can understand Wittgenstein's answers.) Only Pinsent understands Wittgenstein completely. When Wittgenstein, two years his senior, was looking for a guinea pig for his psychological experiments into language and music, Pinsent had answered the advertisement. He soon became his guinea pig in matters of homosexuality and logic too. Wittgenstein will, logically enough, dedicate his *Tractatus* to Pinsent.

Spring Awakening: on 8 March, in Vienna's Café Imperial, Frank Wedekind, Adolf Loos, Franz Werfel and Karl Kraus meet for an early coffee.

Kafka's father is making him suffer like a dog, and he can't bear it when someone coughs in the Prague flat next door or slams the door. He doesn't write his 'Letter to His Father' quite yet. But in 1913 Egon Schiele, the 22-year-old Viennese painter, writes his 'Letters to the Mother'. On 31 March, for example: 'I will be the fruit which, once corrupted, will leave behind eternal living creatures, so how delighted must you be to have brought me into the world?' His mother has a different view of things. She is furious that the grave of her husband, Schiele's father, is becoming overgrown, and writes to him: 'That wretched and neglected grave contains the bones of your father, who sweated blood for you. How much money are you squandering? You have time for everything and everyone, just not for your poor mother! God may forgive you, but I cannot.'

Schiele's father, Adolf, had suffered from early dementia, and little Egon always had to set a place at the table for an unknown person.

Just before his death, the father burned all his money and shares, and since then the family have lived in poverty. Egon's relationship with his sisters Melanie and Gerti is unusually close: he repeatedly draws them naked, takes a gynaecological interest in their bodies as they awaken into puberty. As an adolescent he goes on trips with Gerti, without their mother, and the pictures from their relationship look like the illustrations of the fatal love of the poet Georg Trakl for his sister at the same time.

Gerti then steps out with Egon's friend Anton Peschka, which makes Schiele furiously jealous, but he eventually gives the relationship his blessing when he himself meets Wally, the woman his drawings turned into one of the most familiar bodies of the twentieth century. Yet even though he drew himself and his family stark naked as if working not with a pen but a scalpel – unlike Gustav Klimt, Schiele clearly didn't always go to bed with his models – he gained his glimpses of the depths of physicality only from passive observation. Hardly anyone understood that at the time. Even his dealer, the open-minded Hans Goltz from Munich, writes to him in March 1913, after yet another exhibition at which he hasn't sold a single painting: 'But Herr Schiele, while I am always delighted by your drawings, and while I am happy to go along with your weirdest moods, who is supposed to sell the paintings? I can see very little opportunity for that.' This letter was the first that he received in his new apartment, the one that was to make everything better. No longer the 9th District, no longer 5 Schlagergasse, ground floor, door 4, but, at long last, the 13th District, 101 Hietzinger Hauptstrasse, 3rd floor.

Egon Schiele's mother saw everything exactly as his dealer did – those 'strange moods' could have come from one of her letters. She accuses her son not only of moral neglect but also of ignoring his father's legacy, of failing to pay for his grave and forgetting about her. She writes to Egon again. This prompts the second 'Letter to his Mother', which could find its way into any psychoanalytic textbook: 'Dear Mother Schiele, why all these letters, which end up in the stove anyway? Next time you need anything, come to me, I'm never coming back, Egon.'

The year of parricide, 1913, was also a challenge to mothers. Or, as Georg Trakl writes to his friend Erhard Buschbeck: 'Write and tell me, my dear fellow, whether I am a great source of concern to my mother.' (Trakl had, in fact, just sold his father's bracelet to pay for his brothel visits.) Not bad.

Gustav Klimt, on the other hand, is still living with his mother at the age of fifty-one. After breakfast he goes off to 11 Feldmühlgasse in the 13th District. (Schiele's studio is only four blocks away.) He paints there and he lives there, he has written 'G.K.' on the door in chalk, along with the words 'Knock loudly'. There are sketches scattered over the floor, and several canvases on easels. When he arrives in the morning, the women who long to undress for him are already waiting by the door. As he stands in silence at his canvas, half a dozen naked women or girls are walking about, stretching, lazing around, waiting until he summons them with a little wave of his hand. He wears nothing under his apron, so that he can take it off quickly when desire overwhelms him and the pose of one of his models becomes too seductive for the man inside the painter. But he's home with Mum on the dot for dinnertime, or else he goes to the theatre with Emilie Flöge. When Klimt dies, fourteen former models will come forward with paternity suits.

In the spring of 1913 Georg Trakl is in a pretty odd way. He's drifting through the world, he's only 'half born', he admits to a friend. So he drinks his money away, takes Veronal and other tablets and drugs, drinks again, dashes around, screams like a child, falls in love with his sister and hates himself for it as much as he hates the rest of the world. He tries to be a chemist. Nothing comes of it. He tries to live normally. Nothing comes of that either, of course. But in between he writes the most beautiful, terrifying poems. And letters like this: 'I long for the day when the soul will no longer wish, no longer be able to dwell in this ill-omened, gloom-plagued body, when it will abandon this figure of mockery, of filth and foulness, nothing but an all too true reflection of a godless, cursed century.' This is a letter to Ludwig von Ficker, his patron, father-substitute, even his friend, if one can use such a word about Trakl. His publisher, too, because *Der Brenner*, his magazine, will be the first place in which Trakl's desperate litanies appear. This year he wanders aimlessly and hopelessly between three places: Salzburg is the 'rotted city', Innsbruck the 'most brutal, vulgar city' and Vienna, finally, 'the city of filth'. He can't sit in the train, because it would mean having someone directly opposite, facing him, and he can't bear that. So he always stands in the corridor, his expression shy and hunted. If someone looks at him, he sweats so much he has to change his shirt.

But then, in March 1913, he suddenly receives a letter from Leipzig, from the Kurt Wolff Verlag. They would like to publish a volume of his poems in their new series, 'Der jüngste Tag' ('The Day of Reckoning'). Will things turn out for the best after all?

Rainer Maria Rilke has the sniffles.

On 9 March the profoundly depressive 32-year-old Virginia Woolf sends the manuscript of her first novel, *The Voyage Out*, to her publishers. She has worked on it for six years. It also happens to be the day when her future lover Vita Sackville-West comes of age, having reached twenty-one. But for now Virginia Woolf is trapped in some very old spiders' webs. The publisher to whom Virginia Woolf sends her manuscript is her half-brother Gerald Duckworth. Together with his brother George, as we know now from secret diary entries, he clearly threatened or abused her as a child.

The Voyage Out, the novel about the unmarried, childless Rachel

Vinrace, already contains many of the central elements of Virginia Woolf's later major works. There is an appearance by one 'Mrs Dalloway', for example, who will later achieve independence as the heroine of a novel, and Rachel also has a 'room of her own', the title of an important later essay. In *The Voyage Out* Woolf has her male protagonist give a startling account of the situation in 1913:

> Just consider: it's the beginning of the twentieth century, and until a few years ago no woman had come out by herself and said things at all. There it was going on in the background, for all those thousands of years, this curious, silent, unrepresented life. Of course we're always writing about them, abusing them, or jeering at them, or worshipping them; but it's never come from women themselves.

But that 'silent, unrepresented life' went on. Barely fifty copies of the book were sold in 1913, and by 1929 it was only 479. *The Voyage Out* was a difficult journey for Virginia Woolf.

Franz Marc wants to illustrate the Bible with some artist friends. In March 1913 he writes to Wassily Kandinsky, Paul Klee, Erich Heckel and Oskar Kokoschka. He himself – and this can hardly come as a surprise – chooses the Creation story and creates new animals every day, blue horses that have no need of blue riders.

Terrible things are happening in Prague. On 16 March Franz Kafka actually writes to Felice: 'A direct question, Felice: would you have an hour free for me any time at Easter, on Sunday or Monday, and if you did, would you think it a good thing if I came? I repeat, an hour at any time, I would do nothing in Berlin but wait for you.' Felice immediately says yes. And as the post is quicker in 1913 than in 2013, on 17 March Kafka already writes, as expected: 'I don't know if I'll be able to come.' Then on 18 March: '*Essentially* the obstacle to my journey still exists and will, I fear, continue to exist as an *obstacle*, but it has lost its significance so, as far as that goes, I could come.' Then, on 19 March: 'If I were to be prevented from travelling after all, I would send you a telegram by Saturday at the latest.' On 21 March the uncertainty is cemented: 'Felice! It's still by no means certain whether I'll be coming; the decision won't be made until tomorrow, the millers' convention still hangs over our heads.' Supposedly, and this is his marvellous excuse, at Easter he might be sent by his insurance company to the convention of the Czech Millers' Association. Then new worries – and also, as with Musil, symptoms of neurasthenia: 'But I must have a good sleep before I see you. I have slept so badly this week, much of my neurasthenia and many of my white hairs come from insufficient sleep. As long as I have slept properly when I meet up with you!' Then, on 22 March, the day he is supposed to set off (and will, in fact, set off), he writes these big words on his envelope to Felice: 'Still undecided. Franz.' Three words, an autobiography.

Hard to believe, but the next letter from Franz Kafka to Felice Bauer really does bear the letterhead of the hotel 'Askanische Hof, Berlin', from where he writes in a panic on the morning of Easter Sunday:

> What's happened, Felice? You must have received my express letter on Friday, in which I indicated that I was coming on Saturday night. Surely that letter of all letters can't have gone missing. And now I'm in Berlin, I have to leave at about four or five in the afternoon, the hours pass and I hear nothing from you. Please send me an answer through the boy. If you can do it inconspicuously, you can also phone me for safety's sake, I'll sit in the Askanische Hof and wait. Franz.

He had arrived at Anhalt Station late on Easter Eve, probably hoping to see her on the platform so that they could celebrate their resurrection together. But she didn't come. He paced uneasily back and forth along the platforms. Then sat in the waiting room so that he wouldn't miss her. Then, after endless minutes of waiting, he leaves for his hotel. Can't sleep. As soon as day dawns, he leaps up and shaves. Still no sign of Felice.

It's Easter Sunday in Berlin. Franz Kafka is sitting in his hotel room, gloomy weather outside, he kneads his hands, stares at the door in the hope that a messenger may come, and stares out of the window, in the hope that an angel might.

Then, eventually, she must have called. She has strong nerves. They drive out into the Grunewald. Sit side by side on a tree trunk. That's all we know. It's a strange gap in this double life – after seeing every breath and every day reflected in two to four letters, now all of a sudden: nothing.

On 26 March Kafka writes to her from Prague: 'Do you know that since I got back you have been more of an incomprehensible miracle than ever?' That's all we know about that Sunday in Berlin. An Easter miracle, at any rate.

That's Kafka's life in that March of 1913. But there is also the 'work'. So a letter arrives from Leipzig, from Kurt Wolff, who is at the centre of all German-language literature that spring: 'Herr Franz Werfel has told me so much about your new novella – is it called *The Bug*? – that I would like to meet you. Will you send it to me?' The most famous German short story of the twentieth century, called *The Bug*? One morning when Gregor Samsa awoke from troubled dreams he found himself turned into a bug? Of course not. So Kafka writes to Wolff: 'Don't believe Werfel! He doesn't know a word of the story. Once I've had it written up in a presentable version, of course I would be delighted to send it to you.' And then: 'The next story I have, *The Metamorphosis*, has not yet been copied out.' And that was how *The Metamorphosis* came into the world.

Robert Musil lives with his wife in the 3rd District of Vienna, at 61 Untere Weissgerberstrasse. He is a man with many qualities. He is neatly turned out, fit, his shoes are the shiniest in all the coffee houses of Vienna, and for an hour every day he does sit-ups and knee-bends. He is incredibly vain. But he emanates the quiet power of self-discipline. In a special little notebook he records every single cigarette he smokes, every time he sleeps with his wife he puts a 'C' in his diary, for 'coitus'. Order is all.

But in March 1913 he's had enough. He can bear his dull job as Librarian, Second Class, at Vienna's Technical University no longer. He feels small and weak, and at the same time called to higher things, to a novel of the century. But he is not certain that this isn't just a sign that he's going slowly but surely round the bend. Or whether he should quit his job.

At last, on 30 March, he gets an appointment with the neurologist Dr Otto Pötzl. He waits for two hours. Then the first thing he does is give the doctor a copy of his first book, *The Confusions of Young Törless*. He inscribes it 'To Dr Pötzl, with fond memories'. In the days of his increasing suffering he is consoled by the memory of the times of Dante. He writes in his diary: 'But what is considered mental illness in 1913 might have been mere eccentricity in 1300.' But what would the doctor say? Today they would call it 'burn-out'; in those days they said, 'He's suffering from the manifestations of a serious cardiac neurosis: attacks of pounding heart with a racing pulse, palpitations when falling asleep, disturbances of the digestion with the related psychical phenomena: a depressive state and with high levels of physical and psychical fatigability.' In 1913 this was summed up under the heading of 'neurasthenia'. People mocked, but in the official world of the imperial–royal monarchy the word was immediate grounds for leave of absence. So, at the request of the library, one Dr Blanka writes an 'official medical report': 'Herr Dr. Phil. Ing. Robert Musil Kk. Bibliothekar Wien III unt. Weissgerberstrasse 61 reveals considerable symptoms of neurasthenia, in consequence of which he is incapable of working.'

At the same time as Musil's leave is granted, Franz Blei writes to the Kurt Wolff Verlag in Leipzig and tells them about the great, 'splendid' novel that Robert Musil was working on. If he had a 'library-less summer', it would soon be completed.

🐚

Who am I, and if so how many? In 1913 Otto Dix paints his *Small Self-Portrait*, his *Self-Portrait,* the painting *Heads (Self-Portraits)*, then the *Self-Portrait with Gladioli* and, of course, the *Self-Portrait as Smoker*. Max Beckmann, the great self-portraitist, writes in his diary in 1913: 'How sad and unpleasant always having to spend time with oneself. Sometimes one would be glad to be free of oneself.'

🐚

For Picasso, as always when a new lover came along, life and art have been transformed completely. In this case it was a particularly lovely story: the great odalisque, the sultry beauty Fernande Olivier, lascivious by profession, cheated on Picasso with the young painter Ubaldo Oppi and got her friend Marcelle Humbert involved, one of the most unpopular women in Montmartre. Marcelle was more than happy to distract Picasso during Fernande's rendezvous, because she herself had long been smitten with Picasso. And before he chose her as his new paramour, he gave her a new name: Eva. Above all, he didn't want his girlfriend to have exactly the same name as the lover of his friend, and increasingly his competitor, Braque. So for Picasso, Eva became the symbol of his rejection of the first phase of Cubism and a move to Synthetic Cubism. In his early thirties he seems to have seen in Eva the opportunity to become bourgeois, to get away, at least a little, from the bohemianism that was keeping him from working. And so they both move from Montmartre to Montparnasse, where the new Line 12 of the Paris Métro happened to go. While Montmartre remained the place for the penurious artists, the opium smokers, the prostitutes and the seedy *varieties*, Montparnasse was becoming the new haunt of the successful players in the Paris creative industry.

In the words of the great impresario Apollinaire, 'In Montparnasse, on the other hand, you find the real artists, dressed in the American style. Some of them might dip their noses in cocaine, but no matter.'

In 1912 the 31-year-old Picasso and Eva moved into an apartment and a studio in a complex that was barely ten years old, at 242 Boulevard Raspail. Then, in January 1913, Picasso even introduced his new girlfriend to his father in Barcelona. Don José, formerly a stern paterfamilias, clearly had nothing against either Eva or against Pablo's Synthetic Cubism – but that may have had something to do with the fact that he was by now entirely blind. When Picasso and Eva met, they had escaped to Céret, in the Pyrenees. And now, on 10 March 1913, they did it again. Picasso wanted to flee the city and its art scene so he could finally get some work done. They took a deep breath when they reached the mountain town, sat down at a pavement café and enjoyed a cup of coffee as the spring sun began to glow. They immediately rented the Maison Delcros and prepared to stay there till autumn. Two days later he sends two cheerful postcards to his most important patrons: his art dealer Kahnweiler, with whom he had signed a lucrative exclusive contract in December 1912, which means that for the first time he is earning proper money (and can buy lots of pretty blouses for Eva). And he writes to Gertrude Stein, the salon hostess and great art collector, who had done a lot of work in the background to ensure that Picasso was shown in the Armory Show in February. The postcard to Gertrude Stein, who is trying to throw her brother Leo out of the flat they share, and who is now living with her friend Alice Toklas, shows three Catalan farmers – in a handwritten caption Picasso identifies the one with the beard as 'portrait of Matisse'.

Soon Picasso's good mood evaporates, because his father's health is deteriorating. He hurries to Barcelona, before going on to bury himself away in his studio in Céret again. He is happy when his slovenly friend Max Jacob comes from Paris. Max writes to friends in the city: 'I would like to change my life, I'm going to Céret to spend a few months with Picasso.' But as the painter spends most of his time sitting in his studio stubbornly working away on new possibilities for his *papiers collés*, the collages of Synthetic Cubism, Max Jacob spends most of his time with Eva. As it rains incessantly, they sit inside and sip cocoa and wait until the Master has finished his day's work. In the evening they drink wine together; at night the damp air is filled with frogs and toads and nightingales.

But Picasso's thoughts are with his sick father, the father of fathers, who taught him to draw, whom he loves and whom he hates. When he was sixteen, he had said, 'In art you must kill your father.' And now the time has come. Don José dies, and Picasso is paralysed with grief. But that's not the last of it: that spring Eva falls seriously ill. She has cancer. And then, when his greatest comforter falls ill too, it's the final straw: Frika, his beloved dog, to whom he has paid just as much devoted attention as to his wives (perhaps even more), is on her deathbed. Since Picasso's first days in Paris, Frika, that curious mixture of Alsatian and Breton spaniel, had always been by his side, had lived through many wives and the Blue and Rose and Cubist periods. On 14 May Eva writes to Gertrude Stein: 'Frika can no longer be saved.' No vet can help now, so Picasso asks the local huntsman-in-chief to deal Frika the *coup de grâce*. As long as he lives, Picasso will never forget the name of the huntsman, 'El Ruquetó' – nor how he wept during those days. Father dead, dog dead, beloved terminally ill, incessant rain outside. In the spring of 1913, in Céret, Picasso is having his greatest spiritual crisis.

On 22 March Dr Gottfried Benn receives a welcome piece of news: 'Dr Benn, assistant physician with the Infantry Regiment General Field Marshall Prince Friedrich Karl von Preussen No. 64, is being transferred at his own request to the medical officers of Landwehr Division 1.' Then he switches from the institute of pathology and anatomy of the Westend Hospital to the City Hospital Charlottenburg.

On 29 March Karl Kraus delivers a lecture in the Vierjahreszeiten-Saal in Munich. Among the audience is Heinrich Mann. Warm applause.

On 4 March there is a big dinner at the German Embassy in London. Among those present is, of course, Harry Graf Kessler, that German snob in the white three-piece suit whose address book has 10,000 entries, friend of Henry van de Velde, Edvard Munch and Aristide Maillol, who founded the Cranach Press in Weimar and had to clear his desk as museum director there over some supposedly salacious Rodin watercolours. That same Graf Kessler who commutes between Paris, Weimar, Brussels, London and Munich as one of the great catalysts of modern art and Art Nouveau. It is through him that we become a little better acquainted with the queen of England. At this particular reception he had just introduced the German ambassador, Von Lichnowsky (whose artistically minded, Picasso-collecting, wife liked him), to George Bernard Shaw. Now, at this dinner, she pays him back: Kessler is introduced to the English queen. 'She looked reasonably good, in silver brocade with a crown of diamonds and big turquoise stones.' Otherwise she was rather a trial: 'I couldn't leave her standing on her own, and she couldn't find a way out of the conversation, and you have to keep winding the poor thing up like a run-down watch, but that only works for thirty seconds at a time.' Incidentally, as he confides to his diary, there is no threat of war, or so he has heard: 'The European situation has been completely reversed for a year and a half. The Russians and the French are forced to be peaceful, as they can no longer rely on England's support.' Well, then.

Thomas Mann writes a letter to Jakob Wassermann in March 1913: 'The encounter between negligence and obsessive devotion to duty in wartime is a profoundly poetic invention. And how greatly and severely war is felt as a crisis of moral cleansing, as a grandiose stride

of life's seriousness beyond all sentimental confusions!' The war
Thomas Mann is talking about is the one of 1870–71.

⤜⤛

Now let us switch to Arnold Schönberg, that great charismatic figure
who composed along the fault-line between late Romanticism and
twelve-tone music. He had moved to Berlin because he felt misun-
derstood in Vienna. In the telephone directory it said: 'Arnold Schönberg, composer and composition teacher, consultations 1–2 p.m.' He
had an apartment in Villa Lepcke in Zehlendorf, and he wrote to a
friend in Vienna: 'You wouldn't believe how famous I am here.'

   Then at the end of March he goes to Vienna. And becomes just
as famous there as he was in Berlin. But not quite in the way he
had imagined. On the evening of 31 April, in the great hall of the
Musikverein, he is supposed to be conducting his own chamber symphony, Mahler and pieces by his pupils Alban Berg and Anton von
Webern (who both had portraits of themselves painted by Schönberg
hanging on their walls at home). And it is Alban Berg's music that
creates the greatest stir. 'Songs with Orchestra on Picture Postcard
Texts by Peter Altenberg, *op.* 4', he has called his piece in the best
Pop Art style – performed by a huge orchestra and with great solem-
nity. It rouses the audience to a fury, there is hissing and laughter
and rattling of keys, which everybody brought to Schönberg's last
performance in February but didn't need. Then Anton von Webern
leaps to his feet and shouts that the whole rabble should go home, to
which the rabble replies that people who like such music belong in
the Steinhof. The Steinhof is the mental asylum in which the poet
Peter Altenberg currently resides. The diagnosis of the public: insane
music to lyrics by a madman. (There is, it must be said, a photograph
of Altenberg with his nurse Spatzek from the Steinhof in those days,
Altenberg looking into the camera, cool and relaxed, creating the ery
powerful impression that Spatzek, the nurse, is the one who is mad.
Altenberg captions it: 'The lunatic and the asylum attendant', leaving
it unclear which is which.)

Schönberg stops the orchestra and shouts into the audience that he will have any trouble-makers removed by force, whereupon pandemonium breaks out, the conductor is challenged to a duel and one man clambers over the rows of chairs from the back. When he has reached the front, Oscar Straus, composer of the operetta *The Waltz Dream*, boxes the ear of the president of the Academic Association of Literature and Music, Arnold Schönberg.

Next day in the *Neue Freie Presse*, the following report appears:

> The fanatical devotees of Schönberg and the dedicated opponents of his often extremely alienating sound experiments have often clashed in the past. But hardly ever can we remember having witnessed, in any Viennese concert hall, such a scene as the one that occurred at this evening's concert by the Academic Association. To separate the furiously arguing groups there was no option but to turn out the lights.

Four people were arrested by the police: a student of philosophy, a physician, an engineer and a lawyer. The evening went down in history as the 'ear-boxing concert'.

But contemporaries, above all Dr Arthur Schnitzler, who attended the concert with his wife Olga, responded laconically:

> Schönberg. Orchestral concert. Terrible scandal. Alban Berg's silly songs. Interruptions. Laughter. Speech by the President. 'At least listen to Mahler in peace!' As if anyone objected to him! Intolerable – one voice in the auditorium: 'Little scamp!' The gentleman from the podium, amid breathless silence, smacks him one. All kinds of scuffling.

Life goes on. Schnitzler starts a new paragraph, and then writes: 'Supper with Vicki, Fritz Zuckerkandl and his mother in the Imperial.'

The next day Arnold Schönberg travels back to Berlin, firmly convinced now that 1913 is an unlucky year and the Viennese are unfathomable philistines. As soon as he is back in Berlin, he receives the reporter from *Die Zeit* and explains to him in a wonderfully mean-spirited and self-righteous way:

> A concert ticket only gives one the right to listen to the concert, but not to disturb the performance. The purchaser of a ticket is an invited guest who acquires the right to listen, nothing more. There is a great difference between an invitation to a salon and one to a concert. Contributing to the cost of an event does not grant one permission to behave improperly.

Herr Schönberg closes his interview with the following words for his future behaviour: 'I have undertaken henceforth to take part in such concerts only when it is expressly stated on the tickets that disturbance of the performance is not permitted. It is obvious, after all, that the organiser of a concert is not only the moral but also the material holder of a right that is granted protection in any state based on private property.' This interview is an unsettling document. The advocates of the new music are claiming an inalienable right to an undisturbed avant-garde. But even in this most unusual of years, that was asking a bit much.

At the end of the nineteenth century Camille Claudel had overwhelmed the great Auguste Rodin and created sculptures of singular beauty. She had dictated a contract to Rodin, forbidding him to have any other models but her, and obliged him to win her commissions and pay for her to have an Italian trip – and in return he could visit her four times a month in her studio. He complied. But then in 1893 she left him anyway.

From that moment things went steeply downhill for her. In 1913, twenty years later, she can think of nothing but him. She has grown fat and bloated in the meantime: unwashed, matted hair, confused expression. There is nothing now to recall the young sculptress for whom first Rodin and then Claude Debussy fell head over heels. She is living in a cluttered ground-floor flat at 19 Quai Bourbon, deludedly destroying with accurate blows of her hammer all the works she has created; she feels persecuted by her family and by Rodin and by the rest of the world. She is convinced that Rodin, whom she last saw sixteen years ago, is shamelessly plagiarising her works.

Since she is firmly convinced that everyone is trying to poison her, she eats nothing but potatoes and drinks boiled water, and the shutters are kept closed so no one can spy on her. Her brother Paul Claudel visits her and then notes concisely in his diary: 'In Paris. Camille insane, wallpaper hanging in long strips from the walls, one broken armchair, terrible dirt. She herself is fat and dirty and talks uninterruptedly in a monotonous and metallic voice.'

On 5 March, Dr Michaux issues a medical certificate that authorises Paul Claudel to have his sister committed to a closed institution. On Monday 10 March two beefy nurses break down the heavily bolted door to Camille Claudel's studio and drag the screaming woman outside. She is forty-eight. On the same day she is brought to the Ville-Évrard mental hospital, where the psychiatrist in charge, Dr Truelle, confirms the diagnosis of serious paranoia. Every day she talks about Rodin. Every day she is worried that he wants to poison her, and that the nurses are his accomplices. It will go on like this for another thirty years. As yet no doctoral thesis has been written on 'The Psychiatric Assessment of Camille Claudel'.

In March 1913 Albert Schweitzer graduates as a doctor of medicine. His thesis, 'The Psychiatric Assessment of Jesus', was unsettling but satisfactory. The next day he sells all his goods and chattels. Then on 21 March 1913 he takes his wife, Helene, and travels to Africa. In French Equatorial Africa, he founds the jungle hospital of Lambaréné, on the Ogooué.

Ernst Jünger too dreams of Africa. Under his desk at school he is constantly reading travel tales of Africa. 'I was increasingly filled with the deadly poison of boredom' – so it is clear for him that he must seek out the mysteries of Africa, the 'lost gardens' somewhere in the Upper Nile Delta or the Congo. Africa represents the epitome of all that is savage and primitive. He had to go there. But how? Let's wait and see.

It's the end of March. Marcel Proust pulls his fur over his night-shirt and goes back into the street in the middle of the night. Then he stares for two whole hours at the Saint Anne portal of the cathedral of Notre-Dame. The next morning he writes to Madame Strauss: 'For eight centuries on that portal a much more charming humanity has been assembled than the one with which we rub shoulders.' This is what is known, logically enough, as being In Search of Lost Time.

APRIL

On 20 April, Hitler celebrates his twenty-fourth birthday in a men's boarding house on Meldemannstrasse in Vienna. Thomas Mann is thinking about The Magic Mountain, *and his wife has gone to take the cure yet again. Lyonel Feininger discovers a tiny village church in Gelmeroda and turns it into the cathedral of Expressionism. Franz Kafka reports for voluntary service with a group of vegetable farmers and spends his afternoons pulling up weeds as therapy for his 'burn-out'. Bernhard Kellermann writes the best-seller of the year:* The Tunnel, *a science fiction novel about an underground link between America and Europe. Frank Wedekind's* Lulu *is banned. Oskar Kokoschka buys a canvas as big as the bed of his lover, Alma Mahler, and begins to paint a portrait of them both. When it becomes a masterpiece, Alma will want to marry him. But not before.*

Gefahr im Anzug

(Zeichnung von M. Dudovich)

„Diese ewigen Grenzzwischenfälle sind ja schon ekelhaft genug. Aber unsere Männer werden erst staunen, wenn die Franzosen mit ihren Modeschikanen angerückt kommen!"

How long will Die Brücke remain standing? Ever since the artists Ernst Ludwig Kirchner, Karl Schmidt-Rottluff, Erich Heckel, Otto Mueller and Emil Nolde moved to Berlin from Dresden, arguments had been getting more and more frequent, Kirchner wrote about their 'women issues and intrigues', and by 1912 Max Pechstein had left the group. Each one of them is trying to make his own way, both artistically and financially. They all find lodgings in Berlin lofts, their styles grow apart, and so do they. The unsold paintings pile up in their studios, but they carry on bravely painting.

Like a pair of lovers on the brink, the Brücke painters try to remember the prelapsarian innocence and archaic force of their shared beginnings. They plan to release a chronicle of Die Brücke. It is to contain original wood-engravings and photographs of their paintings. Kirchner, their nimble, egocentric spokesman, is to write the accompanying text. In April 1913 he is working feverishly on it, this text that is to be a manifesto – or he would be if only his anxiety, his drugs, his women, his sketchpads and blasted Berlin would give him a few moments peace to do it in.

'The old collapses, the times change.' This quote from Schiller's *William Tell* is printed in large type in the *Chemists' Pocket Diary for the Year 1913*. Is a revolution looming? Have the German chemists had some kind of premonition of impending catastrophe?

No. They're just announcing some pretty new labels for ointments and cough syrups. Or, as it says in the advert: 'The new labels published by our company were all created by commissioned artists and, with regards to taste, are exemplary and unparalleled. They exceed all others in existence.'

Now that's advertising without false modesty. Unfortunately, though, the name of the company is not quite as catchy and certainly doesn't exceed all others in existence: 'Label printer and publisher for the chemical, pharmaceutical and associated industries, Barmen.'

In 1913 Colonel Mervyn O'Gorman, leader of the British Royal Aircraft Company, is pursuing two technical developments which are also intended to exceed all others in existence. During the week the legendary aeronautical engineer works on the development of powerful fighter planes for use in conflicts. And on Sundays, if the sun is shining, he uses his camera and the autochrome procedure to produce needle-sharp colour images of his beautiful but dour daughter Christina. His aeroplanes go down in world history. And his photographs of the beach near Lulworth Cove in Dorset make art history. An innocent young girl pictured in colour, walking along the beach, leaning against a dinghy. Not a plane in the sky. Only red tones, blue tones, brown tones, waves lapping softly against the shore. Enchanting photographs, created in 1913, but the images look so close you could reach out and touch them.

Thomas Mann wakes up at eight. Not because he's been woken by something or set an alarm. No, it's just that he always wakes up at eight. Once, when he woke up at half-past seven, he lay there for half an hour, baffled as to how it could possibly have come about. It could not be permitted to happen again. His body obeyed him. We still know little about the cold front which was Thomas Mann and Katia Pringsheim's marriage. But it's striking that Katia, after her husband completed *Death in Venice* in 1912, spent almost a year and a half without a break in different health resorts in Switzerland trying to cure her pulmonary condition. What really took her breath away was her husband's concealed homosexuality. She, of course, knew more than anyone else, that Gustav von Aschenbach was a self-portrait of her spouse – and that it was on their holiday together to Venice in 1911, in the Grand Hotel des Bains, that he couldn't tear his gaze from the beautiful young boy Tadzio, whom he describes in the book as 'utterly beautiful', 'pale and charmingly secretive'. Katia had been surprised by the way her husband gazed at the boy at the time, but then she read the novella about the ageing artist unrestrainedly pursuing his love for an adolescent boy, watching him while he was on the beach, while he ate, 'pretty and harsh in a not-yet-manly way'. But Thomas Mann had Gustav von Aschenbach deputise for him in this respect, and ultimately meet his death. During that year of permanent sojourns in sanatoriums, Katia and Thomas must have painfully abandoned what Mann calls the 'severe bliss of marriage'. But they stay together, maintain appearances and build a house.

Katia and Thomas Mann unite in holy matrimony each morning at exactly half-past eight to have breakfast together. Regardless of where they happen to be: Mauerkircherstrasse, their country house in Bad Tölz or, later, in Poschingerstrasse. On the stroke of nine the great writer begins his work. For the rest of their lives his four children will remember their father closing his door at nine precisely – whether they were in their apartment in Mauerkircherstrasse, the country house in Bad Tölz or, later, in the Poschingerstrasse.

It was a very definite, very final closing of the door. The world was to remain outside.

Then he would pick up his writing pad and get started. Like a machine. 'Give us today our daily sheet of paper,' he once said to his friend Bertram.

> I need white, smooth paper, fluid ink and a new, softly gliding pen nib. To prevent myself making a mess of it, I put a sheet of lined paper underneath. I can work anywhere; all I need is a roof over my head. The open sky is good for unbridled dreams and outlines, but precise work requires the shelter of a roof.

Exactly three hours later, on the stroke of twelve, he lays down his pen. Then he goes off to shave. He has tried this one out. If he shaves first thing in the morning, the first signs of stubble will have returned by dinnertime. But if he shaves at midday instead, his cheeks are still smooth even at dinner. After shaving and a few splashes of aftershave, Thomas Mann sets off for his walk. Then he has lunch with the children, treats himself to a cigar on the couch, reads a little, talks a little. Sometimes he even plays with the children. Erika is seven, Klaus six, Golo four and Monika three. Afterwards they are promptly handed back to the nanny, because Thomas Mann wants to have a lie-down. He always sleeps from four to five. And of course, he doesn't need an alarm clock then either. Tea is served at five, then he dedicates himself to what he calls 'incidental tasks'; those who so desire can call him and even visit ('come at around half-past five', he writes to Bertram), and he will be there to receive them. Dinner is at seven. So there we have it: world literature is merely a question of precise planning. This spring he tells his children for the first time about the new book he wants to write, called *Der Zauberberg – The Magic Mountain*. And it is to be a funny one. Erika comes up with a pet name for her father: '*Zauberer*' – 'Magician'. And it sticks, for the rest of his life. He always signs letters to his children with this nickname, and sometimes, affectionately, just with a 'Z'.

And so it seemed he had everything under control with his magic wand: his fountain pen. From A for Aschenbach to Z for *Zauberer*.

Librarian Descending a Staircase. In April 1913, after successfully completing a course in Library Studies, Marcel Duchamp takes on the role of Library Assistant at the Sainte-Geneviève library in Paris. Despite his tremendous success at the New York Armory Show, he is done with the art world. He begins by staying silent, but the value of Marcel Duchamp's silence hasn't yet been over-inflated. No one actually notices. He spends all his time playing chess. Is this the end, perhaps, not just of his art but of art in general? Duchamp, the highly intelligent, highly sensitive lawyer's son who, to his great surprise, found himself celebrated in Apollinaire's book *The Painters of Cubism* in March, thinks he has reached a dead end. The previous year he was in Munich, far away from Paris, where he passed the time being silent, reading and thinking. He also saw the Cranachs in the Alte Pinakothek. He combined the angularity of the naked Eves and the Futurist depictions of the female form in his picture *Nude Descending a Staircase*. In the stagnant medium of oil paint he had found an image of movement. But now his thoughts and his art are stuck in a rut. So perhaps he should just dedicate himself to chess instead? Later he will become a member of the French national chess team and participate in four Olympic Games.

❧

In 1913 defence expenditure accounted for 2 per cent of the gross domestic product of Austria-Hungary, 3.9 per cent in the German Reich and 4.8 per cent in France.

❧

Georg Grosz is in Berlin, sketching the incomprehensible. The explosion of poverty and wealth. The noise. The traffic. The building sites. The cold of the streets and heat of the brothels. Men of Straw. The obese men in hats, the fat women whose flesh is bursting from their clothes. Thrashing bodies, freezing bodies, gaping bodies. A jagged, thin black line captures everything. His sketches scrape, as if he's carving tattoos into skin. 'The periphery of the city, stretching around itself like an octopus, exerted a strong pull on us. We sketched the barely set new buildings, the bizarre cityscapes where rail tracks steamed over subways, waste dump sites bordered on garden allotments, where cauldrons of asphalt stood at the ready next to the newly mapped streets.' Grosz draws and draws. And when he reaches the end of a sketchpad, he goes to a bar, drinks a glass of Pilsner and eats some pickled herring. He finishes up with a *Koks mit'm Pfiff*: potato schnapps with a little cube of sugar, dipped in rum, which you can barely taste. Whenever he's flat broke, he goes to Aschinger's with Kirchner and the other hordes of bohemians. There you can get a huge bowl of pea soup for 30 Pfennigs – and as much bread and rolls as you want to go with it. When the bread basket is empty, the waiter brings a new one, and Grosz tucks some into his pockets for the hungry days to follow. Then he goes out onto the street, into the cafés, the brothels, the bars, and sketches the crown of creation: the pig, mankind.

Vienna lies in Sigmund Freud's shadow. Thoughts of the superego are even spilling from 19 Berggasse and entering people's dreams. On 9 April, Arthur Schnitzler records the following in his notebook: 'Ridiculous dreams. Arrive home from some rehearsal or other, planning to get a shave at Epply's, suddenly in my bathroom, Herr Askonas wants to shave my leg (probably ahead of lancing a carbuncle) – the Freud school of thought might interpret this as some kind of disguised suicide attempt.'

Alfred Flechtheim, the great art dealer and collector, starts to plan his suicide. At this moment he is still a minor corn merchant with a fatal addiction to art. But he has a grand plan: during his honeymoon in Paris with his wife, Betti Goldschmidt, he invested almost all her dowry in contemporary art. Picasso, Braque, Friesz. In his diary he wrote: 'There's something psychotic about art. It has grabbed hold of me.' So he plans to become rich by speculating on corn prices and copper-mining in Spain, so that he can then make his living as an art dealer. But when it comes to the corn trade, he is no expert. Sadly this seems to run in the family. His father and uncle have brought the family business, the Flechtheim Mill, to the edge of ruin through some risky manoeuvres. All the digging for copper in Spain comes to nothing, and before long all Flechtheim's money is spent. He owns five Cézannes, one Van Gogh, two Gauguins, ten Picassos, pictures by Munch and Seurat – and is in debt to the tune of 30,000 Marks. He goes to visit his father-in-law, Goldschmidt – 'dear beau-père', as he addresses him that day – and asks whether he will accept his art collection as 'security'. But the answer given by Goldschmidt, the biggest property owner in Dortmund, is 'No'. Who can say whether Picasso and Cézanne and Gauguin will be worth anything in a hundred years' time? Speechless, Flechtheim gets up and leaves. He cries on the shoulder of the young Nils de Dardel, a stunningly handsome but profoundly untalented Swedish artist. Flechtheim falls in love with him, and Betti threatens to leave him when she finds out. The threat of losing his dignity through divorce and the exposure of his homosexuality and debts prompts Flechtheim to decide, in the absence of anyone he can challenge to a duel, that suicide is the only way out: 'I'm stuck in a quagmire.' He writes to his wife: 'I hope you find a man who is worthy of you.' But he never sends it, instead taking out a very lucrative life insurance policy – to benefit his parents and wife – and planning the 'fatal accident' for 1914. He will dedicate the whole of 1913 to preparing for it. In his diary all his thoughts circle around his impending bankruptcy. 'If I go bankrupt, then I'll flee to Paris, take along as many pictures as I can manage and live there for another eight months.' But then events take an unexpected turn: suddenly he is able to sell his Van Gogh to the museum in Düsseldorf for 40,000 Marks, his friends buy him out of his absurd mine dealings and the corn company is saved from bankruptcy. And so by autumn 1913 Alfred Flechtheim is, with the help of Paul Cassirer, able to open a gallery at 7 Alleestrasse in Düsseldorf. His wife forgives him, and he forgives himself. The carefully laid suicide plans are shelved. He is even able to pay the contributions for the life insurance.

He went on to become one of the greatest gallery owners of the modern movement – even though, in 1913, he exhibited hideous paintings by his former lover, Nils de Dardel, next to works by Cézanne and Picasso. He later founded *Der Querschnitt*, perhaps the most liberal magazine Germany has ever known, and as timeless as the art Flechtheim loved so much.

At exactly half-past seven in the evening of 24 April, the American president, Woodrow Wilson, presses a button on his desk in the White House and sends a telegraphic signal to New York. This triggers the simultaneous illumination of 80,000 light bulbs in the newly finished Woolworth Building, the tallest in the world. Thousands of onlookers are waiting in the New York darkness for the moment of illumination. The tallest lighthouse in the world can be seen from far inland, and by great ships up to a hundred miles out at sea. America is beaming.

On 20 April, Adolf Hitler turns twenty-four. He sits in the men's boarding house at 27 Meldemannstrasse in the working-class neighbourhood of Brigittenau, Vienna, painting in the common room. His room is too small to paint in. Five hundred people have tiny individual cabins there, each containing a bed, a clothes stand and a mirror, in front of which Hitler grooms his moustache each morning. Board costs 50 Hellers a night. Anyone who stays there long-term, like Hitler, gets new bedding every Sunday. During the day most of the residents hang around the city, looking for work or distraction, and in the evenings they come streaming back. Only a few stay there during the day, and Adolf Hitler is one of those. Day after day he perches by the bay window in the so-called study where the day's newspapers are kept, sketching and painting watercolours of Vienna's attractions. He sits there, puny, in his ancient, threadbare suit; everyone in the home knows the story of his humiliating rejection from the art academy. A heavy black strand of hair keeps falling into his face, so he flings it back into place with a frantic jerk of his head. In the mornings he sketches out the picture with his pencil; in the afternoons he adds the colour. Each evening he gives that day's finished piece to another boarder, asking him to sell it in the city. Most of the paintings go to Kühler, a female art dealer in Hofzeile, in the 1st district of the city,

or to Schlieffer, the junk dealer at 86 Schönbrunnerstrasse. Most of his paintings are of the Karlskirche, or sometimes of the Naschmarkt. If a scene comes out well, he paints it a dozen times, getting 3 to 5 Kronen per painting. Hitler puts the money aside, not squandering it all on booze as his fellow residents do; he lives sparingly, almost austerely. Next to the writing room is a branch of an Austrian dairy, where Hitler buys bottles of good milk and Iglauer farmhouse bread. Whenever he wants to relax, he goes to the Schönbrunn Palace Park or plays chess. For the most part he spends the whole day quietly with his paints. But when the talk turns to politics, a spark rushes through him. He throws his paintbrush aside, his eyes flash and he holds blazing speeches about the immoral state of the world in general, and of Vienna in particular. It can't go on, he screams, there are more Czechs living in Vienna than there are in Prague, more Jews than in Jerusalem and more Croats than in Zagreb. He flings back his strand of black hair. He sweats. Then, all of a sudden, he breaks off from his diatribe, sits back down and turns his attention to his watercolours.

In the April edition of the *National Geographic* humanity sees one of the wonders of the world for the first time. Machu Picchu, the Lost City of the Incas, was rediscovered by a collaborative expedition between Yale University and the National Geographic Society. The leader of the expedition, Hiram Bingham, took the very first photographs of the ruins of this magical city, suddenly discovered among the high vegetation at the highest heights of Peru. *National Geographic* dedicates the entire issue to its excavation: the magazine publishes 250 photographs, dazed, enthused and excited, as the introduction to the article states, by this 'wonder'. Then it declares: 'What an extraordinary people the builders of Machu Picchu must have been to have constructed, without steel implements, and using only stone hammers and wedges, the wonderful city of refuge on the mountain top.' In the fifteenth century, when Florence was at the peak of its greatest era and Leonardo was painting the *Mona Lisa*, Machu Picchu came into being, 2,360 metres high up in the Andes. Even today the rain drainage system in the terraced city works perfectly.

The April edition of the Berlin magazine *Die Aktion* issues a call for 'parricide', although the editor, Otto Gross, cannot possibly have known that, in Vienna, Sigmund Freud was working on his own theory of the subject. Gross writes an essay with suggestions for 'Overcoming the Cultural Crisis'. The most important is this: 'Today's revolutionary, who, with the help of the psychology of the unconscious, sees the relationship between the sexes as lying in a free and auspicious future, struggles against rape in its most primal form, against the father and against the rights of the father.' (At the end of the year Gross – quite seriously – ends up being committed to a psychiatric ward by his own father.) This is the same moment when Asta Nielsen can be seen in cinemas in the film *The Sins of the Fathers*. And Franz Kafka writes to his new publisher, Kurt Wolff, in Leipzig, that he's thought of a title for his first collection of stories: *Sons*. Gottfried Benn's second volume of poetry, published in 1913, not by Kurt Wolff, because Wolff doesn't like Benn's poetry, but by the small publisher Meyer in Wilmersdorf, is also called *Sons*. Small wonder, then, that on 3 April, in the Hamburg shipyard Blohm & Voss, the biggest passenger ship in the world, at 54,282 gross tons and 276 metres in length, is christened at its launch *Fatherland*.

On that very same 3 April, Franz Kafka declares himself to be ill beyond recovery – he writes to his friend Max Brod: 'I keep imagining, for example, that I'm lying stretched out on the floor, cut up like a joint of meat, and am slowly pushing the pieces of flesh towards a dog in the corner – thoughts like these are my mind's daily fuel.' And then in his diary: 'This relentless idea of a broad butcher's knife plunging into my sides, at great speed and with mechanical regularity, cutting off these wafer-thin slices, which, due to the speed of the work, fly away in rolled-up form.' Things can't continue like this. His friends are worried, and Kafka himself is genuinely afraid he is going mad. He is hardly sleeping, and has headaches and major digestion problems. He can't write any more – all he can manage are his letters to Felice in Berlin. Even that has become more difficult, ever since his idealised image of his lover from her letters became flesh and blood, since he trembled with despair beside her when they met in Berlin. He's at his wits' end. Another case of burn-out, or 'neurasthenia'. But unlike Musil, Kafka doesn't go to see a doctor. He turns to self-therapy instead. On 3 April he calls by at the Dvorsky market garden in the working-class suburb of Nusle and offers his help with the weeding. Rarely has he made such a wise decision as this: grounding himself as the ground begins to shake under his feet.

He is given a choice between flowers and vegetables. Of course, Kafka chooses the vegetables. He begins on 7 April, in the late afternoon, once he's finished his work in the insurance company. It's raining softly. Kafka is wearing rubber boots.

We don't know how often he went to the gardens. We only know why he fled at the end of April. The gardener's daughter draws him into her confidence, prompting these thoughts: 'I, a man seeking to heal his neurasthenia through work, was forced to listen to the story of how the young woman's brother, whose name was Jan and who was the real gardener and intended successor of old Dvorsky, and indeed already the owner of the gardens, poisoned himself with melancholy two months ago at the age of twenty-eight.' So the very place where he was seeking to be healed from his inner suffering came with the threat of fatal melancholy. Distraught, Kafka leaves the gardens on the Nusle slopes. No sanctuary to be found anywhere.

Lyonel Feininger too is drawn to the country on 3 April, although admittedly his parental genes, nature and fate have conspired to grant him a happier mental disposition. Setting off from Weimar, where his wife, Julia, is studying, he climbs onto his bike and rides up the hill through the spring countryside of Thuringia. 'In the afternoons I scuttle off with my umbrella and writing pad, heading for Gelmeroda; I spent an hour and a half sketching there, picture after picture of the wonderful church.' That's all we know about him. His pictures were his language. And yet this discovery on 3 April 1913 is of central importance for his life's work. He will go on to make hundreds of sketches of the small, inconspicuous village church in Gelmeroda – over the decades twenty paintings in all. Even long after he leaves Germany and the Bauhaus behind him he will still create more and more visions of Gelmeroda from memory. After completing just the first few sketches of the church tower, he writes the following to his wife Julia: 'While working outside over the last few days, I was literally in ecstasy. It goes way beyond observation and discovery, it's magnetic amalgamation, a breaking free from all shackles.' Soon the first painting emerges from around forty studies, named *Gelmeroda I*, as if he knew from the start that many other versions would follow – two more in 1913 alone. It is a very expressive picture, a wild confusion of lines reminiscent of Franz Marc and the Futurists. Or, as Feininger himself saw it: 'For ten days now, an excellent picture has been grinning at me, charcoal on canvas, and I gazed at it with expressions increasingly consumed with longing – the Gelmeroda Church.' That little church becomes a decisive artistic turning point in Lyonel Feininger's oeuvre. And perhaps even the cathedral of Expressionism (although that doesn't stop anyone from turning it into a 'motorway church' a hundred years later).

On 30 April, Frank Wedekind's play *Lulu* is banned by the censors. Thomas Mann, who has just been elected as a member of the Munich Censorship Council, gives it a positive review. But he is outvoted: fifteen out of twenty-three council members vote for the play to be banned on moral grounds. Out of protest, Thomas Mann resigns from the Council.

Again on 3 April, the same day Franz Kafka is starting work with the vegetable farmers, Stefan George calls on Ernst Bertram, a friend of Thomas Mann. At this point in time George was already a mythical figure in Munich and throughout the rest of the Reich. A wonderful poet, a creator of verses of staggering beauty, yet at the same time the sinister ringleader of a circle of adolescent boys. He created an auratic image of himself early on in authorised photographs, always with his hair powdered, a diamond ring on his finger and his head in profile. He thought he looked too rough from the front. From the turn of the century onwards George visited Munich time and again, staying in Karl and Hanna Wolfskehl's guest room: first at 51 Leopoldstrasse, then at 87 Leopoldstrasse and finally, as in 1913, at 16 Römerstrasse, where George was able to arrange two of the rooms as he wished. The Wolfskehls protected George from undesirable admirers and controlled access to him. They knew how to draw attention skilfully to their mysterious tenant's public appearances. On this 3 April, George wanted to meet his youthful admirer Ernst Bertram. But Bertram was in Rome. Instead, the young Ernst Glöckner, born in 1885, opens the door. Confused and shaken, Glöckner writes to his friend Bertram in Rome: 'And now I wish I had never met this person. What I did on that evening was beyond my self-control, it was as if I were asleep, completely under his will, I was a plaything in his hands, I loved and hated at the same time.' Seldom has the direct, diabolical seductive power of the poet and self-declared prophet Stefan George been more honestly portrayed than in this self-accusation from the eighteen-year-old Glöckner. From then onwards, Glöckner, 45-year-old George and his ardent admirer Bertram played out a homoerotic love triangle. At the time George was working on his poetry collection *The Star of the Covenant*. It was an attempt to glorify pederasty and the recruiting of young men to the 'Secret' as if to some sacrosanct cult. *The Star of the Covenant* becomes the constitution of George's circle.

Futurism saunters through the Russian provinces: Mayakovsky, together with fellow Futurists David Burliuk and Vassily Kamensky, is on a reading tour. Out in the countryside it's their style of dress which makes the greatest waves. The maxim at the time seems to have been: 'Futurism is all well and good, but they could at least dress sensibly.' When Mayakovsky climbs up onto the stage in Simferopol wearing a yellow-and-black striped blouse, the agitated onlookers shout for him to get off. On that particular evening Mayakovsky decides against the pink smoking jacket he wore previously in Kharkov. He still insists on declaiming his poetry with a riding whip as a prop, though, even in Simferopol. The response from the local papers is one of horror. But it's all part of the Futurists' carefully calculated plan. Without the opposition of the press they would have felt like they weren't on track. When Kasimir Malevich went out for a walk on Kuznetsky Most, a popular meeting point in central Moscow, he alerted all the local papers so that they could write indignant reports about his provocative stroll. The provocation consisted of him wearing a wooden spoon in the buttonhole of his suit. By so doing, the Futurists wanted to demonstrate against what they regarded as the ridiculous fashion of the degenerate aesthetes who still wore chrysanthemums in their buttonholes in memory of Oscar Wilde. They felt they were on the wrong path. The ideal path, according to the gaudy Futurists, lay in unrestrained celebration of the future.

A small summit meeting at 16 Ainmillerstrasse. Paul Klee visits Gabriele Münter and Wassily Kandinsky, who are united in their desire to drive art forward. At the height of their love affair, in 1906, Münter and Kandinsky travelled together through Italy and France, painting shimmering oil studies of the sea so similar that even today we still don't know which of them painted which. Now, seven years later, their lives are becoming more separate, as are their styles and

– almost – their beds. Kandinsky is drifting away towards his blazingly colourful abstraction, while Gabriele Münter sticks to her weighty painting, with black lines bordering the colours like the lead in stained-glass windows. That's also the style in which she paints Paul Klee when he comes to visit them. A jagged profile, starchy collar, precise moustache, against a backdrop of several Kandinsky and Münter paintings hanging on the walls. Klee is even wearing slippers in the portrait, showing just how at home he feels there. The snow is still thick on the ground that April in Munich, so Klee would probably have got his feet wet as he walked round to see his friends. Comfortably warm now, he tucks his feet into the slippers belonging to the mistress of the house. Perhaps it's that small, friendly gesture that makes him finally give in today when Gabriele Münter asks, yet again, whether she can paint his portrait. His shoes will take another hour to dry anyway, he may have thought, stoically accepting his fate. And so he gazes out at us from the picture, a lasting legacy of this intimate moment from the private lives of the Blaue Reiter.

Austro-Hungary doesn't have a chance against the attack from the French. On 14 April the Frenchman Max Decugis beats the Austrian count Ludwig Salm in three sets at the final of the Madrid tennis tournament: 6–4, 6–3, 6–2.

What's the quickest way to get from America to Europe? In *Telefunken Zeitschrift*, no. 11 (April 1913), there's a report on the 'first radio-telegraphic success between Germany and America'. It says: 'For the first time since the existence of radio telegraphy, radio-telegraphic messages have been successfully sent across the ocean on the New York–Berlin line. The distance spanned was around 6,500 kilometres.'

In April, S. Fischer publishes the biggest best-seller of 1913: *The Tunnel*, by Bernhard Kellermann. Within four weeks 10,000 copies have been sold, and after just six months 100,000. (By way of comparison: Thomas Mann's *Death in Venice*, published in February 1913, sold just 18,000 copies in 1913, and it took until the 1930s for 100,000 copies to have been printed.)

The Tunnel tells the story of the construction of a tunnel from New York to Europe. Deep under the Atlantic, hordes of people burrow towards one another. It's a crazy story: science fiction mixed with realism, social criticism with engineering romanticism, capitalist belief in progress with wearily apocalyptic fantasy. The tunnel collapses, leading to strikes, rage and misery below the earth, and stock market flotations, dreams of marriage and disillusionment above. Then, after twenty-four years, the workers from Europe and America reach out their hands to one another thousands of metres under the Atlantic. Success at last. Two years later the first train travels under the earth between the continents. It takes twenty-four hours, but no one wants to board it. By then development has raced on, and the tunnel, which was once the technological utopia, is now a sentimental piece of history – people are flying from America to Europe by plane, and in half the time.

And so Kellermann succeeds in creating a great novel – he understands the passion for progress that characterises the era he lives in, the faith in the technically feasible, and at the same time, with delicate irony and a sense for what is really possible, he has it all come to nothing. An immense utopian project that is actually realised – but then becomes nothing but a source of ridicule for the public, who end up ordering their tomato juice from the stewardess many thousand metres not under but *over* the Atlantic. According to Kellermann's wise message, we would be wise not to put our utopian dreams to the test.

Crazed with love, Oskar Kokoschka has relinquished common sense. With brute force he tries to put Alma, the personification of his own female utopia, to the test, which in his case is otherwise known as 'marriage'. But Alma is more sensible than that. She doesn't believe in marriage. Nonetheless, she doesn't want Kokoschka to squander all the energy that seems to have arisen out of the intensity of his feelings. So she tells him: I'll marry you if you create a real masterpiece. From this day on her beloved has no other goal but this. He buys a canvas which he cuts to the exact measurements of the bed they share, 180 by 200 centimetres, in order to create his masterpiece.

He heats up the glue, he mixes the colours. Alma is to stand and pose for him, no: lie down and pose. He wants the picture to depict her as he likes her best: naked and horizontal. Alma Mahler – or, the Position of the Woman in 1913. He intends to paint himself lying next to her, but isn't yet sure exactly how to do it. He writes her a letter: 'The picture is moving slowly, but with constant improvements, towards completion. The two of us with strong, calm expressions, our hands entwined, at the bottom a semicircle, a sea illuminated by Bengal lights, a water tower, mountains, lightning and the moon.' It is intended to be Oskar Kokoschka's *Meisterwerk*. And against all expectation, it really is. But will it be enough to make Alma marry him?

In 1913 Walter Gropius publishes his essay 'The Development of Modern Industrial Architecture' in the yearbook of the German Workers' Association. It includes fourteen photographs of American warehouses and silos, which Gropius perceives to be the embodiment of a new architectural language: form follows function. They were built by engineers according to purely functional principles: simple cube formations, no ornamentation, no fuss. Gropius claims that this architectural ethos is a return to 'purity'. Or, to use his words: 'In the motherland of industry, America, large industrial buildings have been created whose unknown majesty towers above even the very best of Germany's industrial buildings. They wear an architectonic face of such certainty that the meaning of the building becomes comprehensible to the onlooker with persuasive force.'

MAY

A warm spring evening in Vienna: Arthur Schnitzler has such a violent argument with his wife that on 25 May he dreams of shooting himself. Nothing comes of it. But that same night in Vienna, Colonel Redl shoots himself after being convicted of espionage. On the very same night in Vienna, Adolf Hitler packs his bags and takes the first train to Munich. The artists' group Die Brücke breaks up. In Paris, Stravinsky celebrates the première of The Rite of Spring *and catches his first glimpse of his future lover Coco Chanel. Brecht is bored at school and has palpitations. So he starts writing poetry. Alma Mahler runs away from Oskar Kokoschka. Rilke argues with Rodin and can't get round to writing.*

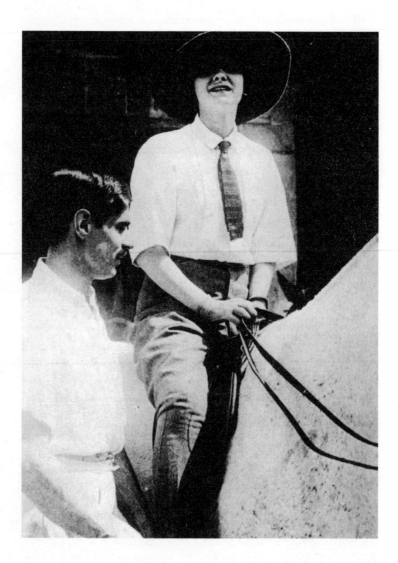

The time has come: Max Weber invents his memorable phrase 'the disenchantment of the world'. In a little essay on fundamental concepts in sociology he writes about what is important for the capitalist structure of society – and that includes the increasingly mechanical, scientific and rational treatment of everything previously considered a miracle. 'Disenchantment of the world' means, in Weber's own words, that humanity believes it can control everything by means of calculation. Still, Weber's own body resists the calculations of diet pills. In the spring of 1913 the 49-year-old had travelled to Ascona without his wife, Marianne, to cure himself of his drug addiction and his alcoholism. In this way, disenchanted, he wants to create an 'outer' beauty. But not a chance. He fasts in Ascona and takes a diet of 'vegetarian fodder', as he writes to his wife. But it's no good: 'The upholstery and the swill won't budge. It's how the plan of creation meant it to be.' So he stays fat, because that's how it was calculated to be. So with him there's clearly more plan than creation involved. Thus his own weight problem becomes the basis for one of the most important slogans of the twentieth century.

※

The month gets off to a difficult start for Oskar Kokoschka. On 1 May he writes to Alma Mahler: 'Today wasn't easy for me, as I didn't get a letter from you.'

※

The love story between the vicar's son Gottfried Benn and the Jewish poet Else Lasker-Schüler, who had published her ecstatic 'Hebrew Ballads' at the same time as his dances of death in the collection

Morgue, lasted throughout the spring of 1913. On 3 May, Else writes to Franz Marc in Sindelsdorf: 'I've really fallen in love again after all.' And she's fallen in love with Dr Benn.

Within a short time Marc, whom she had only met in December 1912 and who had shortly afterwards invited her to join him in his rural idyll in Sindelsdorf, had become Lasker-Schüler's confidant. She called him not only her 'Blue Rider' but also, above all, her 'Half-Brother Ruben'. No one came closer to her in her imaginary oriental realm. Karl Kraus was her 'Dalai Lama'; she changed her husband's name from Georg Lewin to 'Herwarth Walden' (when he left her, he kept the name at least). Oskar Kokoschka is the 'Troubadour' at the court, Kandinsky the 'Professor', Tilla Durieux the 'White Leopardess' – and Benn becomes 'Giselher', the Nibelung, the heathen, the barbarian.

The euphoric, scatterbrained visionary Lasker-Schüler grabbed testosterone-fuelled men by their poetic hearts and propelled them to unsuspected heights. But men afraid of too much femininity – Rainer Maria Rilke and Franz Kafka, for example – were startled by her surging sexuality and tended to run away. And the women of her time despised this unkempt femme fatale by day for her negligence, her irresponsibility, her licentiousness – and secretly admired her in the evening, when their husbands had gone out for a drink and they were left by themselves to flick through a magazine from their lonely armchairs. Only Rosa Luxembourg admired her unreservedly, and pointedly walked down the streets with her in the hot summer months of 1913.

So one May evening Else Lasker-Schüler wrote to Franz Marc to tell him how in love she was with Benn: 'When I fall in love a thousand times, it's always a new miracle, it's the same old thing when someone else falls in love. I have to tell you, it was his birthday yesterday. I sent him a box full of presents. His name is Giselher. He's out of the Nibelungs.' But Marc, whether his wife wouldn't let him or whether he himself was already too exhausted by his demanding Berlin girlfriend, took a few months to write back. To which Else replied by return: 'You are glad about my "New Love" – You say that so easily, and have no idea that you should really be weeping along with me – because – it has already gone out in his heart, like a sparkler, like a burning Catherine wheel – which has rolled over me.' NB: write quickly if you want to congratulate Else Lasker-Schüler on a new love, otherwise it'll be too late.

Between Gottfried Benn and Else Lasker-Schüler, at first, it was as if an inter-city train and an Orient Express had come hurtling straight at one another and locked in a steaming, artistic tangle of steel and blood. But all that remains by the autumn is rubble and stale smoke. The intervening nine months produce some of the most beautiful German love poetry of the twentieth century.

We know everything and nothing about this love affair, because the dates are unclear, disputed; the beginning in Berlin is as obscure as the end in the autumn, probably on the Baltic island of Hidden-see – and yet we know everything about their feelings because they put their love on stage like a public romance, with poems to, for and about each other, published in *Der Sturm*, *Die Fackel* and *Aktion*, the magazines that set the standards of the day. In these poems Benn is the 'Monkey Adam', drawn to the 'Brownest One', to his 'Ruth', the archaic woman. It's an unparalleled attraction that grips both of them, followed by battles, border disputes of the most violent kind, white-hot oaths, injuries, claw-swipes. When it gets going, she writes: 'The august King Giselher/With the tip of his lance/Pierced my heart through.'

With her rare grasp of the essential, she produces one of the quick-est, clearest portraits in existence of Benn, an indian-ink line drawn across the page in a matter of seconds, the hooked nose, the big rep-tilian head, the eyelids with the centuries apparently weighing upon them. And down on his chest the Nibelung wears an oriental star as a piece of jewellery. It appears in the 25 June 1913 issue of *Aktion* with, below it, Lasker-Schüler's piece about 'Dr Benn': 'He goes down into the vault of his hospital and cuts open corpses. Tirelessly enriching himself with secrets. He says, "dead is dead". He is an evangelical heathen, a Christ with the head of an idol, with the nose of a hawk and the heart of a leopard.' Beside this was a poem by Benn, the eighth part of his 'Alaska' cycle, whose very title reveals that this is about a lesson in coldness. And for simplicity's sake his first love poem to the deified poet is called 'Threats':

> I make animal love
> In the first night all is decided
> You grip what you long for with your teeth
> Hyenas, tigers, vultures are my coat of arms.

Else Lasker-Schüler's reply appears in the next eidition of *Der Sturm*, under the title 'Giselher the Tiger': 'I carry you around always/ Between my teeth.' And the whole Berlin art scene watches as the two outsiders celebrate each other in public. The doctor with the good manners and tightly knotted tie, whose hands always smell of the disinfectant with which he washes his hands, which have just been rooting about inside corpses. And the twice-divorced single mother with her tatty robes, her neck and arms hung with fake jewellery, chains and ear-rings. And as she was forever brushing an unruly strand of hair from her forehead, she was forever surrounded by lots of jangling and rattling. 'You couldn't cross the street with her, then or later, without the whole world stopping to look', Benn wrote later. And if they weren't walking down the street together, they were publishing their blazing declarations to one another, their wooing and their rejections. Else Lasker-Schüler's greatest triumph was when Benn refused military service, denied the Kaiser and settled in her personal kingdom. He became King Giselher at the Court of Prince Yussuf – in his military files he imagined he had something called a 'wandering kidney', which made it impossible for him to ride across fields on horseback. Of course, no such kidney existed, either then or now. Benn never suffered from it, and yet this invention helped him turn his inner turmoil into a poetic diagnosis. Benn broke away from his military world, moved through the night with his lover, climbed up to attics and down to basements, learned to love, learned to live. When the winter nights in cafés and lofts and house doorways are over and spring breaks out in Berlin like a feverish virus, it's easy for us to imagine Benn and Else Lasker-Schüler drifting out of the city on one of the many barges that bring fruit and vegetables from the country into the city; they let themselves be carried out into the Havelland, the lakes and rivers of Mecklenburg, to settle on an island, the dark water playing around them. They sit there, the two of them, in the reeds, naked beneath the moon. She plays with his hands, he plays with her hair and then they write poems: 'Oh, I became acquainted with too much bliss from your sweet mouth.'

But in the end, once the battle has been fought, she will write: 'I am a warrior with the heart, he with the head.' The great Protestant–Jewish reconciliation project that they made out of their life, here Yussuf or the Prince of Thebes, as she called herself, there the Nibelungen, is a failure. For her, 'Nibelung fidelity' means being senselessly faithful to something that is false. So she knew from the start what she was letting herself in for with this doctor with the piercing eyes and the receding hair-line. But when it happens, it throws her off track more than any man before or after him. She knew she was the prophetess of the Jewish people – and she needed Dr Benn, with the pomade in his hair and the galoshes on his feet, as the perfect counter-image to her oriental world, as the embodiment of the Germanic. But the young Nibelung moves on and the older Jewess stays behind in despair. She is gripped by a constant fever, abdominal inflammations, pains. In the autumn of 1913 Dr Alfred Döblin will prescribe her morphine against the mental pain caused her by Dr Gottfried Benn.

And so Franz Kafka writes about Else Lasker-Schüler to his distant Felice:

> I can't bear her poems, they make me feel nothing but boredom with their emptiness and revulsion about artistic effort. Her prose irritates me for the same reasons. What's at work in it is the randomly twitching brain of an overwrought city-dweller. Yes, she's in a bad way, her second husband left her, as far as I know, and even here people are collecting for her; I had to hand over 5 Kronen even though I haven't got

the slightest sympathy for her. I don't know the actual reason, but I only ever imagine her as a lush, dragging herself
around the coffee houses all night.

There is still no trace of the *Mona Lisa*. J. P. Morgan, the American
billionaire, receives a letter from a lunatic who signs himself 'Leonardo' and says he knows where the painting is. Morgan's receptionist
throws the letter away.

'Life is too short and Proust too long', Anatole France writes with
wonderful precision in 1913 about the publication of the first volume
of *In Search of Lost Time*. So Proust struck him as 'too long' even
before the remaining six volumes had come out. No one, not even
Proust himself, had any idea where Proust's meticulous search for the
depths of memory would lead. The book as an attempt to capture the
past in language – against the flow of time.

In Vienna, Sigmund Freud is gripped by his own book: 'I'm now
writing *Totem* with the feeling that it is my greatest, best, perhaps my
last good book.' What he's undertaken is quite massive. The last sentence is: 'In the beginning was the deed.' With these words he wants
at last to confront the biblical 'In the beginning was the word' and
establish his new theory of civilisation. The primal moment in the
history of its evolution, Freud thinks in the spring of 1913, is Oedipus'
act of parricide. He writes to a friend in May: 'The thing is due to be
published before the Congress, in the August issue of *IMAGO*, and
it should make a clean break with everything Aryan and religious.'
After his break with C. G. Jung and the Zürich group of psychoanalysts, Freud spends the whole year worrying about September, when

that 'Congress', the Congress of the Psychoanalytical Society, is due to take place, the one that will force the now hostile groups back around a table. And Freud knows that the anti-Christian theory in *Totem and Taboo*, on which he is feverishly working, will seal the break with Jung and his disciples.

In early May, Rudolf Steiner writes to his mother: 'And the war keeps threatening to come.' But he has no time to worry about it. He wants to set up an Anthroposophical Centre at last, known as the Johannesbau.

And after his plans to erect this building in Munich are dismissed by the building commission, he speaks to his devotees in Stuttgart on 18 May and tells them to avoid trying to do anything new in Munich, as something about the city was dying (if Oswald Spengler had heard this in his Munich study, where he was working on his *Decline of the West*, he would have shouted with joy).

So Steiner explains: 'New cultures have never been able to settle in this dying place.' For a long time he has sensed that Dornach, near Basel, is the place for anything new and flourishing. But it was still too early for that.

For a long time the Anthroposophical Centre in Berlin was at the rear of 17 Motzstrasse. Rudolf Steiner lived there with his wife, Anna, but he insisted that his loyal companion and lover Marie von Sivers move in too, which, of course, didn't work well for long. The rear extension was all a bit basic. Hardly any furniture, a few tables, books, a bed. Always the sound of a secretary tapping away somewhere on a Remington typewriter. Under great pressure Rudolf Steiner writes lecture after lecture here, theses elaborated over the course of several hours about the state of souls and the world, Christianity, the spirit of the nineteenth century, and at the same time his 'office' is busy organising lecture tours across all of Europe. Steiner and Marie von Sivers spend almost two-thirds of the year on the road – when Steiner is in Berlin, people make a pilgrimage to Motzstrasse to request help and enlightenment from the master. Consultations go on for days at a time, the atmosphere is unexpectedly informal, visitors wait in armchairs and are then ushered into a little room where Steiner generally sits among the suitcases from his last trip, still unpacked. And yet he wins them all over with his empathy and his approachability. All they want is understanding for their *Weltschmerz*, disguised as neurasthenia. We know that Hermann Hesse was one of those who came in search of enlightenment and who were granted an audience with Steiner, and so, in fact, was Franz Kafka. How their brief meeting went, history, alas, does not record.

Spring is here at last. The teacher Friedrich Braun and his wife, Franziska, are pushing their pram through the Hofgarten in Munich. In December they became the proud parents of little Eva. Eva Braun is six months old when 24-year-old Adolf Hitler arrives in Munich on Sunday 25 May.

On the Sunday morning when Hitler leaves Vienna, the city is frozen with shock: one of the most senior military officers and secret service personnel in the Austro-Hungarian monarchy, Colonel Alfred Redl, has been convicted of espionage during the night and has shot himself in his hotel room at 1.45 in the morning. Strangely, the pistol had been placed in his room, room number 1 at the Hotel Klomser, where he always stayed, in return for his signature on the paper in which he confessed his guilt. And the dishonoured Colonel Redl asks the secret service staff to leave the room quietly, before pulling the trigger. When Kaiser Franz Joseph, on getting up at four o'clock in the morning, learns the extent of Redl's military espionage, he sighs deeply: 'So this is the brave new world? And these the creatures that it brings forth? In the old days, that wouldn't have been imaginable.' An announcement is placed in the newspapers which tries to maintain appearances: 'The General Chief of Staff of the Prague Army Corps, Colonel Alfred Redl, has taken his own life in an attack of mental confusion. The talented officer, who had a great career ahead of him, had been suffering from insomnia for some time.' In that way they attempted to package the terrible news that one of the most influential generals in Austro-Hungary had betrayed all their military plans to the enemy as suicide caused by insomnia. But Vienna hadn't reckoned with Egon Erwin Kisch, the young reporter with the newspaper *Bohemia*. That Sunday, Kisch is waiting in vain, at the away game between his own football team, Sturm, and Union Holeschowitz, for their most dangerous striker, the fitter Hans Wagner. Then, on Monday, when Wagner explains himself to the captain and hems and haws, Kisch learns that on Sunday morning he had been recruited by the military to break into a private apartment in the Army Corps headquarters. He had seen strange things there: ladies' tulle dresses, perfumed draperies, pink silk sheets. Kisch deftly placed an article in a Berlin newspaper about the true background to the death of Colonel Redl, which he had researched with the help of one of his team-mates.

So by Thursday 29 May the War Ministry's military review has to reveal the whole truth:

> In the night of Saturday the 24th to Sunday the 25th of this month, the late Colonel Redl took his own life. Redl carried out the deed when he was about to be accused of the following serious shortcomings, proven beyond all doubt: 1. Homosexual intercourse, which caused him financial difficulties. 2. Sale of classified official information to agents of a foreign power.

Colonel Redl – ironically awarded the 'Order of the Iron Crown Third Class' for his services to counter-espionage, the army's brightest hope, who reported to the Kaiser in person and was in close contact with the General Staff of the German Reich, General von Moltke – this Colonel Redl was suddenly exposed as a character out of an operetta. The small, dapper, red-haired man had spent his entire fortune on his lovers, giving them cars and flats and buying himself perfumes and hair dyes. Having found himself in financial difficulties, he had been selling off all Austria-Hungary's deployment plans, military codes and projects for national expansion. Now it was meltdown. The name 'Redl' became synonymous with a system that had gone rotten, an outmoded, decadent monarchy, the mark of Cain. His brothers Oskar and Heinrich were mercifully granted permission to change their names forthwith to Oskar and Heinrich Rhoden. Along with the name, the case itself was to be eradicated from the memory of the city and the country, but it did no good – whenever Stefan Zweig thought of the Colonel Redl affair, he felt a 'horror in his throat'. But the Redl affair turned Egon Erwin Kisch, the man who uncovered it, into a legendary reporter. In return he received one of the highest civilian decorations that Vienna had to offer: the best table in Café Central was always reserved for him.

One more footnote – a weird one. On 24 May, the night before Colonel Redl shoots himself, Arthur Schnitzler dreams he shoots himself as well: 'A mad dog bites me, left hand, to the doctor, he takes it lightly, I go, in despair – want to shoot self. In the paper it will say: "like a greater man before him", which I find irritating.'

Early on 25 May, Hitler and his friend Rudolf Häusler, with whom he had stayed at the men's hostel in Vienna, flee on the train from Austria, probably to escape the threat of military service. They have no idea that the army has other concerns just then.

On the first day they go walking down the early summer streets of Munich in search of a room. They enjoy the compact size of the city: only 600,000 inhabitants rather than the 2.1 million in Vienna, everything lush and tranquil. At 34 Schleissheimer Strasse, the home of the tailor Joseph Popp, they suddenly see the inconspicuous sign 'Small room to rent'. Hitler knocks on the door, Anna Popp opens it, shows him the room, third floor on the left, and Hitler immediately takes it. In cramped handwriting he fills in his registration form: 'Adolf Hitler, architectural painter from Vienna.' With the piece of paper in her hand Anna Popp goes to her children Josef and Elise, twelve and eight, and tells them they will have to play more quietly from now on, as they have a new tenant.

Hitler and Häusler pay 3 Marks a week in rent for their spartan room. He lives exactly as he did in Vienna: no drinking, no truck with women, a watercolour every day, sometimes even two. Instead of St Augustine's Church he's painting St Mary's. Otherwise it's the old routine. After only two days he's found an easel and set it up in the city centre.

When he's finished a few views of the city, he walks through the big Munich beer halls and tries to sell his views to tourists in the evening at the Hofbräuhaus. The jeweller Paul Kerber sometimes sells his paintings too, as does the Schell perfumery on Sendlinger Strasse.

The minute he sells a watercolour he converts his takings into pretzels and sausages: often he goes for days without eating. But with that amount of money you can get quite a lot: in 1913 a litre of beer costs 30 Pfennigs, an egg 8 Pfennigs, half a kilo of bread 16 Pfennigs and a litre of milk 22 Pfennigs.

Every day at 5 p.m. on the dot Hitler goes to the Heilmann bakery, near his apartment, and buys a slice of plaited loaf for 5 Pfennigs. Then he crosses the road to the dairyman Huber and buys half a litre of milk. That's his dinner.

As in Vienna, Adolf Hitler, the painter who failed to get into the art academy, has no contact with the artistic avant-garde of the city. We don't know whether he saw the exhibitions of degenerate art by Picasso or Egon Schiele or Franz Marc, which caused such a furore in Munich in 1913. The artists of his generation who had made a career for themselves were alien to the art-school reject throughout his life, and he eyed them with suspicion, envy and hatred.

When he comes home, he knocks on Frau Popp's door to ask her to fetch him some hot water for his tea. 'May I?' he always asks, looking trustingly at his pot. This gets on tailor Popp's nerves, and he says, 'Just sit down with us and have something to eat, you look starving.' But Hitler's startled by that, he takes his teapot and flees to his room. Throughout 1913 he never gets a single visitor. He paints by day, and until three or four in the morning he reads political pamphlets and instructions on how to become a member of the Bavarian parliament. The tailor's wife sees that at one point, and tells him he ought to give up those silly political books and paint pretty watercolours instead. Hitler replies, 'Dear Frau Popp, do we know what we need in life, and what we don't?'

'I really dislike Berlin itself', Ernst Reuter writes to his parents. 'Dust and a horrific amount of people, all running as if a minute cost 10 Marks.' A man who understands the mystery of a city so quickly is bound to become mayor in due course.

At the end of May the poet Stefan George comes to Heidelberg and stays, as he always does, in the boarding-house at 49 Schlossberg. He wants to gather all his disciples around him there at Whitsun. But for now it's very hot, so George goes to the swimming pool. Not to swim, of course: the prophet, who is already walking through life like a portrait bust, would never do that. No, to see a beautiful boy with curly hair: Percy Gothein, the schoolboy and teacher's son, barely seventeen, who will become the prototype for the poet's disciple. Three years previously George's eagle eye spotted him on the Neckar Bridge and boasted to the Gundolf brothers that he 'looked so like an antique relief it was worth taking a photograph of him'. The photograph really was taken. Shortly afterwards he visits George at the home of his mother in Bingen. He teaches him – the psychological clichés are pitiful – to tie a tie, and lends him his velvet trousers. But one afternoon in 1913, when Percy is in the lido without his tie and without his velvet trousers, he spots Stefan George lying in the grass by one of the bathing huts. The conversation, Percy trustingly reports, 'soon came back to the ancient Greeks, whom one likes to imagine like that, and even more in the altogether'. And so on. In the evening Stefan George continues to work on his big book *The Star of the Federation*, disguised as a swirling mystery, myth-heavy, somnambulistic verses in praise of boy-love.

In 1913 Albert Schweitzer writes in his diary: 'If only everyone stayed as they were at fourteen.' But then again, perhaps not. At the start of 1913 Bertolt Brecht is fourteen. Reading his diary, you're glad he went on to become someone unlike the person he was at fourteen. He would never have cut it as a disciple of Stefan George: too ugly, too quick-tempered, too self-pitying.

Brecht, a pupil at the Royal Grammar School in Augsburg, complains in his little diary, with its faint blue checked paper, of the 'monotony' and 'banality' of the endless spring days, which he does his best to fill with walks, cycling, chess and reading. He conscientiously jots down his readings of Schiller, Nietzsche, Liliencron and Lagerlöf. And then the young man lets go and confides his wonderfully adolescent poetry to his diary. About the moon and the wind, about forest paths and sunsets. Then comes 17 May 1913. Now – he's just turned fifteen – he experiences a 'miserable night'. More precisely: 'Until eleven o'clock I had a powerfully pounding heart. Then I went to sleep, until twelve o'clock, when I woke up. So powerful that I went to see Mama. It was terrible.' But it soon subsides. The next day he starts writing poetry. As it was warm that May in Augsburg, he calls his verses 'Summer'.

> I lie in the grass in the cool shade
> of a beautiful, ancient linden tree,
> and all the grasses on the sunlit meadows
> tilt gently in the wind.

So in 1913 he's still lying alone under the linden tree. Soon he will be lying with company under the plum tree, as we know from Brecht's poem of the century, 'Memory of Marie A.', that testament to his earliest Augsburg love. Writing poems about trees is already a great source of comfort to Brecht in 1913. One day after he has crept into bed with his mother at night, on 20 May, he reports: 'Morning very good. Now, early afternoon, relapse. – stitches in my back.' With Brecht, it's hard to tell raging hypochondria from genuine disturbance of his cardiac rhythm. He visits a doctor, who diagnoses 'affliction of the nerves'. At the age of fifteen Brecht can proudly suffer the same symptoms as Franz Kafka and Robert Musil.

So in terms of his attitude to life, there are surprising parallels with the two other nervously afflicted poets, as his poem 'The Girlfriend' from that spring reveals:

> You ask what love is –
> I didn't feel it, –
> you ask what joy is,
> it's light has never shone for me.
> You ask what worry is –
> *Her* I know,
> *she* is my girlfriend,
> *she* loves me!

So: worries about worries in Augsburg. Was anyone in a good mood in May 1913? Plainly not.

Die Brücke falls apart. In May 1913 the group dissolves once and for all. The chronicle of Die Brücke, written by Ernst Ludwig Kirchner, provokes Erich Heckel and Karl Schmidt-Rottluff. Kirchner depicts himself as the leading figure in the group, the inventor of the Expressionist woodcut and Expressionist sculpture and generally speaking the guiding spirit of the movement. For the first page of the 'Chronicle' Kirchner had made a woodcut featuring portraits of the members. He had surrounded his own head, on the top left, with a little halo. And the archway of the print, 'Die Brücke', rested on his signature: 'E. L. Kirchner'. From the point of view of the other members of the group, that was egocentric and untrue. But from the point of view of art history it is actually true – Kirchner is the genius in a group of great masters. And in his brighter phases, when his brain wasn't fogged with anti-depressants, he knew it too. There's a big fight – on 27 May 1913, Schmidt-Rottluff and Heckel draw up a letter informing the passive members of Die Brücke about the group's dissolution. Max Pechstein had been excluded a year before, because he had exhibited in the Berlin Secession without their permission, which Kirchner saw as a 'breach of trust'.

'We hereby inform you that we the undersigned have decided to dissolve the artists' group "Die Brücke" as an organisation. Cuno Amiet, Erich Heckel, E. L. Kirchner, Otto Mueller, Schmidt-Rottluff. Berlin, 27 May 1913.' Four signatures follow. Kirchner doesn't sign.

Immediately after sending off the letter Karl Schmidt-Rottluff packs his bags. He has to get out of Berlin, that city which always remained alien to him, given that his art always retained a wonderfully rustic quality, and which afflicted him and his sense of beauty. Unlike Kirchner. He only became himself in the city. Kirchner's art is urban, Schmidt-Rottluff's always rural. He wants to go to the sea and as far away as possible, so he drives to Nidden, on the Curonian Spit. To the hotel run by Herman Blode, the only villager to rent out rooms. Soon Schmidt-Rottluff finds a simple, empty fisherman's hut on the beach, where Max Pechstein spent two summers. When he has unpacked his painting equipment, he writes a postcard to his friend, on 31 May: 'It would seem that I've landed here in Nidden for a time. It's a curious area!' Schmidt-Rottluff, exhausted by the quarrels around Die Brücke and the advancing, wearying metropolis of Berlin, revives on that spit of land. Heaths, pine trees, the lagoon behind him, and then: sand, sand, sand – an endless dune, which he turns into his paradise in watercolours and oils, in which the first humans look innocently at one another. *Sun in the Pine Forest* is the name of one of the paintings, and you could imagine you were in the South Seas. For the first time he paints big nudes, groups of women in the dunes, ink drawings, woodcuts – it's an artistic liberation. He paints the fishermen's wives and children, naked and uninhibited. Schmidt-Rottluff's art may never again have been as sensual as it was that early summer on the beach. He paints the faces as if they were carved heads from Oceania, but the bodies are full of vitality. It's only when he writes about the nudity in his work that he tenses up again, and the intellectual returns. 'The breasts are quite straightforward. They are an erotic element. But I would like to free it from the fleetingness of experience, establish a relationship between the cosmic and the earthly moment.' You must be joking: 'Disenchantment of the world'. But: cosmic breasts! An anatomical discovery of the year 1913, hitherto overlooked by scientific research.

In May, Berlin is preparing itself for the greatest social event of the young century: the wedding of Princess Victoria Louise of Prussia to Duke Ernst August of Hanover on 24 May. The bridal couple drive along Unter den Linden, where thousands of people are cheering. And then, as the *Berliner Tageblatt* reports, there is a special moment: an unequal coincidence of democracy and monarchy. Or: 'It was truly a heart-rending sight to see the democratic bus having to wait as the aristocratic carriage passed, but then the carriage had to wait to let the bus pass.' Both the Russian Tsar Nicholas II and the English King George V travel to Berlin and Potsdam for the wedding – as do countless crowned and uncrowned heads from all over Europe. The wedding was a diplomatic event above all. As the *Berliner Tageblatt* observed:

> Of course, the visit was not political. But after the agitated political processes of the past winter, it had to be seen as a welcome example of a relaxation in the international situation, that the rulers of Russia and England, the crucial monarchs of the triple entente, were guests of the German

Kaiser. It is in the nature of things that personal contacts of this kind also make their mark on the political attitude of the cabinets, although only in the sense that on all sides the will to peace is being still more keenly accentuated.

So on 24 May the world's monarchs gathered rather oddly at five o'clock for the wedding in the Palace Chapel, which was illuminated by hundreds of candles. Only Franz Ferdinand, the successor to the Austrian throne, was not invited – even in Vienna he had long been shunned because of his unsuitable bride, and even on occasion victimised, but this public humiliation on a European stage is a fresh blow for him. All the others celebrate until the small hours. But then, before breakfast, the kings and tsars are given the news from Vienna by their intelligence services: Colonel Redl has been convicted and shot. But the Tsar gives no sign that he has lost his most important informer. He cuts the top off his boiled egg and chats. Decorum is maintained.

It's an exhausting spring for Rainer Maria Rilke in Paris. Again he can barely write. He must live. Or something of the kind. Friends and acquaintances want to see him, he goes out for breakfast, lunch, dinner, meets André Gide, Henry van de Velde, the Insel Verlag publisher Anton Kippenberg, Romain Rolland and Stefan Zweig. Rilke complains: 'People don't get on with me.' Above all, he has become unpleasantly entangled in a series of misunderstandings with his old friend and hero Auguste Rodin. Once he had elevated him in his book to the status of a god of sculpture, but now the awkward sculptor refuses to comply when Rilke begs him please please please to sit for a portrait bust by his wife, Clara Rilke-Westhoff. Clara, long since separated from Rilke, lives with their daughter, but he feels responsible and wants to help her make her artistic breakthrough. Rodin won't budge, which puts Rilke's nose out of joint. And when Rilke visits him with Kippenberg to discuss photographs for a new edition of his book with Insel Verlag, Rodin eventually takes the photographs back.

Clara is in Paris, in a state of despair. She has no money (she is kept financially afloat by Rilke's close friend Eva Cassirer) and has staked everything on making her bust of Rodin. Then Rilke asks Sidonie Nádherný, the ex-lover and close friend that he has just put up at the Hôtel du Quai Voltaire, to sit for his wife – Rilke alone seems quite comfortable with these arrangements; he is at his happiest when the rough edges of the past are smoothed by the bond of harmony. Sidonie proudly stretches her neck as her lovely features are chiselled into stone. But then, on 28 May, her beloved brother Johannes Nádherný shoots himself in Munich. Sidonie has a breakdown and sinks into a depression, and Rilke joins her. He has, he writes to his publisher Kippenberg, 'had a small breakdown' caused by the death of Johannes, whom he knew well from visits to the accursed castle of the Nádhernýs in Bohemia, 'and just before that, had a new rift with Rodin, just as unexpected as the one eight years ago but, because it could even come to that, probably more final and irreparable'.

In a panic Sidonie leaves Paris; Clara, having nothing to do, escapes back to Munich, and Rilke, somehow relieved that he can love from a distance again, takes them both by the hand, with letters, with words, with consolations; he's good at that. In Munich, Clara goes on working on a bust that is not yet acquainted with grief. By the autumn, when Sidonie sees the bust for the first time, she is visiting Clara with her new boyfriend. His name: Karl Kraus.

To get a sense of the cultural networks in Paris in 1913, and of the life of the German *bon vivant*, aesthete, dandy, cultural commentator and legendary diary author Harry Graf Kessler, you only need to take a look at his entry for 14 May 1913: he sleeps late, then meets André Gide and Igor Stravinsky at the Ritz in the early afternoon, after which they go together to the rehearsal of the new ballet by the legendary Russian dancer and choreographer Nijinsky and Diaghilev – the music is by Claude Debussy. He talks to Debussy and to Jean Cocteau during the interval. Tempers suddenly flare in the middle of the rehearsal: Stravinsky shouts, Debussy shouts, Diaghilev shouts. Then they all make up and have champagne next door. Kessler, as he confides to his diary that night, finds Debussy's music too 'thin'. But he finds the costume of the great Nijinsky even worse: short white trousers with a black velvet border and green braces, which is too 'unmanly and comical' even for Harry Graf Kessler. A good thing, then, that Nijinsky, the Russian with the unreliable taste, had cultured French and German style advisers: 'Cocteau and I persuaded him, before the première tomorrow, to get hold of some sport trousers and a sport shirt from Willixx.' And so he did.

Exactly two weeks later, the next general rehearsal in that very special May in Paris – Stravinsky's *The Rite of Spring* at the Théâtre des Champs-Élysées. This time Harry Graf Kessler doesn't even go to the rehearsal, heading instead straight to the post-rehearsal party at the Larue restaurant – with Nijinsky, with Maurice Ravel, with André Gide, with Diaghilev, with Stravinsky, 'where the general view was that the première tomorrow evening would cause a scandal'. And so it did. The première of *The Rite of Spring* was an event that electrified Paris and sent shock waves as far as New York and Moscow. What happens on the evening of 29 May between 8 and 10 p.m. is one of those rare moments when eye-witnesses sense they're part of a historical event. Even Harry Graf Kessler is ecstatic: 'A new form of choreography and music. An entirely new vision, something never seen before, something gripping and convincing, has suddenly come into existence. Savagery in un-art and also in art: old form is ravaged, new form suddenly arising out of chaos.' What Kessler confides in his diary at three o'clock in the morning is one of the most concise and workable formulations for the thrust of modernity that grips the world in 1913.

The audience on 29 May in Paris is the noblest and most cultivated in Old Europe: sitting in one of the boxes is Gabriele d'Annunzio, who has fled to Paris to get away from his disciples in Italy. In another is Claude Debussy. Coco Chanel is in the auditorium, and so is Marcel Duchamp. For the rest of his life, he will say later, he would never forget the 'shouting and screeching' of that evening. Stravinsky's music brought the primal violence of archaic powers back on the stage – the primordial nature of people from Africa and Oceania, who had served as a model for the art of Expressionism, were now at the centre of civilisation, brought to pulsating life in the Théâtre des Champs-Élysées.

From the first note of the extremely high solo bassoon, roars of laughter can be heard – is that music, or a spring storm, or the noise of hell the outraged audience wants to know. Drumming everywhere, up on stage the dancers are in ecstatic motion – there's laughter, then, when the Parisians realise it is meant seriously, shouting. The devotees of the Modern, on the other hand, applaud from the cheap seats, the music rages on and the dancers get tangled up; they can no longer hear the music for all the noise. From somewhere or other Maurice Ravel is shouting 'Genius!' into the auditorium. Nijinsky, who wrote the choreography for the ballet, hammers out the rhythm with his fingers – against the furious whistling of the audience.

The dancers seem to be intoxicated, and the theatre manager turns off the lights in the middle of the performance to avoid an escalation of the chaos, but the dancers at the front keep going, and when the lights come back on the people in the auditorium have the unsettling feeling that they're the stage and the dancers are the audience. It is only thanks to the stoical calm of the conductor, Pierre Monteux, who keeps going just as the dancers do, that they manage to carry the performance to the final bar. *Le Figaro* writes the next morning:

> The stage represented humanity. On the right, strong young people are picking flowers, while a 300-year-old woman dances around like mad. On the left-hand edge of the stage an old man studies the stars, where here and there sacrifices are being made to the god of light. The audience couldn't swallow it. They roundly hissed the piece. A few days previously they might have applauded. The Russians, who aren't entirely familiar with the manners and customs of

the countries they visit, didn't know that the French start protesting at the drop of a hat once stupidity has reached its nadir.

Stravinsky is horrified by these words. He is deeply disturbed by the events of the evening. And yet he guesses he has written a work that will define an era. And he may have been reinforced in this view by Coco Chanel, whose little millinery salon in Paris has been attracting a great deal of attention, and who sees the great Russian composer for the first time this evening. And then becomes his lover.

Two journeys to the centre of the earth: Piero Ginor Conti, in Larderello in Tuscany, manages to use water from the earth's core to produce electricity. Geothermia has been discovered. At the same time Marshall B. Garner writes his book in which he claims that mammoths still live inside the earth. They didn't die out at all, he claims, they just withdrew to warmer climes.

In Vienna, Oskar Kokoschka goes on working on the canvas that is the same size as the bed of his lover Alma, the widow of Gustav Mahler. He is in great pain because Alma has just aborted their child. He cannot forgive her for destroying the fruit of their love. Again and again he paints accusatory pictures of Alma with that child, whose life he imagines through art. He was present at the abortion in a Vienna clinic and took the bloody cotton wool back to his studio, repeatedly mumbling to himself, 'This will be my only child.' (Tragically he was right.)

And yet he's still sexually obsessed with Alma; he can only work when she has granted him her favours. So day in, day out, he stands in his studio in Alma's bright red pyjamas, which he tore off her at the start of their affair and which he always wears when he paints. In

1913 he paints her almost a hundred times: Alma. It's an adventurous passion, full of rage, raving, happiness – 'so much hell, so much paradise', as Alma calls it. He used to want Alma to beat him during the act of love, which she didn't enjoy, but in his daily letters Oskar pleads with her 'to strike me with your beautiful dear little hand'.

Between kisses he shouts out his murderous plans and his fury. It must have given him an almighty kick.

Kokoschka's jealousy is so colossal that, when he leaves Alma's flat at night, he sometimes waits in the street until four o'clock, until he's sure no other man is climbing the stairs to his beloved. 'I shall tolerate no other gods before me', he writes, beautifully and idiotically at the same time. His jealousy also extended with particular intensity to Gustav Mahler, Alma's late husband. So time and again they have to make love right under the composer's death mask. And Kokoschka pleads with Alma, who with her infallible knack of spotting artistic genius and the *genius loci* has, of course, been in Paris this particular May: 'Please, my sweet Almi, shield your sweet body from prying eyes and further strengthen my feeling that every strange hand and every alien gaze is a blasphemy against the sanctity of your beautiful body.' Then, at the end of May, worship turns to magic. Oskar Kokoschka writes pleading letters to her at her hotel in Paris: 'I must soon have you as my wife, or else my great gift will perish miserably. You must bring me back to life in the night like a magic potion.' Alma starts to get worried. She decides to stay an extra week in Paris after all.

In Carl Sternheim's play *The Snob*, on which he is working in the summer of 1913, he hides dozens of allusions to Walther Rathenau, the great chairman of AEG, romantic, author, politician, thinker. And also one of the most narcissistic figures of his time. At the première of *The Snob*, Sternheim's wife, Thea, sits next to Rathenau, worrying that he might know he's the one being depicted on stage. But narcissism can also act as a form of protection. Rathenau is unmoved.

At the end he says only that he would like to read the play through carefully once more.

The 27-year-old Ludwig Mies van der Rohe comes back to Berlin and sets himself up as an architect.

Max Beckmann writes in his diary: 'Man is and remains a first-class swine.'

JUNE

This is the month when it becomes clear that war is simply not an option. Georg Trakl is searching for his sister and deliverance from damnation, while Thomas Mann is just looking for some peace and quiet. Franz Kafka makes a marriage proposal of sorts, but it doesn't come across well. He seems to confuse it with an oath of disclosure. D. H. Lawrence publishes his Sons and Lovers, *then runs off to Upper Bavaria with mother-of-three Frieda von Richthofen, who becomes his inspiration for Lady Chatterley. Other than that, nerves are raw everywhere. In cinemas, Asta Nielsen destroys an unknown masterpiece in* Sins of the Fathers. *The German army is set to grow and grow. Henkell Trocken celebrates Franco-German friendship.*

There couldn't possibly be another war, Norman Angell was sure of that. His 1911 book *The Great Illusion* became a worldwide bestseller. In 1913 he writes a well-received 'Open Letter to German Students', through which his theories reach an even greater audience. At the same time the fourth edition of his book is published. As ever more vexing noises push their way northwards from the Balkans that early summer, the intellectuals in Berlin, Munich and Vienna are able to calm their nerves by reading the British publicist's book. In it Angell expounds his theory that the era of globalisation renders world wars impossible, because all countries are now economically interlinked to such a high degree. He also says that, alongside the economic networks, close international ties in communication and above all in the world of finance mean that any war would be preposterous. He argues that, even if the German military wanted to pit its strength against England, there is 'no establishment of significance in Germany which would not suffer greatly'. This, he claims, will prevent war, because 'the entire German financial world would exert its influence over the German government, thereby putting a stop to a situation which would be ruinous for German trade'. Angell's theory convinced intellectuals all over the world. David Starr Jordan, the President of Stanford University, utters these great words after Angell's lecture in 1913: 'The Great War in Europe, that eternal threat, will never come. The bankers won't come up with the money needed for such a war, and industry won't support it, so the statesmen simply won't be able to do it. There will be no Great War.'

❧

At the very same time Wilhelm Bölsche's epic three-volume work *Die Wunder der Natur* is published, with the lovely title *The Triumph of Life* in the 1913 English-language edition. Bölsche, a divine writer, toned down Modernity, or more specifically the findings of modern science, for the bourgeois public, sprinkling on a fine dusting of sugar to make it more palatable. Instead of providing supporting evidence for Darwin, his intention was to depict the 'Mysteries of the Universe's Splendour'. This gave rise to some unusual biological and moral theories. The public responded enthusiastically in 1913 to Bölsche's reasoning, for example, that all higher beings are, in essence, nice to one another. He claimed that conflict only arises in the animal kingdom when an opponent is deliberately provoked. So not only would countries no longer wage war in the future, but animals wouldn't either. This, at least, was Wilhelm Bölsche's comforting message. Small wonder that his book was prominently displayed on all respectable imperial bookshelves. Kurt Tucholsky described the basic configuration of the upper-class library as follows: 'Heyse, Schiller, Bölsche, Thomas Mann, an old book of verse ...'. In essence, Bölsche's work was a book of verse as well – in that he inscribed peaceful verses into the album of Modernity, dreaming up a world in which the animals behave as peacefully and affectionately as they do in Franz Marc's paintings.

Restless and sweating, the morphine-addicted poet Georg Trakl travels back and forth between Salzburg and Innsbruck in June 1913. He can't wait to see Grete again, his beloved lover, sister, his own flesh and blood, but he misses her; he wants to meet with Adolf Loos, the esteemed anti-ornamentalist, but he misses him too. He rushes to Vienna, where he starts an unpaid internship at the war ministry, only to call in sick a few days later. He vaguely suspects, perhaps even knows for certain, that Grete, who in his mind is allowed to be only with him, is betraying him with his friend Buschbeck. He writes to him: 'Perhaps you know whether my sister Gretl is in Salzburg.' Trakl retreats into drugs, suffering and alcohol, and descends into a 'hell of self-made pain'. He writes and destroys; his corrections on the sheets are like stigmata, scratched into the paper as if it were raw flesh. He writes the poem 'The Damned', which includes the verse:

> The night is black. Ghostly blows the mountain wind
> The sleepwalking boy's white nightshirt
> And quietly, reaching into his mouth the hands
> Of the dead. Sonja smiles, mild and lovely.

Ludwig von Ficker, his fatherly friend and patron, in whose houses and castles Trakl finds shelter that year, immediately prints the poem in the June edition of his magazine *Der Brenner*. But not even that makes Trakl feel proud. He plunges ever lower.

Edvard Munch paints his picture *Jealousy*.

Meanwhile Thomas Mann is sitting in his country home in Bad Tölz, and wants to start writing. He has an idea for a new story, to be set in Davos, in the sanatorium he got to know while visiting Katia. A self-contained universe. The book is to be a counterpart to *Death in Venice*, currently on sale, but this time, as he writes in a letter, the story will be 'easy-going and humorous (even though death will be a favourite once more)'. The working title is *The Enchanted Mountain*.

He wants to get started. The children are playing catch outside in the meadow, watched over by the nanny. But he can't start. He keeps glancing at the rug in his study, and each time he does so he's overcome with rage at the rug trader, Schönnemann, who ripped him off. He asked another Munich dealer to take a look at it, and he valued the rug at a third of the price he paid. But Herr Schönnemann refuses to reimburse him, so Thomas Mann takes the matter to court. He looks out at the Alpine peaks, then lays his fountain pen aside. The enchanted mountain will have to wait. He writes to his lawyer, instructing him to pressurise the rug trader into paying up.

Harry Graf Kessler, dressed, as always, in a white three-piece suit, travels by train from glittering Paris to turbulent Berlin, falling for Westphalia's charms en route. 'Journey through Westphalia', he notes in his diary on 3 June.

> Fields of flowers, green rye and corn as far as the eye can see; softly swelling hills, a golden-blue summer haze over mountain and valley. There's something voluptuous, heavy, expansive, maternal to the mood, a stark contrast to the intimate beauty of the French countryside. This Germanness of the German countryside will have to invent a style for itself, just like the French countryside made Impressionism its own.

These were the words of Harry Graf Kessler – exactly a week after Die Brücke disbanded in Berlin, a group of artists who had spent eight years capturing the voluptuous, heavy, expansive and maternal qualities of the German landscape in German Expressionism. And a group to which Kessler paid no attention whatsoever.

Franco-German relations in 1913 in the publication *Simplicissimus*, featuring an advert for Henkell Trocken sparkling wine: 'From the grape to the cask in Rheims. From the cask to the bottle in Biebrich, where the preparation of our brands Henkell Trocken and Henkell Privat is complete. We are the only German sparkling wine maker which is at the absolute peak of organisation, both in the Champagne region and in Germany.' You turn the page. On the next, you see a caricature of a completely Frenchified German in magnificent clothes, spending the afternoon reading the illustrated journals. The caption reads: 'These relentless incidents on the border are horrendous enough already. But our men will be flabbergasted once they see the French approaching with all their elaborate fashions.'

On 29 June the Reichstag passes a military bill (put forward by the government) at the third reading, approving the increase of peace-time troops by 117,267 men to 661,478.

On a not very pleasant day in 1913 Franz Marc suddenly reaches for his paintbrush and paints a picture that contrasts wildly with the rest of his oeuvre. The painting in question doesn't depict the usual paradise, where animals are as mild as angels and human beings are redundant. No. This time it's all about hell. Franz Marc, horrified by the newspaper reports from southern Europe and the increasingly bloody carnage there, paints a sinister, snarling picture. He calls it *The Wolves (Balkan War)*.

On 20 June 1913, at midday, the unemployed thirty-year old teacher Ernst Friedrich Schmidt, from Bad Sülze, walks into the Sankt-Marien School in Bremen draped with weapons. Brandishing at least six loaded revolvers, he forces his way into the classrooms on a shoot-ing rampage. When one revolver runs out of bullets, he reaches for the next. Five girls between the ages of seven and eight die, while eighteen children and five adults are severely injured. Eventually a passer-by manages to overpower him. He later claims he was protest-ing about not having found a teaching position.

The year 1913 sees the publication not only of the first volume of Marcel Proust's *In Search of Lost Time* but also of a work of revolu-tionary force for twentieth-century philosophy: Edmund Husserl's *Ideas Pertaining to a Pure Phenomenology and to a Phenomenological*

Philosophy. Husserl's great paradigm shift for philosophy was a turning away from the positivist realities of the surrounding world and a move towards the facts of consciousness. And 1913 was the year in which every aspect of the world within became a reality: as a picture, as a book, as a house, as an illusion.

Or as a red book. During this year C. G. Jung starts noting down his dreams and experiences in a red leather-bound notebook – and begins to analyse himself with it. At the beginning of the year he, the President of the International Psychoanalytic Union, committed an act of parricide against Sigmund Freud. He not only rejected the libido theory as the central belief system of modern psychology but above all, as he said in his letter, 'tugged the prophet's beard'. Parricide, however, destroys not only the father but also the perpetrator. While Freud sinks into depression and suppressed rage, Jung descends into a severe crisis, because he no longer has the father figure he looked up to adoringly for so long. He relinquishes his teaching position at the University of Zurich and – just like Freud – becomes nervous about the encounter looming ever closer. The two enemy camps are due to meet in September at the Congress of Psychoanalysts in Munich.

Jung's sleep suffers, and he is tormented by nightmares. One of them is the catalyst for the 'Red Book'. Bathed in sweat, he awakes after having a vision of Europe sinking beneath the waves of a massive flood. Murder and manslaughter and corpses and devastation everywhere. By day he lectures on schizophrenia, but by night, in his unsettled dreams, he fears that he himself is becoming schizophrenic. The nightmare with the apocalyptic vision, in particular, torments him for so long that he tries to overcome it by writing it down. His dreams have been fraught with confusion ever since he managed to establish a very unusual love triangle in his life: he successfully convinced both his wife, Emma, and his lover, Toni Wolf, to accept their ménage à trois. On Sunday evenings Toni even comes to dinner at the family villa in Küsnacht on Lake Zurich. There are no records, however, as to exactly how those evenings played out after dinner. All we know is that both Emma and Toni were analysts, and that the relationship between the three would endure for many decades. And that Jung himself rummaged through the events of the days and nights in his dreams, recording them hurriedly and feverishly in his 'Red Book'. 'Debate with the Unconscious' was the name he gave to this experiment on himself. And, just like the masses of water flooding Europe in his dreams of 1913, Jung's inner being unleashed a storm tide: 'All of my later activities consisted of formulating what emerged from my unconscious, drowning me at first, during those years. It was the primary substance for a lifetime's work.'

∾✺∾

Elias Canetti, at nearly eight years of age, moves with his mother from Galicia to Vienna and starts to learn German.

∾✺∾

And 1913 is the year when D. H. Lawrence becomes *Lady Chatterley's Lover*. His Lady Chatterley is thirty-four years old, and he ran away from England with her after a brief, barely five-week-long affair. Her real name is Frieda von Richthofen – now Weekley, but her husband, a professor from the University of Nottingham and Lawrence's lecturer, is unable to tame either her Prussian nobility or her temperament. The 27-year-old Lawrence, however, the miner's son who has just submitted his manuscript for *Sons and Lovers* to his publisher, is impressed that she is 'the daughter of a baron, from the ancient and famed lineage of von Richthofen'. Frieda is green-eyed, intelligent, blonde and devoted to living life to the full. She believes that paradise on earth can only be realised through free love. Lawrence takes her at her word and flees England with her, heading for Europe. In the spring of 1913 they find shelter in a love nest belonging to Frieda's sister Else, in Irschenhausen in Upper Bavaria. The small, cosy, wooden summer house had always been a retreat for Else, the wife of the Munich professor Jaffé, and her lover Alfred Weber, brother of Max Weber, with whom Else studied for her doctorate. When Frieda arrives there from England, Else gives her a stylish dirndl as a moving-in present, intended to show off her feminine charms to their best advantage. The sisters were always of one mind on these matters, even while they were both lovers of Otto Gross, a Freud disciple, cocaine addict and legendary seducer. Admittedly Else was the only one to have a child with him, named Peter, just like the son born in matrimony that very same year to Otto Gross and his wife, a woman called Frieda, just like his other lover. It seems the paradise of free love was a confusing place at times.

Lawrence and Frieda Weekley, *née* von Richthofen, have to fight for their love even after they flee – they are united by, as Lawrence once wrote, 'a bond of affection, knotted from pure hatred'. But this early summer in Irschenhausen is their happiest time together. Isolated from the rest of the world in the Isar Valley, with fir trees and mountains behind them and the great expanse in front of them, they recover from their flight and summon new energy. It's not long before Lawrence is singing the praises of Frieda's 'genius for living'. He clearly enjoys her genius for love just as much, for when he later goes on to release his most famous book, the erotic tales of *Lady Chatterley's Lover*, the aristocratic seductress bears a strong similarity to Frieda von Richthofen. Irschenhausen, however, is not mentioned by name; it's not romantic enough for a novel of that kind.

But by June 1913 they are both growing restless. Lawrence wants to go back to England to enjoy the success following upon the publication of *Sons and Lovers*. And his lover wants to see her children again. She abandoned three offspring, aged thirteen, eleven and nine, to run off with the young author. And now it's breaking her heart. At the end of June they set off for England, after which Lawrence barely manages to tear her away from her beloved children. They make plans to meet in Italy. She isn't convinced, however, by his declaration of love, so he promises to walk all the way through Switzerland to Italy. And he does. She believes him, for the time being.

The Innsbruck publication *Der Brenner* carries out a survey on Karl Kraus. In June, Arnold Schönberg writes these fine words in response: 'In the dedication with which I sent my *Theory of Harmony* to Karl Kraus, I said something along these lines: "I have, it seems, learned more from you than one really should if one wishes to remain independent." That sums up, not the extent, but certainly the level of the appreciation that I have for him.' A very rare record of silent admiration, high regard and eloquence from this overheated year.

In June the German Reich celebrates the twenty-fifth anniversary of the reign of Kaiser Wilhelm II. He is a strange emperor, fascinated above all else by ships and decorum. Early in his reign he personally saw to it that court ceremonies were extended and new dress codes introduced. As his jubilee approaches, he takes all the planning in hand – wanting to make decisions not just about the staging of the event but also about the selection of presents. It was even his idea that he should be referred to in the speeches as the 'Emperor of Peace' – despite the fact that, just two weeks later, the Reichstag passes a bill approving the expansion of the army. And even though the old seating arrangements were retained at the gala tables – for example, placing the Reich Chancellor behind the Imperial family and the Federal Prince, and other representatives even far behind insignificant court officials – power relationships within the Reich itself hadn't been that clear for quite some time. If the hierarchy was not reflected in the table, Wilhelm needed to fight hard for his political position within the constitutional monarchy. He didn't have a genuine instinct for power. Instead, he turned his attentions to his strong point: public appearances. He would behave in a down-to-earth way, as if he were one of the people, a friend of the military, of simple pleasures, and an enemy of modern French art. He loved ships, the North, the marines. For him the greatest thing about the colonies was that they were accessible only by ship. Even when he went hunting for wood grouse in the Hessian mountains with his lover, Countess Görtz, he spent the evenings, before the hunter's horn sounded, etching little warships into the wood of the hunting lodge.

❧

There are over 200 cinemas in Berlin by 1913. Most of them show productions from the film studios founded in Babelsberg the previous year: for example, Asta Nielsen's *The Sins of the Fathers*. It tells the story of a painter's muse who, to her adored, paternal hero, is a model for allegories of beauty. Then he leaves her, and she becomes an alcoholic. The painter encounters her again later and is transfixed, but doesn't recognise her. He invites her to his studio, intent on painting an allegory of alcoholism which he intends to be his masterpiece. And it is. But when the muse sees that she, her love and her beauty are to be sacrificed on the altar of art and career, she destroys the canvas in a sensational act of protest. Asta Nielsen's outbreak of rage makes her face a much-admired icon.

❧

When the survivors of the *Terra Nova* expedition return to their homeland in June 1913, the brigade's scientific achievements attract a great deal of attention. This is intended to distract from the fact that Scott, exalted as a national hero, was in fact the second to reach the South Pole. For when the last members of the expedition finally arrived at the South Pole in 1912, the freshly erected Norwegian flag was already standing proud. Roald Amundsen was a few days ahead in this ruthless race against ice and time. The morale of the British expedition members was broken. Scott was not the only one to lose his life in the endless ice on his way back. Even today Captain Lawrence Oates is revered as a martyr in Great Britain, for committing suicide so as not to be a burden to his four comrades. His last words as he left the tent are legendary: 'I am just going outside and may be some time.' A sentence like that makes a man immortal in England. The title of Apsley Cherry-Garrard's legendary report on the catastrophic expedition is just as fitting: *The Worst Journey in the World*. So the Brits may not have discovered the South Pole, but at least they didn't lose their sense of humour.

'The Worst Marriage Proposal in the World': on 8 June, in Prague, Franz Kafka has finally begun to ask for Felice's hand in marriage. But he breaks off mid-sentence, and it's not until 16 June that he is able to bring himself to finish the letter. It ends up being over twenty pages long. Kafka begins with a detailed account of how he needs to look for a doctor – what exactly he wants him to certify, perhaps fertility or sanity, is unclear. Or maybe it's all just a laboured pretext to delay the inevitable marriage and its consummation: 'Between you and me there stands, apart from everyone else, the doctor. It is doubtful what he will say, because medicinal diagnoses are not really the crucial factor in such decisions, and if they were, then it wouldn't be worth taking them into account. I was, as I said, not really ill, but I am.' Hmm. Then follows a passage in which Kafka, that wonderful, sensitive stylist, establishes a form of written stuttering:

> Now bear in mind, Felice, that in the face of this uncertainty it is hard to say the words, and it must sound peculiar. It's simply too soon to say it. But afterwards it will be too late, and then there won't be any time for discussing such things as you mentioned in your last letter. But there isn't any time to hesitate for too long, at least that's how I feel about it, and so that's why I'm asking: in view of the above premise, which is sadly ineradicable, do you want to consider whether you want to become my wife? Do you want that?

In fact, what he probably wanted to write was: 'Do you *really* want that?????'

Then, in a rare moment of clarity, he presents Felice with the cost-benefit calculation of a potential marriage:

> Now give some thought, Felice, to how marriage would change us, what each of us would gain and lose. I would lose my – for the most part, terrible– solitude and gain you, whom I love more than anyone else in the world. But you would lose your former life, with which you were almost entirely content. You would lose Berlin, the office you love, your friends, little pleasures, the prospect of marrying a healthy, cheerful, good man, and of having beautiful, healthy children, which you, if you stop to think about it, really long for. And on top of this inestimable loss, you would gain a sick, weak, unsociable, taciturn, sad, stiff, pretty much hopeless human being.

Who could turn down an offer like that? A proposal of marriage disguised as a confession.

Kafka is still uneasy, for he suspects he has stuck his neck out on this occasion, even though he tried, with hundreds and hundreds of words, to cover up and mask his question. But he knows that, somewhere in the middle of the letter, he did ask her to marry him. He hems and haws before putting the letter in an envelope, then goes on a laborious search for a bigger envelope, because the letter is now so thick. Then he goes out on to the street, but dawdles, waiting so long that all of the post offices have closed for the evening. Then he is suddenly overwhelmed by the desire for Felice to have the letter on her desk first thing in the morning, so he runs to the station, where urgent post can be put on the fast train to Berlin. On the way, sweating and in a panic, he meets an old acquaintance. Kafka tries to excuse himself, saying he's in a hurry and has to get the letter to the station. What kind of letter is so urgent, asks the acquaintance in amusement. 'A proposal of marriage', says Kafka, amid laughter.

On 8 June, the day when Kafka began writing his proposal, the German Stadium, built for the 1916 Olympic Games, is officially opened by Kaiser Wilhelm II. The German builders completed it three years ahead of schedule. Ah, the good old days.

On the occasion of the twenty-fifth royal jubilee, fifteen-year old Bertolt Brecht writes the following verse in his diary:

> And if, in the evening, we set
> and die a hero's death
> then the flag will wave consolingly
> black white and red.

And then another verse:

> The wind shall sing within it
> Your duty you have done!
> You died in battle
> as a loyal German man.

Interesting.

In Wuppertal-Elberfeld there are already five paintings by Picasso hanging on the walls. Two still-lifes from 1907 at the home of the painter Adolf Erbslöh, a *Mother and Child* from 1901 at the home of Julius Schmits, as well as a *Man in Coat* from the same year and a watercolour from the Rose Period at the home of the banker August von der Heydt.

The War of the Roses in two Viennese marriages. Fur is flying between Arthur and Olga Schnitzler, with Schnitzler confiding in his diary that he's lying on the balcony as if paralysed. And on 10 June, Robert Musil writes the following after an argumentative walk with his wife: 'Martha, in a foul mood, fired unnecessary accusations at me that left me cold. You're going to leave me, and then I'll have no one. I'll kill myself. I'm going to leave you.' But she didn't.

Someone left, though: Leo Stein. After months of arguments he walked out of 27 Rue des Fleurs, the Parisian apartment he shared with his sister Gertrude and which he had made into *the* salon of the avant-garde. Picasso and Matisse and Braque kept passing through, and the *jour fixe* on Saturday evenings was a central gathering point of Parisian creativity. But it was more than that: over the years the salon had become the first museum of modern art in the world. In the tightest of spaces masterpieces by Picasso, Matisse, Cézanne, Gauguin and all the other great French masters crowded together, collected by the Steins early on and with sound judgement. Gertrude, dressed as ever in brown sackcloth, sat in a dark Renaissance chair and stretched her feet out towards the fireplace. She always felt the cold. Next to her stood Leo, explaining his understanding of modern art to the dozens of guests. His captive audience included English aristocrats, German students, Hungarian painters, French intellectuals and, somewhere in the crowd, Picasso with his lover *du jour*.

But then there's an argument. Leo Stein can't bear his sister's preference for Cubism any longer – nor the fact that she quite clearly regards Alice Toklas, who lives there with them, to be not just a cook, teacher and secretary but also a lover. Leo Stein can't understand any of it. He takes the most beautiful Renoirs, Cézannes and Gauguins and flees from Paris to art's Promised Land, settling down near Florence. Gertrude Stein immediately fills the empty spaces on the walls with Cubist paintings by Picasso, Braque and Juan Gris from 1912 and 1913. From that moment on Alice Toklas takes Leo Stein's place at the Saturday evening salons. The brother and sister whose combined energies created the most important collection of modern art ever assembled in such a short time never spoke another word to one another.

Leo sends offers of reconciliation from Florence, one after the other. But Gertrude doesn't answer. Later, she attempts to deal with their separation using the method most intellectuals favour in trying to deal with things that trouble them: she writes a book about it. She calls it *Two: Gertrude Stein and her Brother*. She believes this will proclaim her independence in black and white. Instead, of course, the main thing it shows is that she never came to terms with the separation from her brother.

In the June edition of the *Neuer Rundschau* a text is published by 25-year-old author and Mann disciple Bruno Frank. The topic is 'Thomas Mann: A Study following *Death in Venice*'. It includes, alongside a beautiful, detailed interpretation of the novella, these extraordinary lines diagnosing the era:

> When metaphysics still existed, it meant comparatively little to be a hero. But now, with an inanimate floor of rock beneath us and an empty sky above, where we have no faith, only hunger for it, where we are so disconnected from one another, thrown back into ourselves, probably more than any preceding generation, it is at this very moment that Thomas Mann appears, wakefully and courageously placing this writer into a completely godless world.

So there you have it. Gustav von Aschenbach, the last tragic hero of Modernity.

On 16 June the wakeful and courageous writer in question sets off on a three-week vacation to Viareggio, on the Tuscan coast, with his wife, who has just returned from another spa cure. There, in the Hotel Regina, he lays aside *Felix Krull*, having toiled away on it for a while, and begins work on *The Magic Mountain*, as he had unsuccessfully

tried to do in Bad Tölz, but only by the sea does one have an uninterrupted view of the soul – and of the mountains before it.

JULY

Holiday! Egon Schiele ad Franz Ferdinand, the Austrian successor to the throne, play with the model railway. The Prussian officers swim naked in Lake Sacrow. Frank Wedekind goes to Rome, Lovis Corinth and Käthe Kollwitz go to the Tyrol (but stay in separate hotels). Alma Mahler escapes to Marienbad because Oskar Kokoschka has called the banns. He consoles himself by boozing with Georg Trakl. Constant rain. Everyone goes half-mad in their hotel rooms. But still: Matisse brings Picasso a bunch of flowers.

On 10 July the highest temperature ever recorded is measured in Death Valley: 56.7° C. On 10 July it rains in Germany. It's barely 11°.

❧

This July, August Macke and Max Ernst, his young admirer, become closer friends. Macke even uses a notebook with a few lecture notes by Ernst as a sketchbook. Together they organise an exhibition called 'Rheinland Expressionists', which, for want of a suitable gallery, they open in Cohen's bookshop in Bonn. Hanging from the shop's first-floor window is a huge poster that the participating authors have inscribed together. Max Ernst also makes sure that news of the exhibition reaches the right audience: under a pseudonym he writes a review in the Bonn *Volksmund*, chiefly praising the art of his friend Macke, whose abstractions 'provide expression for the spiritual through their form alone'. So in 1913 everybody is fighting over the unconscious.

❧

The psychological, the transcendental, is in the air. In 1913 the Italian artist Giorgio de Chirico paints his first proper 'metaphysical landscape', in Guillaume Apollinaire's phrase. It is called *Piazza d'Italia* and shows: nothingness.

If you know that de Chirico studied in Munich for a long time, you can tell from the yellow of the buildings and the width of the streets that the metaphysics in the art of this strange, Greek-born Italian is all Munich. In this way Leo von Klenze's classical architecture appeared between the Hofgarten and Wittelsbacherplatz in 1913. Böcklin and Klinger were de Chirico's artistic forefathers, Schopenhauer and

Nietzsche his intellectual ancestors – and de Chirico no longer needs them for his studies in the loneliness of the lonely individual. Because that is the viewer himself, who is irrevocably drawn into the meaninglessness of the new century. Or, as de Chirico himself says: 'Art was liberated by the modern philosophers and poets. Nietzsche and Schopenhauer were the first to teach the deep significance of the non-meaning of life, and how that meaninglessness could be transformed into art. The good new artists are philosophers who have overcome philosophy.' So de Chirico reduces perspective to a state of absurdity. And soon becomes a revered authority in Paris, Berlin and Milan, on increasingly shaky foundations.

From 16 July, Egon Schiele spends his holidays with his patron and sponsor Arthur Roessler in Haus Gaigg in Altmünster on the Traunsee. He announces his arrival in a long letter – he's coming either at three or four o'clock, or at five or six. But he doesn't come. And his host walks the half-hour journey from the station back to his house, shivers, drinks tea with rum and then rum with tea. It's bucketing down. Eventually Schiele knocks on the terrace door – he has arrived at a different time and from a different direction. And not alone, either, but with Wally Neuzil, whom we know today from the great watercolour *Wally with a Red Blouse* – but who was nobody at the time.

The next morning his luggage is to be picked up from the station. Roessler asks him what it comprises exactly. To which Schiele replies: only the bare necessities. Then they collect from the station: a few clothes, cracked clay jugs, colourfully glazed peasant bowls, thick tomes, art books, primitive wooden dolls, tree trunks, painting and drawing utensils, a crucifix. Schiele assembles all these things as inspiration in the guest room, to work. But he works for: not one minute. Instead he hikes through the wonderful landscape of the Salzkammergut. Enjoys being with his girlfriend and being looked after by Roessler's staff. His host hoped that Schiele would paint, and that he could use one of the paintings for the living room of the summer house. But Schiele just doesn't paint. One morning Roessler goes into Schiele's room and sees Schiele sitting on the floor watching a little clockwork train set go around in a circle. Schiele switches tracks, couples and decouples while loudly imitating the noises. He can do perfect imitations of train whistles, coupling, shunting, squealing. He asks Roessler to join in. Someone has to do the announcements at the little station.

The London *Times* reports that the successor to the Austro-Hungarian throne has sulkily withdrawn to his Bohemian castle near Konopiště, and is lying on the floor in the nursery. He orders every guest who comes to visit to lie down on the floor and help him add on extra tracks. The Kaiser is supposed to have brought in psychiatrists in plain clothes a long time ago, to observe and treat Franz Ferdinand as inconspicuously as possible. Franz Ferdinand hides all summer in his castle; he wants to be far from Vienna, the strange old Kaiser and, above all, the General Chief of Staff, Conrad von Hötzendorf, who is constantly trying to carry out a preventive strike against Serbia.

Franz Ferdinand can't bear the abuse of the court any longer. Everyone there was against his friendship with Sophie Countess Chotek, because she was beneath his dignity and naturally his class. The court only agreed after wife and children had renounced all claims. So Sophie was condemned to a life in the shadows. She might have had three children by Franz Ferdinand, but she was shunned in Vienna; she was even forbidden to sit next to her husband in the imperial box at the Burgtheater or the Hofoper. She was not forbidden to go for walks with him around Konopiště Castle. That was why her husband had renamed it the 'Upper Way of the Cross' early in their relationship. But with his wife, Sophie, and three children, Franz Ferdinand is clearly what you would call happy. Because he isn't actually needed in Vienna, the archduke, who is seen in the capital as a short-tempered, uncontrollable power-politician, is a loving husband

and father. He spends hours playing with his children in the gardens of the Bohemian castle, and it is his purest joy when they know the names of all the flowers whose blossoms spill opulently over the box tree hedges. Next door, in Janovice Castle, Sidonie Nádherný is in mourning.

Picasso was seriously ill. But on 22 July Eva Gouel writes to Gertrude Stein: 'Pablo is almost well again. He gets up every day in the afternoon. Henri Matisse keeps dropping round to ask after him. He came today to bring Picasso flowers, and spent the whole afternoon with us.' What a wonderful, consoling idea: one of the two most important artists of his time bringing a bunch of flowers to the other most important artist of his time. No wonder Picasso was completely recovered a few days later.

Robert Musil is not seriously ill, but he is given sick leave so he doesn't have to perform his duties as a librarian at the Technical College in Vienna but has time to write. On 28 July, Dr Pötzl writes a new sick note for Musil, whom he has been treating for 'serious neurasthenia' for six months (lest we forget). So Pötzl writes: 'The high level of prevalent nervous exhaustion calls for a much longer period of recovery, and from today's neurological standpoint it calls for a suspension of professional activity of at least six months.' And so, referring to this document, Musil writes to request 'six months' leave'. The university sends him to the official doctor, and one Dr Blanka establishes: 'He is suffering from a serious degree of general neurasthenia involving the heart (cardiac neurosis).' Neurasthenia involving the heart – it is hard to think of a better summation of the malady of the modern age.

At the end of June, Harry Graf Kessler had travelled to Berlin for large-scale military exercises with his old regiment. The great aesthete joined in without demur. He loved life in the officers' mess and the aristocratic officer corps in Potsdam, he loved the soirées and suppers that accompanied manoeuvres. So in July he is staying with Princess Stolberg in Potsdam, although she confesses that she 'grew up in a castle surrounded by woods' and still can't tell the different Prussian uniforms apart. 'I said: Well, she could easily tell a hussar from a garde du corps. Yes, she said, but it was so terribly hard to tell a general from an NCO.' Kessler leaves it like that, so that we understand how terrible it is that in Prussia in 1913 there's actually still a princess who can't distinguish a general from an NCO.

On 25 July, when it has finally stopped raining, some of those who are very aware of where those differences lie – intellectually, morally and as regards the uniform – drive out with Kessler to Lake Sacrow. More precisely: Major Friedrich Graf von Kliknowström, born in 1884, 3rd Uhlan Guard Regiment since 1905; Lieutenant Thilo von Trotha, born in 1882, also in the 3rd Uhlan Guard Regiment; and cavalry captain Eberhard Freiherr von Esebeck. 'When we came to the bathing spot, a lonely meadow lined with forests, where we wanted to swim, Krosigk suddenly rose up right in front of us out of the lake and the reeds, stark naked.' Afterwards, Graf Friedel von Krosigk organised a naked race on the meadow. 'Diagonally opposite, on the other bank, a white figure, also swimming.' The white figure: who might that have been? Princess Stolberg, perhaps, wanting to double-check the differences between generals and NCOs? Asta Nielsen taking a break from filming in Babelsberg?

Male fantasies, Part II: two chimeras after a train journey: Oswald Spengler, the old sexist, doesn't take a holiday, he's thinking about the 'Decline of the West', and about all these women all over the place. 'I can bear intellectual intercourse with women only in small doses. Even if a girl is as narrow-minded as a suffragette and as tasteless as an art-filly.' He is back at home in his flat in Munich, and thinks it's ugly, particularly the furniture: 'Any piece of furniture must be able to bear comparison with a Manet or a Renaissance palace. Old furniture can do that. The design of new furniture makes it look like five-finger exercises.' But then he remembers his train journey and adds: 'The only good things are the ones in which these stylistic idiots haven't stinted on their "ability": locomotives etc.' Gottfried Benn takes the train that summer as well. He too gets a testosterone boost from the women in his compartment. In his little notebook he writes these great lines about his experiences on the fast train between Berlin and the Baltic: 'Meat that walked naked./Into the sea-tanned mouth.' And later: 'Men's brown pounces on women's brown:/A woman is a matter for a single night. And if it was fine, for the next one too!/Oh! And then alone again!' So Benn too can bear the company of women only in small doses. Then he too descends happily back into the basement of his solitude.

Kaiser Franz Joseph doesn't want to be alone. Arm in arm with Frau Katharina Schratt he walks through the extensive parkland of Bad Ischl, for many years his resort of choice. And Frau Schratt has been his companion for many years too: they know each other from the days when Sissi was still alive. And yet – and this is the imperial wish – she will never become his lover, only ever his companion. So the two of them, separated by an age difference of thirty years, spend their days together. At night the Kaiser would like to be alone. However, at about seven o'clock in the morning he leaves his imperial villa and walks over to see Frau Schratt in her villa 'Felicitas', where they take tea together. Then he mingles with the spa guests. He generally goes unrecognised, because he doesn't wear his decorations on holiday, dispenses with his bodyguard and looks like any knobbly old retired officer. He wants to be entirely ordinary. But sadly he is the Kaiser. So he goes along with that. But he writes letters of wonderful ordinariness to Fau Schratt. Oh, he laments at one point how his bunions hurt when he has to stand up at the banquet and raise a toast to the king of Bulgaria.

The king of Bulgaria himself has quite different concerns: the dispute between Serbia and Bulgaria about territories in Macedonia escalates on 3 July. Serbia declares war – and the Turks, Greeks and Romanians also stand up to Bulgaria. The Second Balkan War has arrived. New dispatches are constantly reaching the Kaiser in Bad Ischl. But he doesn't want to be disturbed by those hotheads in the Balkans. He walks over to Frau Schratt and drinks some tea.

On 13 July, Freud goes to Marienbad with his beloved daughter Anna to convalesce and gain inner strength for the great battle. The Fourth International Psychoanalytic Congress in Munich early in September, where he will meet up with Jung and the renegade Zurich analysts for the first time since their disagreement. And, of course, Marienbad doesn't help Freud at all. Either with the rheumatism in his right arm or with his depression. He writes: 'I can hardly write, we've had a bad time here, the weather cold and wet.'

In July, Rilke goes briefly to Berlin and sees the newly discovered head of Amenophis in the city's museum: 'A marvel, I tell you', he writes excitedly to Lou Andreas-Salomé. These are the excavations from Tell el-Amarna, from the expedition financed by James Simon. The whole city is in Egypt fever about the beauty of the sculptures. The *Berliner Tageblatt* writes excitedly about Amenophis: 'A true modern, in the boldest sense of the word.' Advice is suggested to the avant-garde: 'Futurists, lower your heads!' Else Lasker-Schüler comes to the museum, falls to her knees with enthusiasm; her paintings of

Prince Yussuf soon bear the features of Amenophis IV, also known as Akhenaten. And the greatest marvel, the head of his wife, Nefertiti, is even in the basement of the museum. The archaeological expedition initially decided not to show their most beautiful item. The curators of the exhibition guess that if everything taken from the country in January 1913 were put on display, the Egyptians would soon start demanding the return of their works. So Nefertiti stays in storage.

Anyone who has spent a thousand years under Egyptian soil can wait a few years until the world is at her feet.

So it's July, everyone's convalescing, Rilke has Egypt fever, a bit of money and nothing to do. So one might think it obvious for him to take a few days' holiday by the sea in August. But for someone who must justify himself daily to his lady patrons and his superego for his cultivated leisure, 'holiday' is a dirty word. So it's quite obvious that it seems 'frivolous' to Rilke to go to the coast in August. He leaves Lou in Göttingen and then writes to her from Leipzig immediately: 'I have had the frivolous idea of going to the sea for eight days at the end of the week (to Heiligendamm, where the Nostitzens are). There are supposed to be lovely beech woods there, and suddenly my soul is filled with the idea of the sea. So perhaps I'll do that.'

Frank Wedekind is in Rome, where on 8 July he finishes his play *Samson*, which he began on 26 January. He has gone to Rome to be alone and to recover from the chaos surrounding the ban on his play *Lulu*. A nymphomaniac who destroys the world of men, that's not allowed. But Wedekind senses that with his Lulu he has created a new heroine for the twentieth century. He consoles himself with the heroes of the past for the ignominy of the present – and in Rome he reads Goethe's *Italian Journey* and Burckhardt's *Culture of the Renaissance in Italy* and visits the Sistine Chapel. The censors in Munich would have rubbed their eyes in amazement at this troublemaker's *haut bourgeois* ambitions. He writes to his wife, Tilly Wedekind: 'The loveliest thing I have experienced here was my walk among the ruins of the Monte Palatino.' But then he warns her: Rome is fast asleep, no theatre, no *variété*. 'For my own purposes Rome leaves nothing to be desired. But if we want to enjoy ourselves together, we would probably be better off going to Paris.' Because this is worth establishing once and for all: 'Paris is the most beautiful city in the world, then comes Rome, and just below that, Munich.'

Lovis Corinth is sitting in the Villa Mondschein in the Tyrol, with his children, his wife and his mother. He hasn't quite recovered from his stroke, but here in Sankt Ulrich in the Grödner Tal he slowly starts feeling better. It is raining so hard that Corinth can hardly paint outside. So his family has to sit for him. First he paints himself, in local costume, his heavy green loden jacket and his hat decorated with a feather (he looks cheerfully growly again). Then his wife, Charlotte, also as a Tyrolean. He applies the paint thickly onto the canvas, as if to demonstrate that he's alive again. And when the world sinks back into fog and rain, he brings the green and red and brightness of the costumes into his art. His son Thomas doesn't want to be painted; he is freezing, and is soon in bed with flu at their boarding house.

Corinth receives the post from Berlin each morning as 'manna in the desert'. Most of the letters concern the big dispute in the Berlin Secession, which has been raging since Paul Cassirer, the dealer, was made its chair. For the next exhibition he has uninvited all thirteen artists who didn't vote for him, which led to a big falling out. Now the association belongs to the remaining Secessionists around Corinth, but the limited company, the owner of the exhibition house at 208–9 Kurfürstendamm, is controlled by Cassirer and Liebermann. So the association around Corinth has to erect a new building to regain its space and fame. When Corinth, in the Tyrol, learns of the idea that this is to be constructed by Peter Behrens, the architect and designer of houses, lamps and tables for the AEG electrical company, he admits he doesn't like him, but he recognises the possible improvement in the association's profile, because Behrens is 'modern'. In fact, amid the driving rain here in the Tyrol, all those quarrels in his distant homeland are far too much. He thinks 'with horror of Berlin', and spends days immersed in Bernhard Kellermann's book *The Tunnel*, about which Corinth writes the shortest and most concise review of the year: 'Good book, I'd like to go to America.' But it's no use: in August, Corinth has to go back to Berlin.

Käthe Kollwitz is in the Tyrol too, with her husband, Karl. They are forever arguing, the rain cascades down, they can't get out into the freedom of the landscape, they sit there dully on the chairs in their pension and are profoundly unhappy with each other. After the summer holidays she falls into a 'great depression'. She has suicidal thoughts, is in despair about her life and her artistic work, is unsatisfied with her first attempts at sculpture. And then she asks her diary: 'Karl and me?' Answer: 'Such a love I have never known.'

Karl no longer interests her. 'Always the same, you already know every nuance, slack sensuality can no longer stimulate it. Quite different fare is needed to revive the appetite.' That is Käthe Kollwitz's declaration of freedom in 1913. She seeks comfort in Strindberg, plunges into his dramas: wild hatred between the sexes, dull togetherness, it helps her, she doesn't feel alone. She tells her son about it, says Strindberg is about the way couples 'maul and hate each other'. Kollwitz sits listlessly at the window, gazes into the rain and writes in her diary: 'Summer is passing and I don't feel it.'

In Vienna, Oskar Kokoschka has called the banns for his marriage to Alma Mahler. It is scheduled for 19 July, at the town hall of Döbling, the district where the bride's parents live. He has gone to the Hohe

Warte to see Carl Moll and ask for Alma's hand. Moll has no objections. But when Alma learns of Oskar's plans on 4 July, she panics, packs her bags and flees; she wants to go to Marienbad. Kokoschka chases after her, catches up with her at the station, shouts, rages at her to open the window again, Kokoschka shoves a self-portrait at her and orders her to hang it in her hotel room to ward off all the other men. And as soon as she's gone, he sends her his first letter: 'Please, my little Alma, don't look at anyone, the men there will always stare at you.' And then: 'Why did you laugh when I said: stay healthy! I would have loved to ask you, but you'd already gone.' Yes, why did she laugh? In the few clear-sighted moments of their relationship (which were also the darkest) Alma probably felt that they could not be healthy together because they were sick with love. Or, as Kokoschka puts it two days later in his next little letter: 'For example, I'm uncomfortable with a thug of a doctor feeling you up, a waitress seeing you partially undressed or in your bed and so on.' She puts up with all these letters, perhaps even enjoys them, but she writes to him from Franzensbad that she's only coming back when he's finally finished his masterpiece. She calls him a 'weed' and 'Jewified'; he's that too. Kokoschka is furious and goes straight to Franzensbad – when he arrives at the hotel, Alma isn't there. And his self-portrait isn't hanging over her bed, as he had ordered. When she comes back from her walk, he erupts. He rages against Alma, drums his fists on her bed and jumps on the next train back to Vienna. The date of the wedding passes. And then, with the smell of Kokoschka's sweat still lingering in her hotel room, Alma, the great tactician, writes a letter to Berlin. She would like to know what chance she has with Walter Gropius, her serious, strict former lover, who withdrew disappointed when he saw the double portrait of Alma and Kokoschka in the Secession exhibition. So Alma writes to him on 26 July: 'I may marry – Oskar Kokoschka, a man both our souls know intimately, but I will remain bound to you throughout all eternity. Tell me if you are alive and if this life is worth living.'

Kokoschka still has no idea that Alma has been putting out feelers again. He is still in Vienna, painting for dear life. But also wondering if this life is worth living. He works away at the huge canvas of their double portrait. He works away on his masterpiece. Perhaps only his visitor keeps him from despair that July in Vienna. Because compared with Georg Trakl, Kokoschka's soul is still in pretty good order. Trakl is staying temporarily in Vienna, at 27 Stiftsgasse, and between his alcoholic and drug-induced stupors he has taken an unpaid job in Vienna, as an accounts clerk at the war ministry. It is hard to imagine a more absurd job for Georg Trakl. He holds it down for only a few days. But during that time, as soon as work is over, he steals away to Kokoschka's studio. The painter is standing in front of his canvas, hopping nervously back and forth, sunk in wild inner dreams about Alma's infidelity, cigarette in his mouth and paint on his palette, painting with brush and right forefinger. Behind him, Trakl sits on a beer barrel, rolling back and forth for hours on end. Kokoschka, the lunatic, finds that calming. Every now and again a faint growl is heard from Trakl's corner. He is starting to recite his poems, talking about crows, fate, corruption and decline; he cries out desperately for his sister, then sinks back into eternal silence and rolls mutely back and forth, back and forth. Trakl is there every day while Kokoschka is painting the double portrait. And it is also Trakl who gives the painting its name: *The Wind-Bride*. In a poem by Trakl written during his chaotic Vienna days, 'The Night', he writes:

> Golden flicker the flames
> Around the peoples.
> Over deep black cliffs
> Death-drunken plunges
> The glowing bride of the wind.

So Wind-Bride Alma glows in the studio and on the easel, but in real life she is beginning to cool off. Or perhaps it is precisely the other way around, that because Kokoschka sensed with his neuraesthenic imagination that Alma was threatening to slip away from him, that she was distancing herself from him, precisely because a cloud had fallen over their symbiotic love, that he is even in a position to paint a portrait of them both that is a work of art rather than a declaration of love. It is only when Alma bears the title 'Bride of the Wind', only when he has imbued his bride with the fleeing evanescence of the wind that he is able to make a portrait of her. You can't marry a 'Wind-Bride'. Only paint one.

AUGUST

Is this the summer of the century? Who knows, but it is *the month when Sigmund Freud has a fainting fit, and when Ernst Ludwig Kirchner is happy. Kaiser Franz Joseph goes hunting and Ernst Jünger spends hours on end sitting in a hot greenhouse with a winter coat on. Musil's* Man without Qualities *begins with some inaccurate information. Georg Trakl attempts to take a holiday in Venice. So does Schnitzler. Rainer Maria Rilke is in Heiligendamm and receives a lady visitor. Picasso and Matisse go horse-riding together. Franz Marc is presented with the gift of a house-trained deer. No one does any work.*

Venezia Lido 1913
592

Georg Trakl

In Heiligendamm, sitting out on the hotel terrace, Rainer Maria Rilke slowly pulls off his dark grey gloves and loosely grasps the hand of Helene von Nostitz, who is sitting next to him drinking an Austrian *mokka*. She gazes into his eyes, his gentle, deep blue eyes, the depths of which always make women forget the rest of his face. Rilke was with Lou Andreas-Salomé in Göttingen when he received Helena's letter asking him to come and join her. To the great surprise of all involved, bound together as they were by a tightly interwoven, confusing network of affection and jealousy, Rilke accepted the invitation. As he wrote in a letter from Göttingen while Lou was off somewhere lying down, exhausted from all their mutual silence, talking, arguing, pining, reading and more silence, he had an 'intense need for some sea air'. But when Rilke arrives in Heiligendamm, he is confronted by the colourful chaos of horse-racing, for the racetrack on the small hilltop between Heiligendamm and Bad Doberan is hosting its big, traditional derby. The hotel in Heiligendamm is overflowing with chic urbanites and fat stud farm owners whose waistcoats practically burst at the belly every time they stand up. There are horse boxes everywhere, women with big hats, businesslike hustle and bustle, conversations about wagers – Beppo is the big favourite today, or so he hears. Distraught, Rilke asks at the reception for some writing paper.

He writes a hasty note to Helene von Nostitz, informing her that he plans to set off again within the next half-hour. When the bellboy delivers the letter to her room, she is in the middle of an argument with her husband about her reasons for inviting the poet. After reading Rilke's lament, she quickly gets dressed and hurries out, finding him in the Kurhaus dressed in his white summer suit, but looking 'grey and exhausted'. The clouds rage outside, towering up to form mighty black mountains. A powerful wind starts up, blowing across from the sea. The women hold tightly onto their hats, while the first wilting leaves are swept from the tall beech trees up into the air.

Helene von Nostitz links arms with Rilke and marches him energetically out of the Kurhaus, past the little path to the newly built cottages, all the while firing out greetings to left and right, everyone hunched over against the stormy wind. Helene and Rainer reach the beech forest. They keep going; it gets calmer and calmer; the wind drops. Behind them, over Kühlungsborn, the sun pushes its way through the clouds and bathes the coast in glistening light. The beech trees rise up majestically into the Baltic Sea sky, their trunks rubbed completely smooth and their crowns pushed up high by the salty wind. Despite being many decades old, they still look so innocent. How do they do that? Rilke feels like he's strolling among enormous stilts. The trees tear their gaze away from earthly moss formation and tree stumps up to the skies. He leans against a tree trunk and takes a deep breath. Helene von Nostitz gives him an encouraging glance, but all he can see is the blue sea, shining out from between the beech trunks, here and there a tiny frothed peak, but otherwise just blue, blue, blue.

Later, once his thoughts have come back to earth, he sits down and writes to Lou Andreas-Salomé: 'This place is the oldest seaside resort in Germany, popular for its forest by the sea, and for its clientele, who consist almost entirely of the landowning nobility from the surrounding areas.' The letter is surprisingly cool, given the newly rekindled relationship between Rilke and Lou, who only recently were holding hands in that Göttingen garden as if renewing their old bond. Then they parted ways – Lou decided to open a psychoanalytic practice in Göttingen, and Rilke decided to attempt a holiday. But, as always, he seems to feel under immense pressure to be suffering at least a little, as though Lou should never feel he can be happy when he's not with her. This forms the basis of all the innumerable letters he sends to his faraway benefactress and admirer. So in Baedeker style he writes another few lines about Heiligendamm in 1913:

The Grand Duke has a villa here, but apart from that there's only a Kurhaus with a lovely columned hall, a hotel, and around a dozen villas, everything still rather pristinely presented in the tasteful style of the early nineteenth century. The people are driven over from their mansions in the most exquisite of horse-driven carriages, providing these wonderful, lively reliefs against the backdrop of the sea. And yet it's so peaceful in the forests and even on the beach, and all in all, it's a ...

Here the reader expects Rilke to let another enthusiastic or at least relatively positive adjective slip out, but the Chief Risk Officer of Happiness manages to rein it in just in time, and continues with: 'all in all, it's a reasonable little place.'

What a shame he can't let himself go even here. For Rilke, that ardent lover of tender unhappiness, high priest of the inexpressible, even Paradise was probably only a 'reasonable place'. But he cannot deny that he grows increasingly fond of Heiligendamm, helped by the fact that the weather is better here than anywhere else in the country, for the sea wind always drives the clouds away, and the most beautiful of sights play out on the beach before Rilke's eyes, with fluttering garments and Impressionist gatherings of people. It pleases him to sit there on a deckchair, his legs crossed, and read poems by Goethe or Werfel, that young hothead he is currently so in awe of. And so he becomes increasingly fond of the place, but this has little to do with the presence of Helene von Nostitz, who, like all his women, he finds very alluring from a distance but demanding and irritating at close quarters. He knows how to escape her without being choked by her jealousy, though, and declares the following: 'The Unknown is drawing me in.' That must have delighted Herr von Nostitz, who was seriously bothered by the goings-on between his wife and the strange poet. So Rilke goes to his room and tries – in complete earnest – to make super-sensory contact with his 'Unknown'.

He got to know her at the séances held by Marie von Thurn und Taxis in Duino, when she, this unknown lady, instructed him to throw a key or ring from the bridge into the river in Toledo. And because he was planning to travel to Spain at some point anyway, he took this order very seriously and had the princess pay his first-class fare for the journey. Rilke's restless and lavish lifestyle depended on permanent contributions from a circle of powerful women – in order to keep them sweet, he developed an intense correspondence with each of them. Every day he sent off many dove-blue pages to the palaces and hotels of Central Europe. He wooed them to solicit money, understanding, affection, even a wife. But he shied away from it too – not from the money, understanding or affection – he was perfectly happy to take all that. It was just the wife he wasn't sure about. He preferred to keep them at a tender distance through his letters. He even became the German champion at doing so. And this is what he is doing now, in Heiligendamm. On 1 August he writes one of his epic letters to Sidonie Nádherný, who is drowning in grief since her brother shot himself. Rilke dries the tears of her soul with his pen, as if it were some exquisite handkerchief, and urges her to turn her mind to practical grieving: she should play some Beethoven on the piano, he instructs, for that will help, and she should do it 'this very evening'.

Then he turns his attention back to his super-sensory relationship. Unfortunately, we don't know what the 'Unknown' told Rilke to do in Heiligendamm. We do know, however, that he stayed on there even after Helene von Nostitz's departure. But that's probably for sensory, rather than extra-sensory, reasons: for he met Ellen Delp, one of Lou Andreas-Salomé's 'adoptive daughters', a young actress favoured by Max Reinhardt, who was recuperating in nearby Kühlungsborn. No sooner has Helene set off to Bad Doberan by train than Rilke writes the following on the afternoon of 14 August: 'Dear Lou's daughter, I've come to extend my hand to you in greeting.' And he does: far away from their social circle and from convention, Rilke seems to achieve a relatively uncomplicated affair with Ellen Delp here in Heiligendamm. After their first walk together beneath the tall beeches, he writes the following poem:

'Behind the Guiltless Trees'

Behind the guiltless trees
the old fate slowly forms
her silent face.
Moths draw towards it ...
A bird's cry here
rebounds there as a train of sorrow
against the hard soothsaying mouth.

O and those soon-to-be-lovers
smile at one another, still farewellless,
their destiny soaring and falling above them
like a constellation,
inspired by night.
Still not near enough for them to experience,
still it dwells
floating in its heavenly course,
a bright figure.

The 'soon-to-be-lovers'! This state of affairs is Rilke's second favourite. His favourite is that of 'having once loved'. Because then he no longer needs to exert himself and can just get on with writing his letters. The in-between state, normally called the present, love and uncertainty – he's not too fond of that one; it overwhelms him. But here in Heiligendamm, behind the innocent trees, he seems to feel freer than usual.

He reads poems out loud to his 'matutinal Ellen', Franz Werfel mostly. They go to the beach together, Rilke letting the fine Baltic Sea sand glide through his long, slender fingers. After that, they probably go to his room. The day after, Ellen has roses sent to the poet's room. And he sends a thank-you letter on his dove-blue paper: 'The roses are beautiful, beautiful, bountiful, and cheer, the way they stand there, one's own heart boundlessly. Rainer.'

To increase the strength of the armed forces, a search begins through-out Austro-Hungary for deserters from military service. As part of the campaign, on 22 August the police publish this missing persons notice: 'Hietler [!], Adolf, last known residence in a men's hostel in Meldemannstrasse, Vienna, current residence unknown, enquiries under way.'

It's a beautiful August day in 1913. Or, to be more precise:

> There was a barometric low over the Atlantic; it moved east-wards towards a high-pressure area situated over Russia, not yet showing any inclination to bypass that high by heading northwards. The isotherms and isotheres were functioning as expected. The air temperature was in the appropriate pro-portion to the mean annual temperature, to the temperature of the coldest and the warmest months and to the aperiodic monthly temperature fluctuations. The rising and setting of the sun and the moon, the changing phases of the moon, of Venus, of the rings of Saturn and many other significant signs all corresponded to the forecasts in the astronomi-cal almanacs. The water vapour in the air was at its high-est buoyancy level, and air humidity was low. To sum it up more briefly in a way that corresponds to fact, despite being a little old-fashioned: it was a lovely August day in the year 1913.

These are the opening lines of Robert Musil's *Man without Qualities*. Alongside Proust's *In Search of Lost Time* and James Joyce's *Ulysses*, this was the third classic of the modern era, saturated with the explo-sive power of the year 1913.

But what was the weather really like in Vienna during these August days of 1913? A detailed article was printed in the *Neue Freie Presse* on 15 August, with the lovely headline 'Persistent bad weather'. In it, Dr O. Baron von Myrbach, assistant at the Central Institute for Meteorology by trade, offers little comfort: 'As feared, this year's summer weather loyally retained the characteristics it possessed from the very beginning. Its harshness has relented a little. But that is not saying much, for the start of the summer was so unusually bad that even the period that followed, despite the improvement, must still be described as bad.' In other words, there was not one single beautiful August day in the year 1913. No, in Vienna the average temperature was 16°. It was the coldest August of the entire twentieth century. Perhaps it's a good thing that people didn't know that back in 1913.

Franz Marc has gone to East Prussia with his sister to stay at her husband's property in Gendrin. After dozens of horse paintings and horse sketches, now Marc himself is in the saddle. A lovely photograph taken that August shows him out riding with his brother-in-law Wilhelm. The horse, a grey, stands to attention, knowing that he's carrying him, the horse whisperer. And Marc hardly dares to press his thighs against its flanks through sheer respect for the animal's elegance. On the day of their departure Wilhelm presents Marc with a tame deer. The deer is sent by train to Sindelsdorf, survives the journey and lives from then on in the garden, named Hanni (not to be confused with the Sindelsdorf cat of the same name). To save it from the loneliness of roaming the meadow in front of Marc's studio by itself, Hanni soon gets a life partner, a doe named Ruth. Captivated by their brown, shy beauty, Marc creates picture after picture of the two animals as symbols of paradise.

On 16 August a moving assembly line is installed at the Ford automobile factory in Detroit for the first time. In the 1913 business year Ford produces 264,972 cars.

While Alma Mahler stayed in Franzensbad, letting her wedding date pass by, Kokoschka finally carried on with painting *The Tempest*, turning in despair to his black paint and transforming his entire studio into a coffin. But then Alma comes back, and they fall for each other all over again. On 22 August, her birthday, they celebrate at the Tre Croci Hotel in the Dolomites, not far from Cortina d'Ampezzo. The next morning they set off early into the dense forest and stumble upon a clearing where foals are frolicking. In spite of his panic-ridden fear of being alone, Kokoschka sends Alma away, takes out his pencils and sketches the horses as if in a frenzy. The young horses come over to him, eat from his hand and rub their beautiful heads against his arms.

And what about Golo Mann? His mother, Katia, writes this in her memoir, *A Youth in Germany*:

> Summer 1913: Golo is gabbing on even more than Aissi. He'll often talk all day long without uttering one sensible word, nothing but nonsense, about his friends, about Hofmannsthal and Wedekind, about the Balkan War, a mixture of things he's picked up or invented, so I really have no option but to rebuke him […] one of the children's favourite games, following on from all the military concerts this summer, is to pretend to be conductors. Golo does it in such an indescribably comic fashion, with those unsightly enraptured expressions, that feeble pathos summoned up from deep within, and given that he's never even seen a proper conductor before, I can hardly believe what I'm seeing.

Golo, Thomas Mann's son, was four at the time. Where did it all come from?

Like father, like son: in Germany, *jus sanguinis*, right of blood, becomes the basis for citizenship in 1913.

Ernst Jünger is bored during his summer holidays in Rehburg, on the banks of Lake Steinhude. Tall oaks rustle next to the family's country house in Brunnenstrasse, the view stretches for miles. But Jünger feels imprisoned in the house, with all its little turrets and alcoves. Dark wood panelling from Germany's industrial era set the tone for the entire property; the windows hardly allow any light in through their stained-glass panes. Magnificent wood-carvings sit enthroned on the door frames. The hunting room is always gloomy, the windows painted over with the scene of a belling stag and a skulking fox. This is where Ernst's father sits with his friends, smoking fat cigars and hoping to shut the world out. Ernst Jünger feels his room is suffocating him, he lies on his bed up in the loft and goes back to reading adventure stories set in Africa. It's raining. But as soon as the sun appears, its sheer summer-like energy warms the air outside in minutes. Jünger opens the window. His parents are setting off on an excursion. The water rolls down the hard leaves of the huge rhododendron bushes in the garden and drips heavily on the ground. He can hear it. Plop, plop, plop. Other than this, it's deathly quiet this August lunchtime. Eighteen-year-old Ernst walks down the wide, dark brown steps to the cloakroom and searches for his warmest winter coat, the one that's lined with fine fur. He takes the fur hat down from the hat rack too, and then sneaks out of the house. It's a humid 31° outside. Jünger walks through the rhododendron bushes along the narrow path leading to the greenhouses. This is where his father cultivates his tropical plants and vegetables. As Jünger opens the door to the cucumber house, musty, stale heat hits him in the face. He quickly shuts the door behind him, pulls on the fur cap and winter coat and sits down on a wooden stool next to the flowerpots. The cucumber shoots snake wildly up in the air like darting green tongues. It's two o' clock in the afternoon. The thermometer inside the greenhouse is showing 42°. Jünger smiles. It can't be much hotter than this even in Africa, he thinks.

On 3 August an artist suffocates inside a pile of sand at Berlin Jungfernheide. His art form consisted of being buried alive for up to five minutes. Today, however, the director of the artists' group was immersed in conversation and forgot to start the excavation until ten minutes had passed.

On 11 August, Sigmund Freud continues his journey with his wife, sister-in-law and daughter Anna from Marienbad on to San Martino di Castrozza. This small mountain village in the Dolomites is home to a branch of Dr Von Hartungen's legendary Riva sanatorium. Freud plans to spend another four weeks recharging here before he has to go to Munich at the beginning of September for that confounded Congress of the Psychoanalytical Society. Freud summons his friend Josef Ferenczi to his hotel; Ferenczi is more than happy to come, and together they work on a strategy for Munich. In the afternoons he goes for his daily constitutional with Anna, arm in arm through the cool forest. A picture of them on one of their walks shows Anna in traditional garb, staring jauntily at the camera, full of confidence, and her father next to her, proud but morose too, even a little anxious. During his stay at the mountain sanatorium he receives treatment for his migraines and chronic cold. Christl von Hartungen prescribes strict abstinence from tobacco and alcohol, and plenty of fresh air. But Freud struggles to re-charge at all. The nearer the event in Munich gets, the more distracted he becomes. Then, in the middle of the night, just one day before his departure, Dr Freud sends for Dr Von Hartungen; he has suffered a fainting fit and requests urgent medical assistance via a calling card.

At the beginning of August, having recovered from the shock caused by the deaths of his father and his dog Frika, Picasso travels to Céret. But his fame is now such that on 9 August the local newspaper *L'Indépendant* runs the following report: 'The small town of Céret is rejoicing. The Master of Cubism has arrived, ready to enjoy a well-earned rest. So far, the artists Herbin, Braque, Kisling, Ascher, Pichot, Gris and the sculptor Davidson have joined him in Céret.' All this fuss is a source of anxiety to Picasso. His greatest concern is Juan Gris, for he has mastered the Cubist technique almost as well as Picasso by now, and has the ability expertly to create a whole new world from fragments, wallpaper and scraps of newspaper. Before long, his old friend Ramon Pichot also comes to Céret, attempting to convince Picasso to give money to his most recent lover, Fernande, to help her get by. But Picasso hates being pressured like that, and they come to blows. Picasso and Eva, who stole him away from Fernande, leave in a panic. They head back to pulsating Paris in search of some 'peace and quiet', as Picasso – in all honesty – writes in a letter to his art dealer Kahnweiler in Rome. Eva and Picasso move into their new apartment and studio at 5 Rue Schoelcher in Montparnasse.

From there it's only ten minutes on the new railway line to Issy-les-Moulineaux, where Henri Matisse is now living. Scarcely back from Céret, Picasso and Eva drive out there and spend the summer horse-riding with Matisse. This is such an extraordinary event that it is immediately reported twice to Modernism's head office, Gertrude Stein. First, a note from Picasso: 'We're riding through the Clamart forest', on 29 August. And then, on the same day, this from Matisse: 'Picasso is a horseman. We're out riding together, which comes as a great surprise to everyone.' The news of the two heroes' reconciliation quickly becomes the most important topic of conversation in Montparnasse and Montmartre – in other words, the whole world.

'We are each passionately interested in the technical problems of the other. We undoubtedly profited from one another, it was like an artistic brotherhood', writes Matisse about the man who was once his greatest rival. And to Max Jacob, Matisse says: 'If I didn't do what I do, I would love to paint like Picasso does.' And Max Jacob replies: 'It's crazy, but Picasso just said the very same thing to me about you.'

Georg Trakl is furious. He wants to see his sister Gretl, but can't find her. His appointment as a clearing officer in the Viennese war ministry was, of course, a complete joke. He stops turning up and drinks his first five carafes of red wine by midday every day. He takes drugs. His friends Adolf Loos and his English wife, Bessie, prescribe him an immediate dose of: holiday – holiday from himself. They are due to travel to Venice. On 14 August he writes to his friend Buschbeck: 'On Saturday I'm supposed to travel to Venice with the Looses, which inexplicably makes me somewhat nervous.' The next day, a second letter, this time with a rare trace of euphoria ignited by the prospect of his first ever holiday: 'Dearest Buschbeck! The world is round. On Saturday, I will be falling down towards Venice. Further and further – towards the stars.' Of course, the whole thing turns out to be a failure: a displeasure trip. He who once reached for the stars has ended up with a handful of jellyfish. Even his adored Karl Kraus, who goes to the lido with them, even the caring attention of Adolf Loos, Ludwig von Ficker and their wives can't brighten Trakl's mood, which is further clouded by the presence of Peter Altenberg on this 'staff outing' of the Austrian intelligentsia. It's mid-August, and Georg Trakl is walking aimlessly across the Lido in Venice. The sun is shining, the water is warm and the author is the unhappiest person in the entire world. A photograph from those days of 1913 shows him wandering tentatively across the sand, his hair brittle and shorn, his skin as pale as that of a moloch living in a hole deep under the earth. His left hand is curled upwards like a flower bud, his lips are pursed. He has his back to the sea, clearly feeling like a pitiful sight in his bathing costume, lost, homesick and may be mumbling poetry to himself. At night, in the hotel, he writes them down:

Black swarm of flies
Darkens the stone room
And the head of the homeless man
Gazes tormented at the golden day.

Venice, the sinking city, exerts an irresistible pull on the morbidly inclined Viennese intelligentsia in the summer of 1913. As well as Trakl, Peter Altenberg, Adolf Loos and his wife and the Von Fickers, Arthur Schnitzler and his wife, Olga, also arrive in Venice on 23 August. They have travelled from Brioni, and are staying in the Grand Hotel. On the beach they meet more old acquaintances: Hermann Bahr, a bearded giant of a man, and his wife. The very next day, after a gondola ride with Olga, Schnitzler meets with his publisher Samuel Fischer to discuss forthcoming publications. The Fischers are in Venice with their best friends to celebrate their son Gerhart's nineteenth birthday. Richard Beer-Hoffmann is there, the actor Alexander Moissi, and Hermann Bahr and Altenberg come along too. There's no mention of Trakl. Unfortunately, they are all ailing from something: Gerhart, the birthday boy, is scrawny and feverish, and Samuel Fischer has an inflammation of the middle ear. But they celebrate anyway, toasting young life and its rich prospects. At the end of August the Schnitzlers set off in leisurely fashion via St Moritz and Sils Maria, where on 28 August in the 'Waldhaus', they celebrate Goethe's birthday and also, just a bit, their tenth anniversary.

We can't forget Kafka, or his bride! So how did Felice Bauer react to reading the most preposterous marriage proposal of all time? She was distraught. But even she, hardened as she is by now, probably hadn't thought Kafka capable of surpassing that disastrous note of self-incrimination masked as a marriage proposal. But then Kafka writes his 'Letter to the Father'. It never became as famous as the one he wrote to his own father. But it deserved to, because it's simply incredible. On 28 August, Goethe's birthday, Kafka asks Felice's father whether he would entrust his daughter to him. Or rather: he implores him desperately *not* to entrust his daughter to him:

> I am taciturn, unsociable, morose, selfish, a hypochondriac and genuinely in poor health. Among my family, the best, most loving of people you could ever encounter, I live as a complete stranger. In recent years I've spoken an average of less than twenty words a day to my mother, and I've barely ever exchanged more than a few words of greeting with my father. I don't speak to my married sisters and their husbands at all, unless I have something bad to say. I have no sense of how to co-habit normally with my family. And yet your daughter is supposed to live alongside a person like this, a healthy girl like her, whose nature has predestined her for genuine marital bliss? Is she supposed to bear it, leading a cloistered existence alongside the man who, admittedly, loves her as he's never been able to love anyone else, but who, by virtue of his unalterable destiny, spends most of his time either shut away in his room or wandering around alone?

Marriage as a stroke of fate. Issue 21 of *Die Gartenlaube* has something to say on the matter:

> In some regions of our Fatherland, there still exists a beautiful custom long forgotten elsewhere. The bride, when crossing the threshold of her parents' house as a girl for the last time before setting off for her wedding, is handed a handkerchief made of new linen by her mother. The bride clasps this handkerchief in her hand during the ceremony, in order to dry her bridal tears. On the wedding night, the young woman then stashes away the little handkerchief in her linen closet, and there it stays – unused and unwashed – until the day when it will veil the face of its owner, its

features now frozen by death, and follow her into the grave. This handkerchief is called the 'Cloth of Tears'.

These are lines from *Die Gartenlaube*. They read like one of Kafka's short stories.

Marcel Duchamp travels to England with his eighteen-year-old sister Yvonne, who wants to study English at a language school in Herne Bay, on the north Kent coast. Duchamp, on the other hand, is just on holiday, and writes: 'Delightful weather. Playing as much tennis as I can. A few French people here, so I don't even need to learn English.' He still doesn't feel like making art.

As he does every year, Max Liebermann sets off at the beginning of August for the Dutch coast, this time staying at the chic beach hotel Huis ter Duin in Noordwijk. But he doesn't see any reason to relax. All he wants to do is paint. Among the dunes of the coastal resort he once again paints the huntsmen, the horse-riders in the water, the women playing tennis. The sky is always grey in these pictures from the summer of 1913, but Liebermann, unlike the other holiday-makers, isn't bothered by that in the slightest, for it offers a beautiful contrast against the sandy beige and white of the clothing. On 18 August he writes to his friend and patron Alfred Lichtwark in Hamburg: 'I've been here again for a week now, the place where I know every person, every house, almost every tree, where I've painted practically everything. My weeks here alone are like therapy for my inner self.' Day after day he sets off with his paints and his easel, and on this particular day he and Paul Cassirer, his friend, art dealer and the former chairman of the Berlin Secession, plan to visit a tobacco magnate in his summer house in Noordwijk. Or, more specifically: his kennel. A huntsman opens the door, upon which eight rather small grey or white shaggy-haired spaniels appear, yapping wildly over one another as their droopy ears jiggle excitedly back and forth. The owner informs Liebermann that spaniels are excellent for hunting rabbits. They set off into the dunes together. Liebermann takes his easel with him in order to paint a picture of the hunter with his dogs in tow. Soon, the first shot rings out through the air. Every single report startles Liebermann, and it bothers him that his models have to make such a racket. He tries to paint the dogs as quickly as possible, their silhouettes standing out on the crest of the dunes against the rosy, setting sun. Then Liebermann starts to sketch the hunter placing the rifle over his shoulder and organising the dogs into pairs, but the sun is already sinking into the sea and Liebermann has to break off mid-sketch. He makes plans to return the following morning – and the hunter promises to just pose rather than shoot. And so *A Hunter in the Dunes – Trainer with Dogs* is born.

On 28 August, Kaiser Franz Joseph joins in the last Hochleiten hunt on Steinkogl, near Bad Ischl, and shoots a goat.

On 14 August 1913, Hugo von Hofmannsthal loses his cool in a letter to Leopold von Andrian:

> This year taught me to see Austria the way that the thirty previous years had taught me *not* to see it. I've completely lost both the trust I had in the highest class of society, the high nobility, and the confidence that it had something to give in Austria, especially in Austria. Vienna has been left at the mercy of mob rule, the worst there is, that of the wicked, stupid, vile petty bourgeoisie.

A new man takes to the stage of 1913: Heinrich Kühn. A middle-class intellectual from Dresden, born in the house 'Nine Muses'. Thanks to his father's financial support, he lives as a gentleman of independent means in Innsbruck, dedicating himself entirely to photography. Kühn is a deliberate eccentric, who wears either a Tyrolean costume or English suits, with a long, rumpled coat over them while he takes his photographs – this can be seen on his bookplate, in which it's hard to tell which is more crumpled, his overcoat or his folding camera. He had an old-fashioned and naïve aura to him. And yet he managed to take photographs of the utmost modernity. His pictures from 1913 are fresh and full of innocence, grace and strength. This is partly down to their composition, the extreme low-angle shots. And then there's his technique, for it was he who perfected the use of Autochrome in collaboration with the great American photographer Alfred Stieglitz. Even in those days he was able to use it to create excellent colour pictures, one after the other, of the Tyrol's alpine pastures and meadows. After the death of his wife, who had always regarded his strange passion with great scepticism, he had only five models: his four children and their nanny, Mary Warner, who became his partner. The villa in Innsbruck became the 'House of the Five Muses'.

In 1913 the family was slowly running out of money: the allowance from Dresden had dwindled to nothing, his brother-in-law had gambled away the family fortune and Heinrich Kühn was desperately searching for a way to earn a living. He had been trying to establish a state teaching position for art photography in Innsbruck – and the prospects were looking very good. But in August he discovered, after two years of negotiations, that the ministry responsible was withholding its signature for lack of funds; all the money had been spent on military matters, for the Balkan War: 'You know how it is, Herr Kühn.'

But Kühn refuses to be discouraged and continues to take photograph after photograph of his private theatrical troupe – in other words, the children: Walter, Edeltrude, Lotte and Hans. And Mary. One photograph (used on the cover of the German edition of this book), shows Mary and his eldest daughter darting across the crest of a hill, the heavy August clouds pressing down from above. White is one of the few choices available to them for their clothing, along with blue, red and green – the father buys the children special 'photography clothes', which are suitable for the pure colour tones of the three layers of the Autochrome plate.

There's the melancholic Walter, with his metal-rimmed glasses resting on his teenage nose, who began painting at a young age; then introvert Edeltrude, who looks like she's suffering greatly from the world in general and her forename in particular; then Lotte, the liveliest and most radiant; and then Hans, the youngest, a patient lad. Heinrich Kühn is a loving father, but a radical artist. If one of the children accidentally hogs the painting, destroying the balance of the image, he rigorously airbrushes them out, even if it took him hours to get all the children in position in the first place. What Kühn wants to depict in his photographs is nothing less than paradise. Children at play, children resting, women in swirling clothes, the innocence of nature. 'The Fall of Man', he writes in a letter 'takes two forms: Social democracy. And Cubism.'

❦

Kaiser Franz Joseph appoints the heir to the throne, Grand Duke Franz Ferdinand, as 'Inspector General of All the Armed Forces', thus extending his authority. The heir subsequently refuses to approve the demand for a preventative war made by the Chief of the General Staff, Franz Count Conrad von Hötzendorf, his arch-nemesis.

❦

In The Hague, the Palace of Freedom is inaugurated in September, built with the help of donations from all over the world, including around $1.25 million from the American multi-millionaire Andrew Carnegie. Preparations begin for a new Hague peace conference in 1915, which is intended to resolve all unresolved issues between nations.

After the dissolution of Die Brücke, Ernst Ludwig Kirchner leaves Berlin, heading for the island of Fehmarn. So eager is he to leave the city, its noise and motifs behind him, that he travels all the way to the south-east tip of the island, to the isolated home of the light-house keeper, Lüthmann – and then right to the top, to the 'Gable Room', where he spent some time last year. The lighthouse, the iso-lated beach, the lighthouse keeper's eight children – these become his motifs for the summer. The bad weather is clearly visible in the paintings, dark clouds moving across the horizon again and again. Down on the beach, the trees stoop over into the water, almost remi-niscent of the South Pacific. Above, the golden rainbow blooms, and Kirchner paints it for days on end, its blazing gold splendour. This time Kirchner brought not just Erna, who is called 'Frau Kirchner' here – even though she's always running around practically naked – but Otto Mueller and his wife, Maschka, too. They take turns paint-ing one another swimming; they relish the freedom, their steadily increasing fame. The Lüthmanns' children and the lighthouse keeper himself welcome the Kirchners into their family circle with warmth and trust. Those summer weeks on Fehmarn may be the happiest days of Kirchner's entire life. 'Oh, Staberhuk, how wonderful you are, a little corner of happiness, so peaceful and beautiful!' he cries out into the wind, again and again. Even Kirchner's style ascends to new heights. The women are no longer broadly sprawled out but reach towards the skies; his brushstrokes are more nervous, slender, lengthy figures, his sketches and paintings dominated by Erna and Maschka naked on the beach. He is addicted to the body's form, he complains jovially, utterly addicted to it. Whenever he is dissatisfied with a pic-ture, he throws it into the sea in a fit of rage – only to plunge in after it, rescue it from the waves and put it back on his easel, to paint it all over again, but better. The most wonderful driftwood keeps washing up on the beach; a year before, at the same time as the *Titanic*, a ship cap-sized off Fehmarn. The schooner *Marie*. Its wood has become part of art history, for Kirchner swam repeatedly out to the sandbank where the wreck lay in order to pick out especially fine pieces of wood which were suitable for carving. On 12 August he writes to his Hamburg collector and patron Gustav Schiefler: 'The head I sent you is a wood carving (oak), I've made several like it out here.' And in September, in a letter to his student Hans Gewecke, he writes:

> Unfortunately we have to leave soon. You won't believe how difficult this is for us. I can't decide whether the sea is more beautiful in summer or in autumn. I am painting as much as I can, so that I can take at least some of the thousand things I would like to paint back with me. On top of that, the oak wood from the stranded ship is becoming more and more appealing for statues. I'll have to take a few unhewn pieces with me, for time is limited now, and the days are getting shorter and shorter.

As fascinated as Kirchner was by the wreck, and as much as he plundered it for his work, it doesn't appear in a single one of his sketches, art works or paintings from Fehmarn, even though he created hundreds of works there in 1913 alone. The ship stranded in the Baltic Sea – he had the classic motif of Romanticism embodied in front of his very eyes, the ultimate Caspar David Friedrich scenario. But Ernst Ludwig Kirchner impudently denied the wreck a place in his oeuvre. There can hardly be a more conclusive sign that German Romanticism is definitively over.

The *Mona Lisa* is still nowhere to be found. In the Louvre a Corot has been hung on the orphaned nail.

Felice Bauer, shocked by Kafka's letters, spends August in Sylt. Innumerable letters go back and forth between her and Prague, about whether Kafka is going to join her there or not, about whether or not the bracing climate will do him good. In the end, of course, he doesn't come. Such a shame, it would have made for such wonderful journal entries: Kafka in Kampen. But it wasn't to be.

SEPTEMBER

A death in Venice shakes Berlin. Virginia Woolf and Carl Schmitt want to kill themselves. The stars look bad on 9 September. Duel in Munich: Freud and Jung cross swords. Rilke has to go to the dentist for amalgam fillings, Karl Kraus falls head over heels in love with Sidonie. Kafka goes to Venice, doesn't die, but falls in love with Riva. The 'First German Autumn Salon' begins, and Rudolf Steiner lays the foundation stone in Dornach. Louis Armstrong makes his first public appearance. Charlie Chaplin signs his first film contract. The rest is silence.

On 9 September, Gerhart, son of the publisher Samuel Fischer, whose birthday had just been celebrated in Venice, and who was already sickly and pale and feverish, dies the titular 'death in Venice' of his father's great 1913 publishing success. He is brought back to Berlin hotfoot by ambulance, but there he succumbs to the disease – the 'Italian disease', as one might call it, because the story of his illness is so similar to that of Gustav von Aschenbach, Thomas Mann's hero, who is carried off by cholera in Venice. And so it is only appropriate that Hugo von Hofmannsthal should learn of the publisher's son's death in Venice and sends condolences from there to Samuel Fischer and his wife on 17 September: 'There, where lies the most grievous of pains, at the very summit of pain, there consolation seems to me to dwell – only there and not somewhere off to the side.'

Gerhart's death is a shock for S. Fischer Verlag and the whole of cultural Berlin – Gerhart was a much-loved, delicate person, now following his own path as a music student after lengthy arguments with his parents. There is a large funeral in the Jewish cemetery in Weissensee, the sun sits ill with the shattered grief on the faces of the attendees. Samuel Fischer, numb with pain, loses his hearing in one ear from shock. Gerhart Hauptmann, after whom Fischer's son was named, just fifty-one and at the peak of his fame, hurries to the funeral, before laconically observing in his diary: '3 o'clock Gerhart Fischer funeral. 5 o'clock big dress rehearsal for *William Tell*: that's Berlin, that's life.'

Rainer Maria Rilke has to be treated at Berlin's Western Hospital, 4 Marburger Strasse, for severe toothache. From there he writes to Eva Cassirer, his confidante and the patron of his wife, Cara, that he has just read Thomas Mann's *Death in Venice*: 'Very surprised by much in the first part and found it wonderfully formed; but the second part rather contradicted this impression, so that I couldn't work out the whole thing, even though it lifted me somewhere within.' Then Rilke has to go back to continue his dental treatment. He is placed in the hands of Dr Charlie Bödecker, a German-American expert in metal inlays, who attempts to combat Rilke's considerable dental decay with amalgam fillings.

Galerie Hermes sends Lovis Corinth a painting at his home in Klein Niendorf on the Baltic. He had painted it in the Tyrol in July, when his son was feeling better again and he was being bathed. *Naked Child in Wash Tub* it is called – and on his way back Corinth had then left it in Munich with the art dealer Oscar Hermes. But Hermes didn't like the nursemaid's nose. So on 2 September he sent the painting to the Baltic for cosmetic surgery. Corinth looks at the painting, looks at the nose, asks the nursemaid in, looks at her nose – and changes the nose in the painting. Then it is sent back to Munich. These are the advantages of being a dealer in contemporary art. Complaints can be dealt with straight away.

In September the first edition of the school magazine *Die Ernte* (40 hectographed copies, 15 Pfennigs) is published at the Königliches Realgymnasium in Augsburg. Most of the contributions are written by a pupil in class 6A called Bertolt Brecht. The rest is by Berthold Eugen. Eugen is Brecht's third Christian name after Friedrich and Bertolt and the pseudonym of Bertolt Brecht. Under this name he also sends poems to the newspaper *Augsburger Neuste Nachrichten*. There they lay beneath a big pile on the arts editor's desk. Brecht is fifteen. Marie Rose Amann is twelve. Unfortunately they haven't yet met; he hasn't yet held her in his arms like a lovely dream, as he will later write in 'Memory of Marie A.'.

That day in September 1913, the only things Brecht is holding in his arms like a lovely dream are the first copies of his new school magazine, which he takes to the headmaster's office.

On 10 September, while on a tour of South America, the dancer and choreographer Vaslav Nijinsky – who had a long relationship with Diaghilev, the director of the Ballets Russes, and celebrated the success of Stravinsky's *Rite of Spring* with him – marries the dancer Romola de Pulszky out of the blue. Diaghilev suffers a shock and fires them both, with immediate effect.

Marcel Duchamp, who still doesn't feel like making art, takes a piece of paper and writes down his thoughts on the question of what is still possible:

> Possible.
> The figuration of a Possible.
> (not as the opposite to impossible
> nor as relating to credible
> nor as subordinate to probable.)
> The Possible is only
> a physical caustic
> that burns up all aesthetics or callistics.

On 20 September Rudolf Steiner lays the foundation stone for the new Centre of Anthroposophy, the Goetheanum, in Dornach, near Basel. He writes a short text that is buried along with the stone: 'Laid by the J. B. V. [Johannes Building Association] for anthroposophical work, on the 20th day of the month of September 1880 a.t.M.G. (after the Mystery of Golgotha), i.e. 1913 a. Chr. b.' This is followed by the

position of the stars on that day: 'With Mercury as the evening star in Libra.' Mercury corresponds to the sound I, and the star sign Libra represents CH, so that the constellation of Mercury in Libra signifies the word 'ICH'. Rudolf Steiner has clearly been waiting for the day when this cosmic rune would stand in the sky. And he has also chosen it because Mercury is the evening star that day. Mercury forms a conjunction with the sun, at a declination of 03° 26' 45. (Not that it does much good: the place burns down ten years later.)

❧

On 8 September, in the Café Imperial, the 39-year-old Karl Kraus, editor of *Die Fackel* and the sharpest-tongued author in Vienna, is introduced to 27-year-old Sidonie, Baroness Nádherný von Borutin, Rilke's confidante. And it is about him that they immediately converse. They talk on and on, fascinated by one another. They stagger out into the night, they take a fiacre through the Praterallee, the stars are shining, and Karl says to her, 'If one could only be where her eyes gaze.' Then they are driven to a hotel bar, she tells him about the death of her brother, who has now joined their parents, about her depression, the spiritual wasteland in which she lives. And Karl Kraus, overwhelmed by Sidonie's beauty, unmanned by her grief, takes her hand. He wants to lead her out of that wasteland. 'He recognises my essence', she thinks after their conversations in the Prater at night. And she even lets Kraus stroke Bobby, her Leonberger dog, which no one else is allowed to touch.

❧

On Odd Fellows' Day Louis Armstrong, who has just turned thirteen, makes his first public appearance as a jazz musician, with the band from the institution whose name, Municipal Boys' Home, Colored Dept. Brass Band, is emblazoned on its big drum. Armstrong stands proudly beside the drum in the band photograph from that year, next to his first teacher, Peter Davis, who handed him the instrument in January. And Armstrong is wearing a police uniform. It was traditional in New Orleans for police to pass on their discarded jackets and trousers to poor young people so that they could use them as band uniforms. The band moves through the city, playing as they go, with an enthusiastic Armstrong on trumpet, following the tunes, setting the note. Then, when the band comes back to the home in the evening, happy and exhausted, and all the others have handed their instruments back in at the music room, Louis Armstrong picks up his trumpet again and looks hopefully at his teacher. 'All right, then,' growls Peter Davis, 'Just this once.' It's warm in his dormitory, the others are still outside, smoking in the hot summer night, dreaming about their new female sports teacher, and the sounds of the Odd Fellows' Day festivities drift over from the distance. Armstrong takes off the old policeman's uniform. And as he sits alone on his bed and a fly flows through the room, he tries to copy its flight with his notes, he follows it, buzzing, stopping, buzzing. And when the fly has found its way out of the window, he just keeps on playing. And never stops. Louis Armstrong is on his way to becoming the greatest jazz trumpeter in history.

A special case of family care: on 4 September in the town of Degerloch, Ernst August Wagner kills his wife and four children because he wants to spare them the consequences of his planned rampage. Then he cycles to Stuttgart, where he boards a train to Mühlhausen. When night has fallen over the city, he sets four houses on fire and waits until the people flee the smoke and flames. Then he shoots them with his rifle, killing twelve, seriously injuring eight more. He is finally overpowered by the police. His further plans for the night were to kill his sister and her family, then go to Ludwigsburg to set the castle ablaze and die in the duchess's burning bed.

On 9 September Albert Einstein delivers a lecture in Frauenfeld to the 'Swiss Society of Natural Research', in which he explains his new approaches towards the theories of gravity and relativity.

On 9 September at about 7.00 p.m. the first Germany naval L1 Zeppelin plunges into the sea off Heligoland after being caught in a whirlwind.

On 9 September, the day Gerhart Fischer dies and disaster is plainly written in the stars, 31-year-old Virginia Woolf is examined by two neurologists after complaining about an 'inability to feel'. Since August, when she delivered her first novel, *The Voyage Out*, she has lost weight so quickly and become so anorexic that she is barely able to travel and has to be tended to by two nurses. The examination by the neurologists is so humiliating, her feeling of pointlessness so great, that only a few hours after the examination, when the nurses are taking a break, she tries to take her own life with an overdose of the sleeping tablet Veronal. Her husband, Leonard, saves her at the last minute, and she is revived in hospital.

He then sends her to Dalingridge Place, the country seat of her stepbrother George Duckworth. This is ridiculous, in that Virginia Woolf's collapse dates back to her childhood abuse by that same stepbrother. But her husband, Leonard, seems to be blind to this difficulty, and that same September he writes of his brother-in-law that 'as a young man he was, it is said, an Adonis'. Virginia Woolf can defend herself only by returning to health. She starts eating again and is able to leave Dalingridge Place in the autumn.

The Fourth Congress of the International Psychoanalytic Association is held on 7 and 8 September, in the Hotel Bayerischer Hof in Munich. It is the meeting that Freud and Jung have feared since their split in the spring. The atmosphere is tense and oppressive; both men are on their guard. There are 87 participants on the first day, only 52 on the next. When Jung stands for re-election as chairman, 22 members abstain. Freud has allowed himself to be persuaded to deliver a short lecture 'On the Problem of Choice of Neurosis'. The next day Jung speaks on 'The Question of Psychological Types'. The atmosphere, Freud says, is 'weary and unedifying'. The main event is not the lectures but the seating arrangement: the 'Freud table' on one side, the 'Jung table' on the other, with icy silence in between. Freud, the father, and Jung, the parricide, barely look at one another – after 8 September 1913 they will never see one another again. Freud is delighted when Lou Andreas-Salomé suddenly appears in the conference room, bringing Rainer Maria Rilke, the poet he knows only from his verses. Freud flees into their arms to escape the atmosphere at the congress, and as soon as the last paper is finished they move on as a threesome, talking non-stop, even joking, and go and eat together. Lou hovers over things, Rilke is beyond Good and Evil. Freud, the patriarch, the great excavator of the unconscious and the repressed, hangs on Rilke's every word. When Freud's daughter Anna hears of this, she writes a euphoric letter to her father: 'Did you really meet the poet Rilke in Munich? Why? And what's he like?'

Yes indeed, what's he like? The next day, after these conversations about the unconscious in which Rilke and Freud were immersed on their walk, Rilke goes with Lou, the woman who took his virginity when he was well on in years, and who has now become his mother-substitute, first to see his mother, Phia, who lives in Munich, and then on to Clara and Ruth, his forgotten wife and his forgotten daughter, helping them move into their new flat at 50 Trogerstrasse. Then Lou Andreas-Salomé and Rilke board the train into the mountains, and she analyses his dreams. They talk with great seriousness about the symbolic differences between a phallus and an obelisk.

Hugo von Hofmannsthal lies in his hotel bed in the Vier Jahreszeiten in Munich and dreams that his house has become a French Revolutionary prison – 'and I am aware that this is the last day of my life: I have been condemned to death.' All around him are clerks busy writing out death sentences. Then his wife appears: 'but she is a creature whose face I have never seen before, but as familiar to me in the dream as the woman with whom one has lived for ten years. In a flash we both say to each other that we must not embrace.' His wife leaves him with the clerks imposing the death sentence. 'I feel I can't watch after her, turn towards the window through which the harsh sunlight is falling.' Hofmannsthal wakes up. He dresses woozily and tries to recover from the dream by going for a walk in the Englischer Garten. But the images won't leave his head; his body still feels as if it has been sentenced to death. It is still very early, and there are hardly any strollers in the park. A warm autumn sun shines over the trees. He is crossing the little bridge over the Eisbach when – and this is no longer a dream – a man comes towards him, looking like the great interpreter of dreams Sigmund Freud. Freud greets his Viennese acquaintance cordially, asks how he is and whether he has slept well, and says he looks a little upset. 'All fine, dear Doctor,' says Hofmannsthal. And then when Rainer Maria Rilke comes around the corner, having agreed to go for a stroll with Freud, Hofmannsthal finally feels as if he is still dreaming. But it is, like everything in this particular year, true.

In an article about first-aid instruction the *Neue Freie Presse* in Vienna writes on 6 September 1913, as if it were the most natural thing in the world: 'Just as the fate of the injured man on the battlefield depends on the quality of the first bandage, so first aid is of the greatest importance to the prognosis in everyday accidents.'

The symptoms of 'neurasthenia', the burn-out syndrome of 1913, are included in the eleven-volume work *Special Pathology and Therapy of Internal Illnesses*. Jung is supposed to write about 'neurasthenia' but refuses, because 'I don't understand enough about it and also don't believe in it.'

Franz Kafka leaves Prague at the beginning of September to be cured of his despair and 'neurasthenia'. His destination is Hartung's sanatorium in Riva, on Lake Garda. He wanted to travel with Felice, but her father still hasn't replied to his letter asking for her hand, so he sets off now because he has to go to Vienna for his job, to attend the Second International Congress for the Emergency Services and Accident Prevention, then by train to Trieste, Austria-Hungary's only port on the Mediterranean, which is enjoying an unparalleled boom. Being a port, its streets and coffee houses are filled with a unique mixture of nationalities, and it is the city where James Joyce lives quietly as an English teacher, spending day after day writing the preparatory studies for his *Ulysses*. So on 14 September, Franz Kafka and James Joyce are in Trieste. Robert Musil is here at this time too, travelling from Rome to Vienna. We can imagine them drinking coffee in the harbour in the late afternoon, before moving on.

Kafka travels on to Venice by ship, and there, at the Hotel Sandwirth, he writes his last letter to Felice Bauer for the time being, after more than two hundred letters and cards since the start of the year. He has recognised that he cannot produce great art if he yields to love and life. In his diary he notes: 'Coitus as a punishment for the joy of being together. To live as ascetically as possible, more ascetically than a bachelor, that's the only option for me.' And then, a few days later: 'I am going to close myself off to everyone else to the point of oblivion. To make enemies of everyone, talk to no one.' So he writes on 15 September on hotel writing paper, with a view of the Grand Canal, oblivious and 'boundlessly unhappy', to Felice: 'What am I to do, Felice? We must say farewell.'

Kafka travels on, suddenly free of the burden of having to be a husband, and when he arrives in Riva, on 22 September, he feels empty and distraught, but also relieved. The brothers Erhard and Christl von Hartungen, who have just tried to cure Freud at their branch in the mountains, now take their next great patient under their wing. There is an introductory therapeutic discussion; the doctors recommend diet, a lot of fresh air and a lot of rowing. In the first week – the sun is shining, and the weather is warm – Kafka is transferred to one of the 'air huts' on the beach, to be completely surrounded by oxygen. The therapy seems to be working, and on 28 September he takes a little trip to Malcesine, from where he writes a witty letter to his sister Ottla in Praque: 'Today I was in Malcesine, where Goethe had the adventure that you would know about if you'd read the *Italian Journey*, which you should do soon.'

On the same day – it's cooler now, and the first snows are appearing up on the mountain peaks – Kafka moves from his air-hut to the main building of the sanatorium. At table, he writes to his friend Max Brod, 'I am seated between an old general and a little Italian-looking Swiss woman.' The little Swiss woman brings Kafka back to life. They devise knocking games between their rooms, play catch in the park. They row out onto the lake together, and drift in their rowing boat: 'The sweetness of grief and love. Being smiled at by her in the boat. It was the loveliest thing. Only ever the demand to die and just surviving, that alone is love.' They are both aware that they have only ten days for their love. Then they travel back: Kafka to Prague, the Swiss woman to Genoa, where her family lives. For the first time Kafka hasn't been thinking about Felice every hour of the day. He has plunged for ten days into a childlike passion that will lead nowhere.

Kurt Tucholsky, the hotheaded postgraduate law student at Jena University, soon to be one of the sharpest-tongued critics on the Berlin magazine *Die Schaubühne*, dreams up the plan of every hotheaded, sharp-tongued journalist. He wants to found his own newspaper, which will be called *Orion*. Tucholsky wants to reach for the stars. It will be a 'yearbook in letters'. Meaning that it will present the great people of the day in their authentic testimonies. A strange idea: three times a month subscribers will receive 'the facsimile of a letter from a great European'. Nothing comes of it. Soon Tucholsky will have to tell the ninety-four interested parties who want to subscribe: 'Orion remains what it was: a constellation, far away and unattainable.' Rainer Maria Rilke and Hermann Hesse, those great letter-writers, had declared their interest early on (Rilke sends a poem on 21 September), as had Thomas Mann. But it isn't enough. However, one extraordinary document survives from the phase of the magazine's foundation: a letter from Tucholsky, in which he tries to recruit prominent collaborators from his room at 12 Nachodstrasse. In it he provides a cross-section of 1913 and the individuals who strike him as 'great Europeans' from a German point of view. The letter is unique in its breadth and concision. From the world of literature he wants to ask 'Dehmel, Hofmannsthal, Brod, Blei, Morgenstern, Werfel, Rilke, Hauptmann, Wassermann, Thomas Mann, Heinrich Mann, Hesse, Schnitzler, Altenberg, Robert Walser, Sternheim, Shaw, Wedekind, Kellermann, Friedell, Keyserling, Hamsun and Kafka' for contributions. But as well as them, 'Mynona, Owlglass, Holz, Schäfer, Willi Speyer, Wied, Hochdorf (Brussels), Irene Forbes-Mosse' – names which were given equal status to the great names quoted first, and which nobody knows today. Equally impressive is his list of the great living philosophers that Kurt Tucholsky wants to ask for help: 'Mauthner, Chesterton, Rathenau, Simmel, Wundt, Mach, Buber, Flammarion, Bergson'. And finally, from visual art: 'Meier-Graefe, Lichtwark, Behrens.' And for the illustrations and drawings Tucholsky thinks, among others, of 'Klimt, Barlach, Kollwitz'. It would have been nice if something had come of it.

There is a second contemporary cross-section of 1913 – an artistic one. The 'First German Autumn Salon' in Berlin, for which Franz Marc from Sindelsdorf and his friend August Macke in Bonn had been doing the groundwork since the spring, opens on 19 September in Herwarth Walden's legendary 'Sturm' Gallery. He has transformed the empty villa at 34a Tiergartenstrasse – actually scheduled for dem- olition – into a spectacular exhibition space.

The list of artists for this exhibition, based on the Paris 'Salon d'Automne', contains everyone who was avant-garde in 1913 – with the exception of the Berlin Brücke artists, who are off at their sum- mer retreats on the Baltic, still licking their wounds after the painful collapse of the artists' association in May, and who aren't yet ready for the next burst of group dynamics. 'If I don't join in,' Marc writes to Macke in Bonn, 'it wouldn't be the greatest disaster imaginable, I just feel sorry for Nolde and Heckel.' Not a word from Kirchner. He is deeply alien to the two warm-hearted Blue Riders. In the end 366 paintings by 90 artists from twelve countries are shown – after the 'Armory Show' in New York, the second exhibition of the year to set new standards. For the 'Autumn Salon' Walden had hired a huge hall at 75 Potsdamer Strasse. Bernhard Koehler, the great patron, donates 4,000 Marks to the organisation, although in the end he has to add an extra sum for transport costs. The 'First German Autumn Salon' is a sensation. Robert and Sonia Delaunay come from Paris for the open- ing, so do Marc Chagall and almost the whole of the Blaue Reiter, and even the Italian Futurists travel specially to the Sturm Gallery. They all know that they are witnessing a historic event. Englishmen, Frenchmen, Germans, Russians, Austrians, Hungarians, Italians, Czechs – all united in their desire for new art. It is an aesthetic alli- ance across all boundaries, a demonstration of the solidarity of the avant-garde beyond all foreign political skirmishes.

Works by Archipenko, Delaunay, Léger, Severini, Carra, Boc- cioni, Jawlensky, Marc, Macke, Münter, Klee, Chagall, Kandinsky and Picabia are on show, and beside them, for the first time in the circle of the avant-garde, paintings by the young painters Lyonel Fei- ninger and Max Ernst. Franz Marc shows his three epoch-making paintings from 1913, on which the paint is not quite dry: the *Tour of the Blue Horses*, then *Wolves (Balkan War)* and finally that picture of intersecting creatures for which he could not find a title, until Paul

Klee at last suggested *Animal Destinies*. Accompanying this is a series of lectures for which Guillaume Apollinaire, the man who gave the Cubists their name, and Tommaso Marinetti, the spokesman of the Italian Futurists, the two most glittering art theorists, come to the Sturm Gallery.

The public reaction ranges from furious to outraged. The newspapers publish terrible insults that seriously wound August Macke after the organisation's endless efforts. He rages at the 'bastards' and 'swinish newspaper rogues', who don't understand the works on show in Berlin. The *Frankfurter Zeitung*, for example, writes: 'It creates the impression that something is on show in a developmental phase. Never has pretention been more presumptuous, never less well-founded.' And the *Hamburger Nachrichten* adds: 'In fact it is rough fiddle-faddle, this great mass of absurdities, of ludicrous scribbles. You think you're coming out of the art gallery of a lunatic asylum.' On the other hand, Franz Marc writes to Kandinsky: 'My guiding idea in the hanging was: to show the massive intelligent absorption and artistic activity that is going on. A person will only go with a pounding heart, full of good surprises. For me personally, the conclusion is also surprising: a significant predominance (also in terms of quality) of abstract forms.' Then Marc, Macke and Herwarth Walden publish a flyer which they distribute on the Kurfürstendamm and in the Zoo. It includes these fine words: 'Art exhibitions must be visited against the will of the art critics!' But it's no good. Hardly anyone comes. The exhibition ends up as a financial disaster. In the end Koehler, the patron, has to stump up almost 20,000 Marks rather than 4,000 to cover the costs of rent and transport.

❧

Like Rilke and Freud, Arthur Schnitzler is in Munich during the first days of September. He is staying at the Hotel Continental and attending the rehearsals of his play *Liebelei*. As chance will have it, his former lover Marie, known as Mizi, has a leading role. This Marie Glümer, 'Mz' in the diaries, is a former patient and one of those 'sweet girls' from Vienna that Schnitzler always loved, who had a grip on their guilty consciences, girls you could take out to dinner, or take on outings, no more than that, and who fitted nicely into the bourgeois lives of their lovers. But now, in Munich, where he is staying with his wife, things become a little unclear.

On 9 September he is invited to Leopoldstrasse, to someone who loves women as much as he does: 'Lieslo takes us to see Heinrich Mann, who lives here with his lover, a Prague Jewess. He introduces her as his wife and insists she be addressed and treated accordingly. Duke and Miss Morena are also there. Coffee on the terrace. Tolerable conversation. I cannot find Frau Mann as bad as other people paint her. Everyone together to the lake.' And the atmosphere? 'There is none.'

In Düsseldorf the lawyer Carl Schmitt waits daily to be discovered. In the evening he goes to bed with his lover Cari and is, as he confides in his diary, 'wonderfully clumsy': 'nice fingering at night'.

So it goes, day after day; there's nothing to do in court and the publishers reject his book *The Value of the State*, which contains Schmitt's big anti-individualist programme. But then on 20 September the time has come. The publisher Mohr wants to publish Schmitt's book, and the author grows an extra three feet tall: 'Wonderful autumn weather. I feel like a great man walking unrecognised through the streets with secret superiority.'

Sadly it is not to last. On 30 September he writes after a visit to a concert: 'The music stirred up all my complexes. I wanted to kill myself. What's the point? No one cares about me, I don't care about anybody. If only my book was there.' Then, according to his wonderfully naïve hope, everything will be fine. But even the lawyer Dr Carl Schmitt cannot enforce such a law.

On 25 September 1913 Charlie Chaplin signs his first film contract

with Keystone Studios. He receives $150 a week during the shoot for his début film, *Making a Living*.

☙❧

Walther Rathenau publishes his book *On the Mechanics of the Mind*, in which he – chairman of the board of AEG and one of the central figures in German business – warns sharply of the dangers of technology and mechanisation to purity and the 'Empire of the Soul'. He dedicates the book to 'the young race'.

OCTOBER

This is the month when Thomas Mann's past catches up with him. In Dresden-Hellerau the avant-garde gather to watch a mystery play. Young Germans go hiking on the Meissner, which has been known as the 'High Meissner' ever since. Emil Nolde leaves Berlin to join an expedition to the South Pacific. August Macke finds paradise in Switzerland, by the shores of sunny Lake Thun. This month's big question: is it OK to feel repulsed by the sight of Franz Werfel? And how much avant-garde can Berlin handle? Completely out of the blue, Ludwig Meidner paints a battlefield, which he calls Apocalyptic Landscape. *Kaiser Wilhelm II inaugurates the Monument to the Battle of the Nations. Freud picks up his hat – and throws it at some mushrooms.*

Between 11 and 13 October the legendary meeting of reformist and youth movement groups takes place on the 753-metre-high Meissner in the Kaufunger Wald. Ever since then, the mountain has been known as the 'High Meissner'. The German Woodstock of the last generation to be born in the nineteenth century is an attempt to unite the Wandervogel hiking associations and the Free German youth groups in the open air. It's a protest against the pompous statement of hyper-German patriotism going on at the same time in Leipzig, with the inauguration of the Leipzig Monument to the Battle of the Nations. A huge camp of tents assembles at the base of the mountain, with two thousand youths taking part. They hike through the forests, sing, take part in debates and listen to a variety of speakers. One of these is Ludwig Klages, who tells the young people that the modern age poses a grave threat, endangering Germany's forests and, by association, the very essence of the German life principle. Klages warns them about technology destroying nature and pleads for a return to a more natural way of life. Titled 'Man and Earth', his provocative speech is a warning against progress and environmental destruction. The logo for the gathering on the 'High Meissner' is created by the reformist Fidus, a painter of down-to-earth yet sublime watercolours, in his dramatic painting *Hohe Wacht*, printed in the commemorative publication: young, naked men, with blades at their belt, stare proudly upwards. These men are also the audience for the young student Walter Benjamin's very first public appearance. Having just switched from Freiburg to Berlin University, he has come to the mountain with his friends. As one of the speakers at the gathering, he explains that there can only be a truly free German youth once anti-Semitism and chauvinism are no longer in the picture. Next, the progressive educator Gustav Wynekens, co-founder of the Wickersdorf Free School and Walter Benjamin's teacher, appeals to the crowd of young people:

Does it have to get to the point when a speaker only needs to call out certain words to you – like 'Germany', or 'national' – to hear your applause and cheers? Should every pushy prattler be able to win you over just by adopting the right vocabulary? When I gaze at the shining valleys of our Fatherland, I only hope the day will never come when war-mongering hordes rage through them. And what's more, that the day will never come when we are compelled to carry war into the valleys of another nation.

The conference's closing statement, the 'Meissner Formula', sworn to by all the participants, is much less dramatic. It states that 'the free German youth bases its life around inner truthfulness.' Conference also rules that 'all events of the free German youth will be alcohol- and nicotine-free.' Alcohol- and nicotine-free: no wonder it never turned into a revolution! Herbert Eulenberg said something along similar lines in his rhyming foreword: 'My greetings to the youth that is no longer drinking/Instead, hiking through Germany and thinking.' But once everyone comes back down from the mountain, returning to the valleys of the Fatherland, disillusionment quickly sets in. For Walter Benjamin too, who draws the following conclusion under the pseudonym 'Ardor' in Fritz Pfemfert's Berlin magazine *Die Aktion*: 'Hikes, festive garb and folk dances are not the ultimate and – in the year 1913 – not yet intellectual. This youth has not yet found its enemy, the born enemy it must hate.' Benjamin misses the uprising against the fathers of the previous, affluent generations. He misses parricide. It's worth noting, though, that he writes these fine words – and hopefully Benjamin disciples will forgive him for this – from his parents' house at 23 Delbrückstrasse in Berlin, having moved back home following his semester in Freiburg.

But let's give him credit for coming back from Freiburg to Berlin. As Else Lasker-Schüler said in 1913: 'The artist will always come back to Berlin: for the clock of art is here, and it moves neither back nor forwards.'

After days of rain, the sunshine is causing mushrooms to shoot up from the ground all over the place. Sigmund Freud, visibly relieved that he managed to handle the gathering of psychoanalysts with dignity and good grace (and with a nice defeat for Jung), goes mushrooming on Sunday with his family. They all have their little wicker baskets with them, covered with checked cloths, and their eyes are fixed on the mossy ground of the Vienna Woods. Sometimes they go to the Semmering mountain too, where everyone whispers about the love nest that Mahler's widow, Alma, is building out there for herself and the chaotic painter Kokoschka. But Freud and his family are drawn to the woods, not the summer residences. The children slip into their dirndls and shorts, Freud into his lederhosen, his green jacket and the hat with the gamsbart, and then the hunt begins. Freud leads the mushroom hunters – and it is always he who, with his eagle eye, finds the best mushrooms in the most hidden of spots. He then takes a few steps forward, pulls off his hat, throws it over the mushroom and whistles shrilly through his silver pipe, bringing his fellow hunters storming out from the undergrowth. Then, once he has the whole family's rapt attention, he finally lifts his hat and lets them admire the booty. Anna, his beloved daughter, is usually granted the honour of laying the mushroom in her basket.

Just when Futurism is once again being proclaimed as the movement of the hour in Berlin, with Tommaso Marinetti speaking at the 'First German Autumn Salon', Dr Alfred Döblin, the great doctor, great author and great friend of Ernst Ludwig Kirchner and Else Lasker-Schüler, publishes his 'Letter to F. T. Marinetti'. It contains these delightful words: 'You tend to your Futurism, I'll tend to my Döblinism.' Döblin is unwilling to accept the destruction of syntax promoted by Marinetti in his *Futurist Manifesto* as the basis of a new literature and art form. Instead, Döblin asks this of writers: don't destroy, but rather get closer to life.

But when writers get closer to life, a collision can easily occur. On 28 October 1913 the following announcement appears in the *Lübeck Nachrichten*:

> In the course of the last twelve years, the publication of *Buddenbrooks*, written by my nephew, Mr Thomas Mann from Munich, has caused me so many difficulties, resulting in the saddest of consequences for me, and these will now be added to by the publication of Wilhelm Albert's book *Thomas Mann and his Duty*. For this reason, I feel compelled to turn to the reading public and ask that they give the aforementioned book the reception it deserves. I'm sure every person in their right mind will find it to be reprehensible that the creator of *Buddenbrooks* is using caricature to drag his closest relatives through the mud and flagrantly expose their lives. It is a sad bird who dirties his own nest.
>
> Friedrich Mann, Hamburg.

These are the words of Mann's then 67-year-old Uncle Friedrich, who is known as 'Christian' in *Buddenbrooks*. Thomas Mann delivers an amused response in a letter to his brother: 'Did he feel he was being passed up in favour of Christian B., and perhaps wanted to remind people of his existence? I pity him, truly. My Christian Buddenbrook would never have written a letter like that.'

After fifteen years of construction, the grandiose Monument to the Battle of the Nations is inaugurated in Leipzig on 18 October, in honour of the hundredth anniversary of the battle against Napoleon.

Kaiser Wilhelm II pays tribute to the fighting spirit of the German people. The 91-metre-high monument, at a cost of 6 million Reichsmarks, commemorating the defeat of the French at the hands of the Prussians and their Russian and Austrian allies, was funded entirely from donations and lottery funding. The dark stone is granite porphyry, quarried in Baucha near Leipzig: 26,500 pieces of granite and 120,000 cubic metres of concrete were used for its construction. The inauguration of Clemens Thieme's monument is attended by the German Kaiser, the king of Saxony, as well as all the rulers of all the German states and representatives of Austria, Russia and Sweden. The inauguration becomes a national, martial celebration with a grand parade. Dignitaries from the three victor countries lay down wreaths at the foot of the monument. Afterwards, there is a celebratory dinner in the Gewandhaus for 450 guests. No toast is made to freedom, only to the indestructible brotherhood of arms between Prussia and Austro-Hungary.

For just five days, from 23 October onwards, this brotherhood is given a test-run: on pheasants. Franz Ferdinand, heir to the Austrian throne, who was in Leipzig for the inauguration of the Monument to the Battle of the Nations, has just achieved the Serbians' withdrawal from Albania in the Second Balkan War through an adept diplomatic initiative. This relieves and impresses the German Kaiser Wilhelm so much that he visits the heir in his castle in Konopiště. The two men get along magnificently. Franz Ferdinand organises a two-day hunt, on which Kaiser Wilhelm II, believe it or not, shoots 1,100 pheasants. Unfortunately, he only eats one for dinner.

In Ludwig Meidner's studio at 21 Wilhelmshöher Strasse in Berlin-Friedenau an illustrious circle gathers every Wednesday evening: Jakob van Hoddis, famed for his doomsday poem 'Weltende', Paul

Zech, René Schickele, Raoul Hausmann, Kurt Pinthus and Max Her-mann-Neisse. First, the master of the house shows the guests his latest works. He calls them 'Apocalyptic Landscapes'. They are in keeping with his motto: 'Paint your grief, your entire insanity and sanctity out of the whole of your being.' In Meidner's landscapes everything is exploding. In 1913 he paints *The City and I*, a picture in which his head seems to be exploding just like the city behind it. The sun hangs there shakily in the background, as if about to fall down.

Meidner is repeatedly overcome by these visions of horror. He works obsessively, day and night, in his little atelier in Friedenau. He writes: 'A painful impulse inspired me to break away from all straight-lined verticals. To spread ruin, destruction and ashes across all landscapes. My brain bled amid these awful visions. All I could see was a thousand-strong roundelay of skeletons prancing around in front of me. Numerous graves and burned-out cities with plains winding through them.'

The cities burn, as do the faces of the people – even his own, albeit contorted with pain – and the landscape is torn apart by bombs and war. An eerie light plays ghost-like above it all. Armed with his paintbrush, Meidner seems to be fighting against the sinister pow-ers threatening him, and he tries to exorcise his nightmares by put-ting them down on paper. He takes Cubism and Expressionism very seriously. He names his traumatic paintings *Vision of the Trenches* or, repeatedly, *Apocalyptic Landscape*. He lives, as we already mentioned, in idyllic Friedenau. These are warm, peaceful October days. And the year is 1913. The friends who visit him on Wednesday evenings see the pictures and grow concerned about their creator. Is he losing his mind?

On 17 October, a month after the airship L1 crashed into the sea by Heligoland, the military airship L2 explodes over Johannisthal, near Berlin, on its maiden voyage. Its thirty-man crew dies as the burn-ing wreck crashes to the ground, sending a nearby pine forest up in

flames, and the bodies of the soldiers on board are burned to a cinder. Their namesake, Count Zeppelin, writes to Great Admiral von Tirpitz that very same day: 'Who could be more stricken or grieve more deeply with the Navy than I?'

Reviews of the re-opening of the Neue Galerie opened in autumn 1913 by Otto Feldmann at 6a Lennéstrasse in Berlin spoke of the state of Picasso's reputation, and that of Modernism in general. This inaugural exhibition is the reason, thus far overlooked, why such greats from the French art world as Picasso and Braque were not on display at the 'First German Autumn Salon', which was being held at the same time. Kahnweiler, their Parisian dealer, was more keen on selling the works than exhibiting them, and sent them to the more commercial rival exhibition in Berlin. If you consider them together, the two exhibitions collected the entire artistic repertoire of the year 1913 and, moreover, its heroes. For next to the Paris artists Neumann also showed 'negro sculptures', Hellenistic sculptures and 'Oriental' pieces. Early works from cultural expeditions to distant lands, which were having such a great influence on artists at the time, were therefore mixed with European works – and Carl Einstein, who would become famous for his book about *Negro Sculpture*, wrote the foreword. It was a fascinating display of the situation of French art around 1913. In the magazine *Die Kunst*, however, Kurt Glaser drew the following surprising conclusion about new art salons in Berlin: 'A still-life by Matisse is exhibited, the colours lacking impact. Picasso has a whole wall to himself, and you get the impression that it's been designated as the exhibition's shrine. Perhaps a little late, too, for one would hope that the fuss that has been made about these decent but nonetheless feeble artists will soon die down.' But Feldmann refused to be deterred by this. In December, straight after his inaugural show, he exhibited sixty-six of Picasso's works, again commissioned by Kahnweiler. The German critics kept up their attack: a review in *Cicerone* stated that Picasso, whose Cubist works were included in the exhibition, 'still doesn't seem very strong, or very independent for that matter'. The great Karl Scheffler gave his judgement in *Kunst und Künstler*: 'And there's really not much that can be said about Picasso.' In the magazine *Die Kunst* the devastating verdict is that 'there can hardly be any doubt that Picasso has reached a dead end.'

There's only one person missing from this line-up: Ernst Ludwig Kirchner. There was no trace of his work in either exhibition, because he was in the process of creating something entirely new and wonderful. He returns to Berlin from Fehmarn at the end of September, happy and laden down with paintings. His months by the sea have produced sixty. Now he wants to leave the old times behind him, as well as the dissolution of Die Brücke and the apartment on Durlacher Strasse. He and Erna Schilling hunt for a new den together, and find one at 45 Körnerstrasse. They are back in Berlin, that 'tastelessly muddled and rather senselessly unfurling city', as Rilke so eloquently described it at the time. Kirchner discovered a new type of woman on Fehmarn, modelled on Erna and Maschka as they emerged naked from the gentle tides of the Baltic Sea. These bodies are almost Gothic, tapering off towards the top, with faces whose features appear carved as if into a piece of wood. While Erna dedicates herself to transforming the Körnerstrasse studio into an art work of sculptures, paintings, hangings and embroidery, with great expanses of cushions for the models and their friends to lie around on in comfort, Kirchner is drawn back out to Potsdamer Platz.

His senses are still so keen from the months by the sea, his perception and pores so open, that the city, its noise, its power and its faces penetrate his soul with elemental force. Only now that his visual nerves have been cleansed by the brisk Baltic Sea air is he able to see entirely fresh images: He begins with *Berlin Street Scene*, the first picture from his 'Potsdamer Platz' series. It depicts urban modernity, the city and its main characters all condensed together, the garishly clad coquettes with their dead faces, promising the men a happiness that not even the whoremonger could believe. Kirchner senses how the physicality which he was able to experience and paint on a pure, natural level in the women and children in Fehmarn is now no longer possible in the urban space of the new era, amid all the garments and the noise, the different glances and different expectations. The city's driving force is its speed, its incessant forward propulsion, its obliviousness to the present. But in those pictures of Potsdamer Platz, Kirchner is pressing the pause button. Suddenly, everything stands still. And by making the viewer of the picture into a whoremonger, the coquettes and the city offering themselves to him in their meaningless disposability and senseless belief that, tomorrow, everything will be different and better, Kirchner succeeds in creating unique pictures of a modern age in which the bodies of the city consist no longer of flesh and blood, but only of longing and nerves.

Emil Nolde simply can't bear to be in Berlin any more. So on 1 October he and his wife, Ada, pack up his painting tools and clothes into numerous large trunks. Then, early on the evening of 2 October, they head to the house of the art collector Eduard Arnhold at 19 Prinzregentenstrasse, in the Tiergarten district.

By 1913 Arnhold has climbed to the top rung of the social ladder. Having made his fortune in the coal trade, he is now on the board of directors of the Dresdner Bank and, that same year, becomes the first and only Jew to be appointed to the Prussian House of Lords by Kaiser Wilhelm II – he is offered a peerage too but turns it down. He invests his money almost exclusively in artists and art and, along with James Simon, is a major untitled patron of the arts, donating the Villa Massimo in Rome to the Prussian state as a cultural institute in around 1913. His own house in Prinzregentenstrasse is a masterful demonstration of the taste and power of a 'Kaiser Jew', as the future Israeli state president Chaim Weizmann scornfully named a group of prominent Berlin Jews, including James Simon, Albert Ballin and Walter Rathenau, because of their closeness to Wilhelm II. Works by

Menzel and Liebermann, and Böcklin's *Prometheus*, were hung up in his home, but there were also portraits of Wilhelm I and Bismarck alongside them.

So, on the evening of 2 October, an illustrious group of travellers have gathered in the Arnhold residence. Emil and Ada Nolde are nervous with excitement. They feast, dine and drink before setting off for Bahnhof Zoo at a quarter to twelve. When they arrive, a little sleepy by now, the night train to Moscow via Warsaw is already on the platform. It departs at 00:32, right on time. The expedition leader, Dr Alfred Weber, claims a sleeping compartment, while the young nurse Gertrud Arnthal, Arnhold's niece, sets up camp next to the Noldes, there to look after the ailing Ada. The 'Medical-Demographic German-New-Guinea Expedition' has begun.

On 5 October the train for the expedition – which was the simplest way for Nolde to get to his adored, distant South Pacific – arrives in Moscow. On 7 October they continue their journey by the Trans-Siberian Railway, over the Ural Mountains and Siberia to Manchuria. As representatives of a German government expedition, they all travel first-class. From Manchuria the journey continues to Shenyang and Seoul. From there the travellers set off to Japan by ship, arriving at the end of October. It's cold, wet and uncomfortable, and there's still no sign of the South Pacific.

On 5 October 1913, Paul Claudel's play *L'Annonce faite à Marie* is performed in Dresden-Hellerau. Lured by the reformist zeal of the Hellerau Dance School, the Dalcroze Method and Heinrich Tessenow's new Festival Hall, the audience is extremely select: Thomas Mann is there, Rainer Maria Rilke with his two closest friends, Lou Andreas-Salomé and Sidonie Nádherný, as well as Henry van de Velde and Else Lasker-Schüler. Max Reinhardt is in Hellerau that evening too, along with Martin Buber, Annette Kolb, Franz Blei, Gerhart Hauptmann, Franz Werfel, Stefan Zweig and the two most prominent young publishers, Ernst Rowohlt and Kurt Wolff.

While Reinhardt and Hugo von Hofmannsthal are staging *Der Rosenkavalier* at the Dresden Hoftheater, the new Festspielhaus becomes the meeting place for the avant-garde. Émilie Jacques-Dalcroze's goal was to create a new unity of body, spirit and music. Through undertaking rhythmic exercises and improvisations to music, the body is supposedly freed from the blocks imposed on it by civilisation. Ernst Ludwig Kirchner would have liked that. Upton Sinclair, the American author, who was probably in Hellerau on 5 October too, later wrote in his novel *World's End*: 'At Hellerau they taught you an alphabet and a grammar of movement. With your arms you kept the time; a set of movements for three-part time, another for four, and so on. With your feet and body you indicated the duration of notes. It was a kind of rhythmic gymnastics, planned to train the body in quick and exact response to mental impressions.'

This new form of Expressionist dance captivated everyone. Combining it with Paul Claudel's *L'Annonce*, however, did not go down so well. That night Claudel made a confused note in his journal about the almost complete absence of applause. Dalcroze even referred to it publicly as a fiasco. Rilke summed up the evening and its irritations beautifully in his letters to Hugo von Hofmannsthal and Helene von Nostitz: 'Like overgrown children, the people of Hellerau are getting involved in something they don't understand, but, God knows, perhaps they'll learn in the process and bypass the bleakness of today's theatre, heading instead straight to something transparent and pure. That would certainly be good for us all.' Fundamentally, therefore, Rilke sees an opportunity in the Hellerau experiments, the secret that all avant-gardes exhausted by the modern era are searching for. Unfortunately Rilke is certain that Paul Claudel's *L'Annonce* is of no use here whatsoever. Or, in his own words, as he writes to Hofmannsthal: '*L'Annonce*, Claudel, I wouldn't know how to describe it precisely, was thought-provoking, but was so intertwined with the Hellerau experiments, which were also thought-provoking, that you couldn't really tell whether the concerns you went home with were the result of one or the other.'

So the production itself didn't go down in the annals of cultural history. But the intermission and the worries which some of the audience went home with certainly did. During the intermission the very first encounter takes place between Rainer Maria Rilke's circle, which he has been swearing in for months now with eulogies about the poetic force of Franz Werfel, and the barely twenty-year-old poet Werfel himself. Rilke will later write a distraught letter to Marie von Thurn und Taxis in Duino, saying that when he saw Werfel he felt the 'falsity of the Jewish mentality' for the first time, 'that spirit which penetrates things like poison, which gets in everywhere in revenge for not being part of an organism'. But then Rilke re-reads Werfel's 'glorious poems' in the *White Pages*, which 'allowed me abruptly to shake off everything which was confusing and restrictive about our personal encounter, and once again I would walk through fire for him'.

During that intermission in Hellerau, clearly distressed and incapable of striking up a conversation, Rilke introduces Werfel to his close friend Sidonie Nádherný – and her reaction is one of both confusion and repulsion. According to Rilke, she whispered 'a Jew-boy!' upon catching sight of Werfel. So maybe he heard her. In any case, the countess treats the young poet with contempt. It's the opening chapter of a monstrous story.

The Prague-born Franz Werfel had, through Kafka's close friend Max Brod, taken an editorial role with Kurt Wolff's up-and-coming publishing house in Leipzig – a particularly avant-garde operation owing, not least, to the fact that the average age of its staff in 1913 was twenty-three. Werfel succeeded in signing the author Karl Kraus up to Kurt Wolff Verlag, and in the summer of 1913 wrote this lovely advertisement for the publisher:

> It is important to point out that, in Karl Kraus, one of the greatest European masters lives among us. The publishing house is releasing this sublime satirist's most shocking essay 'The Wall of China', in a monumental edition adorned with Kokoschka's illustrations. The time has come for a new youth, for all intellectual and just individuals to let themselves be swept away by the apocalyptic force of this rhetorical fugue, lest future generations are ashamed of our own.

Fine words indeed. At the same time they also reveal the twenty-year-old Werfel's obsessive and total adoration of Karl Kraus, then thirty-seven. Whenever they met, he would hang on his every word for hours; his letters are characterised by awe and submissiveness. In June he sent this sentence to Ludwig von Ficker in response to the survey among *Brenner* readers about Karl Kraus: 'I love this man, painfully.' Karl Kraus responded to this love by offering recognition; he regularly printed Werfel's poems in his magazine *Die Fackel*, giving them euphoric reviews.

So when Franz Werfel and Sidonie Nádherný von Borutin met in Hellerau on 5 October, no one knew that Karl Kraus had barely moved from her side for the past month and that they were passionately in love. Sidonie, in turn, knew nothing about her Karl's high regard for the young poet. And so they were both completely uninhibited: Sidonie in her dismissal of him, and the insulted Franz Werfel in spreading rumours about Sidonie – for example, that Rilke had once been passionately in love with her, and that she used to travel around with a circus troupe. When these rumours finally make their way back to Sidonie, and then to Karl Kraus, Kraus is filled with rage and cold fury. He severs all ties with Werfel and picks his poetry to pieces. Disparaging his poems in *Die Fackel*, he writes this devastating judgement of Werfel: 'A poem is good until you know who wrote it.'

We don't know whether Kraus, himself a Jew, ever found out that it was his beloved Sidonie's exclamation of 'Jew-boy' that had so wounded Werfel that he felt his only recourse was to spread rumours about her. Finally, the fact that Rilke, after finding out about her close relationship with Kraus, warned Sidonie, in one of his intimate letters to her, against a potential marriage, arguing that 'one last indelible difference' separated them, means that the events during that intermission on 5 October in Dresden mark a very sad date in German cultural history. In the same intermission, by the way, Else Lasker-Schüler, the great poet of the *Hebrew Ballads*, kept exclaiming, 'Bad, bad!' because the performance displeased her so much – and that distressed Rilke as well, as he found her actions barbaric.

Brief epilogue on the theme: 'Love Comes and Love Goes': In Hellerau, on 16 October, Rainer Maria Rilke has Émile Jacques-Dalcroze and his students dance for him once more, so that he may see exactly what their method of body activation involves. Sitting beside him in the otherwise empty festival theatre are Lou Andreas-Salomé, to his right, and Ellen Delp, to his left: that much-desired 'matutinal Ellen' from Heiligendamm in August whom Lou refers to as her 'chosen daughter'. Rilke, who, as coincidence would have it, is staying in Dresden's Sidoniestrasse (in the European Court Hotel), then writes a joint letter with Lou Andreas-Salomé to Sidonie Nádherný, in which they advise her to turn at once to Dr Friedrich Pineles in Vienna in her time of need – the same Pineles who was more successful as a seducer than as a psychiatrist, and who, as 'Erdenmann', had taught Lou Andreas-Salomé the joys of physical love a few years before. How delightfully confusing things were. It's possible that it all became too much even for Rilke; the following day he sets off in haste back to Paris. From there he writes on 31 October that he wants to file for divorce from Clara.

Parricide again. The young Alfred Bronnen writes his wrathful drama *Parricide*, in which the son kills his father in order to make love to his mother. And then there's Gottfried Benn, who the year before watched helplessly as his fatally ill mother died a painful death after his father, Gustav Benn, the country parson for Mohrin in Neumark, had on ethical grounds denied her the morphine which her son, a doctor, wanted to prescribe to alleviate her suffering. Even pain, the parson preached to his wife and son, is a gift from God. This was the very last time that Gottfried Benn was to obey the world of the fathers. In 1913, a year later, he sentenced his father to execution by verse. The volume of poetry is called *Sons*, the title alone expressing who is in charge now. It is a sign of self-assertion against overbearing fathers. Fathers are being challenged, under torture, only in thoughts at first, but later with words as well. But it will take a while. That autumn Georg Trakl writes this screaming self-accusation in his *Metamorphosis of Evil*: 'What compels you to stand silently on the derelict stair in the house of your fathers?' Kafka will write the 'Letter to the Father'. And Benn extols his mother's memory in his poems. Much later, in his century-spanning poem 'Teils-Teils': 'My father went to the theatre once/Wildenbruch's *Crested Lark*.' In his eyes that was the ultimate parricide, unlike that of Freud's 'primal horde': in other words, camouflaged as cultural snobbery.

Benn's volume *Sons* is dedicated to Else Lasker-Schüler. 'I salute Else Lasker-Schüler: Aimless hand of play and blood', he writes on the endpaper, in what is evidently a last, brief trace of sentimentality before the pathologist's fit of emotion turns truly pathological. From her mattress tomb, made bearable only by her daily opium and the visits of her family doctor and shrink Alfred Döblin, Else sends an update to her 'Blue Rider' Franz Marc in Sindelsdorf on the state of her love affair: 'The Cyclops Dr Benn has dedicated his new poems to me. They are as red as the moon, as hard as the earth, wild twilight, hammering in the blood.' And so this great love ends as it once began: with great words.

On 16 October, Ludwig Wittgenstein journeys with his friend David Pinsent by ship from England to Norway and continues to work on his *Tractatus Logico-Philosophicus*. He records his thoughts neatly in a notebook. First, though, he annotates the first page with these words: 'In the event of my death, please send to Frau Poldy Wittgenstein, Neuwaldeggerstrasse 38, Vienna, and to B. Russell, Trinity College, Cambridge.' Wittgenstein's family and the Cambridge academic are his twin pillars as he attempts to erect a new structure of logic. While still on the crossing he writes Russell a letter with key questions, only to leave it on board by accident. On 29 October he writes to Russell again: 'Did you get my letter? I left it in the boat's dining room and it was supposed to have been sent to you, but perhaps it was forgotten?'

Carl Schmitt, who believed he would be happy just as soon as his book *The Value of the State* was published, writes unhappily in his journal, despite the fact that the book *has* just been published: 'No one writes to me.' And it gets even worse: he has the sniffles. He doesn't know if he will survive, and on 2 October he writes: 'It's hideous, this catarrh; oh God, and some day we will all die.'

First, though, Schmitt wants to get married to his beloved Cari, to whom he dedicated his first book. Even the privy councillor Hugo am Zehnhoff – Schmitt's father figure during these months – agrees, and keeps sending little legal mandates his way. Zehnhoff is the second most important person in Schmitt's life in 1913; he bows to him in constant fear and affection, pleading for his favour, drinking and smoking with him late into the night. Zehnhoff warns Schmitt about the 'music-hall' nature that Cari exudes, but then demands that she at least become Catholic so they can be married in Maria Laach Abbey.

Cari buys herself a hat, and Carl buys a ring; they get engaged. But then Cari suddenly loses her passport, making marriage impossible and Carl furious. Cari, though, remains strangely calm. Given that they now can't move into their new apartment in the Conservatorium as a married couple, and also because they are hard up financially because Carl does not yet have a fixed tenure, Cari has to go and live with Schmitt's parents in Plettenberg until they are able to get married and live together. They travel there by train, then Schmitt has to go back to Düsseldorf in full knowledge of the awful surroundings in which he has left his beloved: 'She is in Plettenberg, in the company of my loathsome and evil mother and spoilt little Anna.' Soon, he writes, he will free Cari from the family hell-hole and lead her to the altar.

He met Cari, a Spanish dancer, in a music hall in 1912, and

promptly fell head over heels in love with her. She said her name was Pabla Carita Maria Isabella von Dorotic. Her passport would never turn up again, and for good reason too. Later, when they divorce, he will find out that his wife was not of Spanish nobility, but an illegitimately born Munich girl by the name of Pauline Schachner.

It may seem unlikely, but there was a place filled with sunshine and happiness in this October of 1913. August and Elisabeth Macke and their two sons move into Haus Rosengarten in Hilterfingen, on the banks of Lake Thun, with a view across the water, and with the steep, snow-capped peaks of the Stockhorn on the horizon. In the foreground a meadow runs gently down to the shore, where the Mackes drink freshly brewed coffee at four o'clock every afternoon in the rose-covered veranda.

For the first time August Macke hasn't brought any old paintings with him; he wants to make a new start here in Switzerland. He is still quite exhausted from the 'First German Autumn Salon' exhibition, and also bitter about his failure and bad reviews. But down here, by faraway Lake Thun and beneath the warm October sun, his mood lightens after just a few days. He buys some paints and makes a start – in a passionate fury, the like of which he has never experienced in his art work before – and manages to create the most important work of his oeuvre in those four weeks by the lake. He finds himself drawn to the lake promenade again and again, and repeatedly sketches the elegant strollers, the men in hats, the sunlight falling warm and bright through the rows of trees. And the blue of the sea beyond, here and there a white boat. In *Sunlit Path*, for example, painted at the very beginning of October, the tree trunk glows in the same tone as the woman's dress, she gazes into the deep, dark blue of the water and the sky can't even be seen for all the flashing bright green and yellow foliage. Here, by the banks of Lake Thun, August Macke paints his versions of paradise.

The Mackes have a small boat there too. Louis Moilliet and his wife, Hélène, come to visit, the painter friend with whom Macke will soon depart on their legendary journey to Tunisia; but first they all set off together on a trip in Thun, out onto the lake. They berth on an island, where they build a small fire and Hélène brews up fine Arabic coffee in a Tunisian copper can that she has brought along with her.

It's an idyllic life, even on weekdays. In the mornings they push open the green window shutters and gaze out into the shimmering blue of the Indian summer.

The days are so warm they are able to eat outside all through October; it's only from the afternoon onwards, when the coolness slowly creeps across the lake towards the meadow, that Macke pulls on his favourite, unevenly striped roll-neck jumper and smokes his first pipe of the day. Then he romps around the garden with the two boys, Walter and Wolfgang.

August Macke has installed his kingdom right at the top of the house, a room with a balcony and a wonderful view over the lake, where he paints whatever he has sketched on the promenades, in the hat shops, the shop windows. Elisabeth Macke will later tell of how her husband would bring the paintings out from the loft studio down to the garden, 'which was flooded in gleaming autumnal colours by the sunlight, and stand them in the middle of this glow: by no means did they pale in comparison, they had their own luminescence. Then he asked me: "What do you think; do I have something here, or is it just kitsch? I really can't tell."' Elisabeth knew what it was. And so do we. They were pictures of such genuine, captivating beauty that sometimes the only way to bear them is to denounce them as kitsch.

NOVEMBER

Adolf Loos says ornament is a crime, and builds houses and tailors' work-shops filled with clarity. It's all over between Else Lasker-Schüler and Dr Gottfried Benn: she's in despair, so Dr Alfred Döblin, currently sitting for a portrait by Ernst Ludwig Kirchner, gives her a morphine injection. Proust's Swann in Love, *the first volume of* In Search of Lost Time, *is published, and Rilke reads it straight away. Kafka goes to the cinema and cries. Prada opens its first boutique in Milan. Ernst Jünger, eighteen years of age, packs his things and goes to Africa with the Foreign Legion. The weather in Germany is disagreeable, but Bertolt Brecht thinks: anyone can have the sniffles.*

On 7 November Albert Camus is born. He will later write the play *The Possessed*.

The lead magazine of the year: in Vienna – what a coincidence – on 7 November the first issue of the magazine *The Possessed* is published. On the front page: a self-portrait of Egon Schiele. Subtitle of the magazine: 'A journal of passions'.

On 7 November, Adolf Hitler paints a watercolour of the Theatinerkirche in Munich and sells it to a junk dealer in the Viktualienmarkt.

In mid-November the fun-loving countess of Schwerin-Löwitz, wife of the president of the state parliament, or Landtag, issues an invitation to a tango tea-dance in the Prussian Landtag. On the floor: dancers in a close embrace with dignitaries and serious military officers. Kaiser Wilhelm II, who finds the tango vulgar, cracks down. On 20 November an imperial bill is passed, henceforth banning officers in uniform from dancing the tango.

Still no sign of the *Mona Lisa*.

For Adolf Loos his greatest year is coming to an end. *Ornament and Crime* was the name he gave to his furious *cri de coeur* against the threat of asphyxiation by wedding-cake architecture on Vienna's Ringstrasse. And now, in 1913, more and more people want their plans and souls and shops and houses to be cleansed by Loos's free spirit and clear vision. His 'Haus Scheu' at 3 Larochegasse has just been finished, as has his 'Haus Horner' at 7 Nothartgasse. And two internal spaces, which he has designed in an inimitably magnificent, minimalist and yet sedate elegance, also celebrate their opening: the Café Capua on Johannesgasse and the Kniže tailor's shop at 13 Graben.

Precisely because Loos and his American wife, Bessie, are close friends with many of Vienna's artistic avant-garde – with Kokoschka, Schönberg, Kraus and Schnitzler – he sees art and architecture as being worlds apart: 'The house has only to please. Unlike the work of art, which doesn't have to please anybody. The art work seeks to drag people from their comfort. The house has to serve comfort. The art work is revolutionary, the house conservative.'

His masterpiece from 1913 is the 'Haus Scheu' in Hietzing, the first stepped house in Europe which, in its plain white elegance and Arabic-looking tiers, enraged the Viennese from the year of its construction. But the clients, the lawyer and friend of Loos, Gustav Scheu, and his wife, Helene, were happy. 'I wasn't thinking about the East at all when I designed this house,' Loos said. 'I just thought it would be very pleasant to be able to step from the bedrooms on the first floor onto a big, communal terrace.' And yet 'Haus Scheu' does have the look of a mirage. The living and sleeping areas open into fresh air, you walk out onto large terraces, the whole house is flooded with light and air. The neighbours and the local authorities protest loud and long, and then Loos suggests a compromise: he agrees that plants should grow over the façades. Loos is primarily concerned with the effect of spaces on people:

but I want the people in my rooms to feel the material around them, that it has an effect on them, that they know about the closed space, that they feel the material, the wood, that they perceive it with their senses of sight and touch, sensually, in short, and that they can sit down comfortably and feel the chair on a large surface of their peripheral physical sense of touch and say: here you can sit perfectly.

Adolf Loos did not make jokes, and meant everything in complete earnest. And yet he came across as incredibly winning. You could tell from all of his internal spaces and each of his houses that they were really made to measure. And also that Loos would prefer not to build anything at all rather than build something unsuitable. Or, as he himself said in his great, true credo: 'Do not fear abuse for being unmodern. Changes in the old building style are only permitted when they represent an improvement; otherwise stay with the old things. Because the truth, even if it is hundreds of years old, has more of a connection with us than the lie that walks beside us.' The provocative innovator as a thoughtful traditionalist – Loos overtaxed his contemporary audience. He had no problem with not being considered modern (whatever that word might actually mean). But we know how modern he was. More so than any other architect working in 1913.

On 8 November, at 10.27 p.m., after an eight-hour train journey, Franz Kafka arrives at Anhalt Station in Berlin. At the end of October, Grete Bloch, Felice Bauer's friend, had stepped in as an intermediary between Prague and Berlin and attempted a reconciliation between the unhappy lovers, who seemed to have been paralysed by Kafka's disastrous proposal.

On 9 November, the German day of destiny, the two of them meet for a second time in Berlin. Again it is a tragedy. In the late morning they walk through the Tiergarten for an hour. Then Felice has to go to a funeral, after which she says she will call at Kafka's hotel, the

Askanischer Hof. She doesn't. It rains slowly and incessantly. Again Kafka sits in the hotel, as he did in March, waiting for news from Felice. But nothing happens. At 4.28 p.m. Kafka boards the train for Prague. And he informs Grete Bloch, the intermediary: 'I departed from Berlin like someone who went there quite without justification.'

On the same 9 November in Berlin, the well-known psychoanalyst and author Otto Gross is arrested by Prussian police officers in Franz Jung's flat and extradited to Austria. There his father declares him insane, and he is committed to the sanatorium at Tulln. From Heidelberg, Max Weber vehemently campaigns in favour of his friend Frieda Gross, Otto's wife. From Berlin the magazine *Die Aktion* protests with a special issue. It is a battle between father and son, a generational conflict of a very different kind. Controlling the uncontrollable son by declaring him unfit to handle his own affairs.

In the Minerva Hall in Trieste, the southernmost harbour city of Austria-Hungary, James Joyce delivers a series of lectures on *Hamlet*. He has previously tried to make some money by opening a cinema in Dublin and has toyed with the idea of importing tweed from Ireland to Italy. But it came to nothing. His attempts to earn money with his books have been a disaster too. Now he is scraping a living as an English teacher in the morning – and in the afternoon he gives private lessons, notably to the future author Italo Svevo. And in the evening he talks about *Hamlet*. The local newspaper *Piccolo della Sera* is enthusiastic: with its 'dense but clear thoughts, with a form at once sublime and simple, with its wit and vividness the lecture revealed genuine brilliance'.

'Those who touch you are bound to fall', wrote wise, wild Else Lasker-Schüler when she met Gottfried Benn. Now he has left her. And she is laid low with unbearable abdominal pains. Dr Alfred Döblin, who has just sat for a portrait by Ernst Ludwig Kirchner, drives out into the Grunewald and gives her a morphine injection. He can think of no other way to help her.

On 13 November, *Swann's Way*, the first volume of Marcel Proust's great novel *In Search of Lost Time*, is published. After the book was turned down not only by the Fasquelle and Oldenbourg publishing houses and the *Nouvelle Revue Française* but also by André Gide, the then editor at Gallimard, Proust had the book published by Grasset at his own expense. No sooner does he hold the first copy in his hands than his chauffeur and lover Alfred Agostinelli splits up with him. Everyone else falls for the author. Rilke reads the book only a few days after its publication. It begins with the golden words '*Longtemps, je me suis couché de bonne heure*' – 'For a long time I went to bed early' – and in saying this, Proust touched the nerve of an exhausted avant-garde who, from Kafka to Joyce, from Musil to Thomas Mann, boasted in their diaries whenever they managed to go to bed before midnight. Going to bed early – to the ever weary pioneers of the modern age it seemed like the bravest struggle against depression, drinking, senseless distraction and the advance of time.

In Munich, Oswald Spengler goes on feverishly writing his mammoth work *The Decline of the West*. The first part is finished. Spengler's state of mind: similar to that of the West. His diary: a tragedy. He notes: 'I have never had a month without thoughts of suicide.' And yet: 'Inwardly I have experienced more than perhaps any other human being of my time.'

Alma Mahler always piled her hair up high so that it often came tumbling down in conversation or while dancing. She had made an art of letting the dark tendrils fall into her face at precisely the right moment, sending men out of their minds. Today she grants this joy to Kokoschka again. Because he has just completed the double portrait of them both, the painting that has stood on his easel since the start of the year, and which shows Alma and the painter on a stormy sea. He originally wanted to call it *Tristan and Isolde*, after the Wagner opera from which she sang to him the first time they met. But then Georg Trakl gave the painting the title *The Bride of the Wind* – and that was the one that stuck. In November, Kokoschka, deeply in debt, writes to his dealer Herwarth Walden in Berlin:

> In my studio is a large painting I have been working on since last January, *Tristan and Isolde*, 2 ½ × 3 ½, 10,000 Kronen, finished for several days. I must receive a security of 10,000 Kronen before 1 January, because my sister is engaged to a man and getting married in February. The painting will be an event when it is made public, my strongest and greatest work, the masterpiece of all my Expressionistic efforts: will you buy it for yourself? It could make you an international success.

Modesty has never been Oskar Kokoschka's strong point. But the surprising thing is: Alma Mahler actually sees *The Bride of the Wind* as Kokoschka's long-awaited masterpiece. 'In his large painting *The Bride of the Wind* he has painted me lying pressed trustingly against him in a storm amid high winds – entirely dependent on him, a tyrannical expression on his face, radiating energy as he calms the waves.' She liked that. It was how she saw herself: full of energy, reposing, calming the waves. Alma, the ruler of the world. That was how she had imagined her lover's masterpiece. A blind homage. She studiously ignores the fact that she once promised to marry him for it.

But as a reward he is allowed to come out to Semmering, because her new house is ready. And he is allowed to paint a new picture there.

In Breitenstein, Alma has had a curious house built for herself, on the land that Mahler bought three years previously. The house looks like an over-sized chimney, dark, with larch shingles still being fitted to the roof; the verandas running along the outside make all the rooms dark and gloomy. A temple to melancholy. Hanging in the sitting room is Kokoschka's portrait of Alma as the poisoner Lucrezia Borgia. And beside it, in a glass case, Mahler's unfinished Tenth Symphony, open at the page where the dying composer wrote his cries: 'Almschi, dearest Almschi.'

Kokoschka's only reward for his *Bride of the Wind* was to paint the sitting room in Semmering, a fresco above the fireplace, 4 metres wide. The subject is, surprisingly enough: Alma Mahler and Oskar Kokoschka. Or as Alma puts it: 'showing me, pointing in spectral brightness at the sky, while he appeared standing in hell, wrapped in death and serpents. The whole thing is based on the idea of a continuation of the flames in the hearth. My little "Gucki" stood next to it and said: "Can't you paint anything but Mami?"' Good question. Answer: No.

Rilke sits in Paris, thinking distractedly about summer and autumn in Germany. As he travelled uneasily back and forth between all his wives and *über*-mothers, between Clara, still his wife, his ex-lovers Sidonie and Lou, his summer love Ellen Delp, his mother, his helpless admirers Cassirer, von Nostitz and von Thurn und Taxis. Keep everything open, don't go down any one path, wherever it may lead: that is what Rainer Maria Rilke is thinking on 1 November. As an attitude to life it's disastrous. As poetry it's a revelation:

Paths, open

That this no more before me lies,
failing, I rein myself back:
paths, open, heavens, pure hills,
leading past no dear faces.

Oh, the pain of love's possibilities
I have felt day and day after night:
to flee to one another, slip from one another's grasp,
nothing has led to joy.

In Augsburg, Bertolt Brecht is suffering: it is November, and the sea-son of colds. And the fifteen-year-old schoolboy is suffering from eve-rything going: his diary records headaches, sniffles, catarrh, stitches, back pains, nosebleeds. There are short daily bulletins about his own 'condition'. He observes his pains with relish and works himself up to a secondary state of illness: 'Morning Doctor Müller came. Dry Bronchitis. Interesting illness. Anyone can have sniffles.'

The phrase 'An apple a day keeps the doctor away' appears in Eng-land for the first time in 1913. It comes from the book *Rustic Speech and Folklore*, by Elizabeth M. Wright.

Emil Nolde works his way towards the South Sea. On 6 November he crosses the Yellow Sea to China. The steamer *Prince Eitel Friedrich* takes five days to reach Hong Kong, passing by Taiwan. From Hong Kong the expedition group then continues on the steamer *Prince Wal-demar* across the South China Sea to German New Guinea. But when he comes ashore in the far-off German colony, he is perturbed. He finds not an untouched paradise but an enormous car boot sale. In November 1913 he writes home, 'It is depressing to note that all the countries here are swamped with the very worst European knick-knacks, from paraffin lamps to the coarsest cotton materials, dyed in inauthentic aniline colours.' To see that, he complains, he didn't need to make the journey. He leaves his painting equipment in his suitcase and flees.

On 2 November, Burt Lancaster is born.

When Georg Trakl comes back from Venice to Austria, the declining city becomes a source of retrospective inspiration. In the last months of 1913 poetry assails him with unanticipated force, so much so that his skull almost shatters. A linguistic frenzy reveals his internal inferno.

'Everything is breaking apart', he writes in November. What happened there will never be quite explained, but we may assume that his beloved sister Grete is pregnant. Whether by her husband (who really existed, in Berlin), by himself or by his friend Buschbeck, whom he suspects of having a relationship with her, is completely unclear. We know only that in a poem by Trakl from November the word 'unborn' appears, and that he will write three months later that his sister has had a miscarriage. But who knows? He had such a tortured soul that life alone was quite enough to tear him in two.

Out of gratitude to his patron and saviour Ludwig von Ficker he allows himself to be persuaded to make a public appearance, in spite of his desolate state of mind. He reads at the fourth literary soirée of Ficker's magazine *Der Brenner* in the Innsbruck Musikvereinssaal. And the poet must have spoken as if he were still mumbling as he walked along the beach of the Lido in Venice: 'Unfortunately the poet read too faintly, as if from things hidden, things past or yet to come, and only later could one discern from the monotonously prayer-like murmurings the words and phrases, then images and rhythms that form his futuristic poetry.' So wrote Josef Anton Steurer in the *Allgemeiner Tiroler Anzeiger*.

Between these two disastrous appearances, at the Lido and before the Musikverein, one of the central chapters of twentieth-century German-language lyric poetry is produced. A total of fifty-nine poems, including the major works 'Sebastian in a Dream' and the 'Kaspar Hauser Lied' (one devoted to the Venice-lover Adolf Loos, the other to his wife, Bessie), and 'Transformation of Evil'. In fact, he produces 499 poems, or 4,999, because Trakl's poems are never finished; there are countless versions, over-writings, rewritings, corrections and variants. Again and again he picks up his pen, changes the manuscripts; again and again he writes to the publishers of the magazines that publish his poems, that this word must be changed to that, and that to this. A 'blue' can become a 'black', a 'quiet' a 'wise'. You can see him dragging motifs around with him, trying to capture them verse by verse and, if it still doesn't work, crossing them out again and then carrying them on to the next poem, to the next year. 'In an elevated sense unimprovable', Albert Ehrenstein wrote of Georg Trakl. But that is incorrect. Even he still needed improving. But only by himself. His poems are montages of things heard and things read (above all, Rimbaud and Hölder-lin), and things sensed. But it may also happen to him, as in the poem 'Transfiguration' from November 1913, that what begins as a 'blue spring' that 'breaks from the dead rocks' turns finally into the 'blue flower', 'which sounds quietly among the gilded rocks'. Romanticism is always the starting-point, but it is also the longed-for destination of Trakl, the quiet musician. Nine times the blue flower blooms in Trakl's poems in autumn 1913 alone. But in his inscription for the grave of the nineteen-century poet Novalis it already blossoms in an early version. But no sooner has the 'blue' faded and been crossed out than many new verbal experiments follow. Then the flower can be anything: first 'nocturnal', then 'radiant' and finally 'rosy'. In their bid to sound prophetic, Trakl's poems lack concision. Instead, what glimmers here in all its magnificence, in all its power, is the vocabulary of the German language of the Salzburg late Baroque, before Trakl opens the door to the engine room of his inspiration and allows the pestilential breath of death to blow over it, the icy breath of his soul. Everywhere flowers are dying, the forests darkening, the deer fleeing, voices falling mute.

A dead man visits you.
The self-poured blood runs from his heart.
And in his black brow there nests unspeakable moment;
Dark encounter
You – purple moon, appearing in the green shade
Of the olive tree.
After him comes everlasting night.

These everlasting *vanitas* experiences seem too existentially lived to be accused of verbal frenzy, even kitsch. Trakl could only express himself through poetry; his corrections and rewritings are his autobiography. He saw the dark, he captured the fleeting, he interrogated the intangible. He looked within himself and thus became the witness of the invisible, with an imagination only truly liberated through introspection.

Trakl hones his words, battles with his language until he knows he can release it into the world. A world in which he himself cannot survive. His poems – even those about the last days of mankind – do not herald disaster. In them history has long since taken what Friedrich Dürrenmatt calls 'the worst possible turn', precisely because it has now been thought and written down as poetry.

Robert Musil is tired and goes to bed before his wife. But he can't get to sleep, and eventually he hears her going to the bathroom to get herself ready. Then he takes his notepad, which always lies on his bedside table, and his pencil, and simply writes down what he is experiencing:

> I hear you putting on your night dress. But it doesn't stop
> there by any means. Again there are a hundred little actions.
> I know you are hurrying; clearly it is all necessary. I under-
> stand: we watch the mute gestures of animals, amazed that
> they, who are supposed to have no soul, line up their actions
> from dawn till dusk. It is exactly the same. You have no
> awareness of the countless moves you make, above all those

that seem necessary to you, and remain quite unimportant. But they loom widely into your life. I, as I wait, feel it by chance.

Love is also apparent in feeling, marvelling, enthusiastic, tender hearing and observing.

On 1 November, King Otto of Bavaria is officially declared insane. The doctors diagnose the 'final stage of a long-lasting psychical illness'. This makes the accession to the throne of the Prince Regent Ludwig as Ludwig III a legal possibility.

Woyzeck is mad and hallucinates: 'Everything is in flames above the city! A fire blazes around the sky and a roar as if of trombones.' On 8 November in the Residenztheater in Munich the unfinished drama *Woyzeck*, written in 1836 by Georg Büchner, who was born in 1813, is given its première, after years of lobbying by Hugo von Hofmannsthal. It belongs wonderfully in this year and has chosen exactly the right moment to enter the public consciousness. What a play, what language, what pace! Almost eighty years old, and still quite contemporary. It is a parallel story to Heinrich Mann's novel *Man of Straw*, except much more violent and archaic. Woyzeck is abused by a doctor for medical experiments, and then by the army captain, who humiliates him. When his beloved Marie betrays him with the brash 'drum major', he can no longer control his aggression and stabs her. The victim becomes the perpetrator. 'The central point becomes', in the words of the critic Alfred Kerr – 'tormenting humanity, not the tormented human being.' It is a proletarian drama, a play of revolt and rebellion. Rilke is speechless with enthusiasm: 'It is a play like no other, that abused human being standing in his stable-jacket in the universe, *malgré lui*, in the infinite procession of the stars.

That is theatre, that is what theatre could be.' But it is above all the celebration of a unique kind of language that runs around between hallucination and fairy tale, the gutter and poetry, and comes down on you like a buzzard. At the end of the play a fairy tale is told about a lonely child:

> And since there was no one left on earth, it wanted to go to heaven, and the moon looked down on it so kindly and when at last it came to the moon it was a piece of rotten wood and then it went to the sun and when it came to the sun it was a withered sunflower. And when it came to the stars, they were little golden flies, stuck on the way the shrike sticks them on the blackthorn and when it wanted to go back to earth, the earth was an upturned pot and the child was all alone.

This was a fairy tale very much in line with the taste of 1913. Unconsoling, beyond any utopian thoughts but full of poetry.

Ernst Jünger has 'inwardly made excessively great preparations'. His desire for danger drives him to Bad Rehburg, the spa town that smells of cows and turf and old people, and out of the parental home, whose bull-glass windows the light barely penetrates.

In August he had climbed to his father's greenhouse in his winter clothes to prepare his body for extreme conditions. Now he feels ripe for Africa. For years he has read adventure stories of journeys into the heart of darkness under his desk at school. Now he wants to go there himself. 'One damp and misty autumn afternoon I went into a junk shop with much fear and trembling to buy a six-shooter revolver with ammunition. It cost 12 Marks. I left the shop with a feeling of triumph, before going immediately into a bookshop and buying a fat book, *The Secrets of the Dark Hemisphere*, which I considered indispensable.'

Then, with book and revolver in his bag, he sets off on 3 November without telling a soul. But how do you get from Rehburg to Africa by train? Unfortunately geography has never been his strong point. Now Ernst Jünger buys a pipe so he feels grown up and to strengthen his adventurous heart, and then he buys a fourth-class ticket and travels south-west from station to station. He travels on, first to Trier and then through Alsace-Lorraine; Jünger keeps on going and eventually, after an aimless odyssey, on 8 November he has reached Verdun, where he joins the Foreign Legion. He is assigned to the 26th Instruction Regiment as number 15,308, and taken to Marseille, where he boards a ship for the promised land: Africa. The local newspaper reports:

> Bad Rehburg, 16 November. The sixth-former as Foreign Legionary. Jünger of the lower sixth, a son of the mine-owner Dr Jünger, applied to join the French Foreign Legion and is already on his way via Marseille to Africa. The father of the unfortunate young man has applied to the Foreign Office in Berlin for help. The German embassy has been instructed to contact the French government to release Jünger.

After their wedding in May, Victoria Louise of Prussia and Prince Ernst August of Hanover move to Braunschweig. For the first time in almost fifty years there is once again a member of the Guelph family as ruling count of Braunschweig. The young couple are very happy and go on to have five children.

In the small garrison town of Zabern in Alsace-Lorraine, which has been part of the German Reich since 1871, something horrendous happens on 28 November. In the evening a few dozen demonstrators turn up outside the German army barracks, protesting that the regiment commander Baron Günter von Forstner has declared that all

Frenchmen are 'Wackes' – a term of abuse for the Alsatian French – and that 'you can shit on the French flag'. These words had reached the local newspaper and provoked shock among the population. When the demonstrators hold up placards and ask for respect, the commander of the regiment has three infantry units advance with live ammunition and bayonets at the ready. Panic breaks out among the demonstrators, but the German soldiers lay into them and arrest more than thirty people, including some innocent passers-by. They are locked in a coal cellar without light and toilets. Then commander Baron Günter von Forstner says the following words: 'I consider it a great fortune if blood flows now […] I am in charge, I owe it to the army to create respect.'

Five days later he is recognised with a troop of soldiers, and some workers at a shoe factory call him 'the Wackes Lieutenant', whereupon he loses his temper and brings his sabre down on the head of a disabled hostage, who cannot run away quickly enough, making him collapse in a pool of blood.

The very next day the Reichstag in Berlin discusses events in Zabern. The 'Zabern Affair' threatened peace between France and the German Reich more than any previous event. The German war minister, Erich von Falkenhayn, refuses to be diverted by this open flouting of the law by the German army. He claims that 'noisy rioters' and 'provocative organs of the press' are responsible for the intensification of the situation in Zabern. In response there are fights in the Landtag, and the opposition opposes any illegal actions by the military. The centre-party member Konstantin Fehrenbach: 'The army is also subject to the law, and if we place the army outside the law and abandon the civilian population to the arbitrary rule of the army, then, gentlemen: *Finis Germaniae*! … It will be a disaster for the German Reich.' But the real disaster is yet to come, because the German head of state, Wilhelm II, actually approves of the spirited response of the German military and cannot find anything really dramatic in the so-called 'Zabern Affair'. But the reaction in the European press reached a furore when the sentence of Commander Forstner, which initially carried a prison term of only 43 days for grievous bodily harm, was reduced on appeal in the higher military court to acquittal. Forstner, the judges ruled, had acted in 'putative self-defence' and was consequently innocent. The left-liberal *Frankfurter Zeitung* acknowledges the frightening message of this acquittal: 'The bourgeoisie has suffered a defeat. That is the actual, visible sign of the Zabern trial […] In the argument between military force and civilian force, the court martial has laid down the right of the unrestricted dominion of the former towards the bourgeoisie.'

In 1913 Prada is founded and opens its first shop, selling high-class leather goods in the Galleria Vittorio Emanuele in Milan.

In mid-November, Kaiser Wilhelm takes the train to Halbe, to the 'Kaiser Station', then continues on into the forest of Dubrow, south of Berlin. The hunt begins at half-past one in the afternoon, in an area spanned with cloths and nets. By the time the horn is blown again at a quarter to three, a total of 560 animals have been killed. Kaiser Wilhelm II alone has killed ten stags and ten boar. At the hunt dinner in the evening he asks that a memorial be erected to his marksmanship forthwith.

November 1913 produces the most intimate, sympathetic and perhaps most honest correspondence between Thomas and Heinrich Mann. Thomas Mann is not in a good way right now. His wife, Katia, isn't getting any better; her cough, which she has been trying to heal for months, even years, in sanatoriums, is there again, more hacking than ever. And for the first time he is in debt, having over-reached himself with the construction of a house on Poschingerstrasse, now almost completed. He asks his publisher Samuel Fischer for an advance of

3,000 Marks for his next novel. And to his brother Heinrich he writes: 'I have only ever been interested in decay, and that is precisely what prevents me from taking an interest in progress.' And then:

> But what nonsense is that. Things are serious when all the wretchedness of the times and of the fatherland weigh down on one, and one does not have the strength to shape it. But that is part of the wretchedness of the times and of the fatherland. Or will it find shape in *Man of Straw*? I look forward more to your works than I do to my own. You are spiritually better off, and that's the crucial thing.

And then, with unusual warm brotherly love: 'It is of course crassly tactless of me to write to you like this, for what can you reply?' But Heinrich Mann, who will conclude his great novel of the times, *Man of Straw*, in the next few months, clearly knows what to reply. We don't know his reaction. But we do know Thomas's: 'For your intelligent, tender letter I thank you from the bottom of my heart.' And again, a kind of sudden declaration of love to his sibling: 'In my fondest hours I have long dreamt of writing another long and faithful book of life, a continuation of *Buddenbrooks*, the story of us five siblings. We are worth it. All of us.' Never again will he grant his brother so deep an insight into his soul, so tortured by weariness and doubts.

Still no sign of the *Mona Lisa*.

Marcel Duchamp still doesn't feel like making art, but he has an idea. 'Can one,' he wonders, 'create works that are not art works?' And then, in the autumn, in his new flat on Rue Saint-Hippolyte in Paris, the front wheel of a bicycle suddenly appears, and he mounts it on an ordinary kitchen stool. Marcel Duchamp mentions it quite casually: 'It was something I wanted to have in my room, the way one has a fireplace or a pencil sharpener, except that it was not in any way useful. It's a pleasant device, pleasant because of the movements it made.' Duchamp finds it so calming to spin the wheel with his hand. He likes its endless rotation on its own axis. While in Paris and Berlin and Moscow artists are still fighting about whether Cubism, Realism, Expressionism or Abstraction is the royal road, the young Duchamp just puts a bicycle wheel in his kitchen and thus creates the first 'ready-made'. It's the most casual quantum leap in art history.

On 20 November, Franz Kafka notes in his diary: 'Went to the cinema. Wept.'

Emotional overload in the cinema brings the youth protection officers out in force. The pedagogue Adolf Sellman writes in the foreword to his book *Cinema and School*:

> The teaching body is prepared to draw attention to all the dangers posed by bad cinema, and to protect our young people against them. School must work to enlighten, in such a way that within and without its walls it will be apparent what bad intellectual nourishment is available in cinemas, even today. School must ensure enlightenment in the press, at parents' evenings and conferences. It must urge that legal measures and police regulations be passed so that our young people are granted protection against all the corrupting influences that the cinema can exert.

In Fulda the German Episcopal Conference draws up special guidelines for the clergy to protect against the negative effects of visiting the cinema. No longer was anyone to weep at trashy tales! The demand is made that children under the age of six should not be allowed into the cinema. And adults should also avoid morally inferior films.

That is what is known as a pious wish.

What a lovely name: Albert Duke Mensdorff-Pouilly-Dietrichstein. Thanks to the marriage of one of his ancestors to a princess of Sachsen-Coburg long ago in the nineteenth century, Albert Mensdorff, known as Duke Ali, was related to almost all the courts of Europe, a fact that delighted him anew every day. The cousin of the British king, and Imperial Ambassador in London, pulls off his masterstroke in November 1913. King George V writes to him, hoping that the archduke and duchess will be able to come to Windsor in November for a few days' shooting. Can they? It's the first official invitation to the successor to the Austrian throne and his wife, Countess Sophie, hitherto subjected to an endless series of official humiliations. Duke von Mensdorff-Pouilly-Dietrichstein knows what he has succeeded in doing, and therefore writes to Archduke Franz Ferdinand: 'As you know, such official occasions, with dinners, toasts, receptions, theatres etc. etc., where one becomes half sick and plagued to death, have always been a horror to me.' It is a bad joke, because the duke is really the biggest party animal in the world of Austro-Hungarian diplomacy – he keeps the menu from each of his dinners and the next morning draws a seating plan, marking on it who was sitting next to him. His reason for denouncing the social aspect of the archduke's visit has entirely to do with the fact that he and the successor to the throne cordially dislike one another. But the archduke couldn't care less. He is enjoying making his first official trip abroad with his wife. And he is enjoying the fact that barely two weeks after the hunt with Kaiser Wilhelm he is now able to go pheasant shooting with King George V near Windsor Castle. Franz Ferdinand and the king are accompanied by three English earls, while the ladies chat in Windsor Castle and listen to concerts. On Tuesday 18 November a thousand pheasants and 450 wild ducks are brought down by the marksmen after being driven into the line of fire by beaters. On Wednesday 19 November, in the loveliest sunshine, they shoot 1,700 pheasants. On

Thursday they shoot about 1,000. And then on Friday, with rain lashing the faces of the royal hunting party, 800 pheasants and 800 wild ducks are slaughtered. A bloodbath.

DECEMBER

Everything is open: the future, and the lips of beautiful women. Kasimir Malevich paints a black square. Robert Musil finds Germany to be very dark. The Mona Lisa *is found in Florence and becomes the most important painting in the world. Rainer Maria Rilke would like to be a hedgehog. Thomas Mann makes one thing clear: 'I'm not writing* The Sorcerer's Apprentice, *but* The Magic Mountain!' *Emil Nolde finds only disturbed people in his South Pacific paradise, while Karl Kraus finds happiness in Janowitz. Ernst Jünger is found in Africa and celebrates Christmas in Bad Rehburg. And what do the stars tell us?*

In December 1913 the first 'ready-made', the bicycle wheel on the wooden stool, is turning at the hand of Marcel Duchamp in Paris, while the first 'Black Square' comes into being in Moscow – the twin starting-points of modern art.

At the 1913 Futurist Congress in Uusikirkko, in Finland, Malevich introduces the term 'Suprematism', which for him represents 'the beginning of a new civilisation'. He throws aside the burden of representational art, which still held even Cubism under its spell. He wants to move forward, and to a place where nothing is needed: no reality and no colours. In December 1913 he presents thirty-five of his latest works at the '0,10' exhibition in St Petersburg, including his *Suprematist Manifesto* and even his unprecedented painting *Black Square on a White Background*. The picture is an all-out provocation, and a revelation. For Malevich the square embodies the 'zero state', the experience of pure abstraction. And the elementary contrast between white and black creates a universal energy for him. It is an end-point for art – and yet, at the same time, the beginning of something completely new. It is the rejection of all demands made on artists and art – and, in the process, one of the greatest self-assertions of artistic autonomy. We should always think of the *Black Square* when we think of 1913.

The second masterpiece that defines 1913 is 400 years old and painted on a 77cm by 53cm wood panel made from Lombard white poplar. The *Mona Lisa*, by Leonardo da Vinci. There has been no trace of her since she was stolen from the Louvre two years ago.

But at the beginning of December the Florentine art dealer Alfredo Geri receives a letter. This portly, broad-shouldered and gregarious gentleman caters to Florence's upper classes from his antiques shop in Via Borgo Ognissanti. His clients include Eleonora Duse, known as 'La Duse' for short, and her lover, Gabriele d'Annunzio. The letter he is holding in his hands disturbs him. Is it the truth, or simply a letter from a lunatic? He reads it again: 'The stolen painting by Leonardo da Vinci is in my possession. It is quite clear that it belongs to Italy, because the painter was Italian. It is my desire to give this masterpiece back to the country it came from and by which it was inspired. Leonardo.'

Geri manages to arrange a meeting with the ominous sender for 22 December in Milan. But on 10 December, when Geri is about to close up his shop at half-past eight in the evening, a man comes up to him from among the last customers: 'My name is Leonardo.' Geri looks at the man, aghast: he has a dark complexion, pomade-black hair and, all in all, makes quite a greasy impression with his twirly little walrus moustache. He had, the man told Geri, come a little earlier after all, and was staying at the Albergo Tripoli-Italia in Via Panzani under the name of Leonardo Vincenzo. In other words, just one block away from Borgo San Lorenzo, where, 400 years previously, Lisa del Giocondo had sat and modelled for Leonardo.

Leonardo went on to say that Signore Geri could come to see the *Mona Lisa* in the guest house at three in the afternoon the following day. Geri subsequently alerts the director of the Uffizi Gallery, Giovanni Poggi, and the three of them go from the antiques shop to the run-down guest house. As they walk through the streets, Geri and Leonardo agree that he will receive 500,000 Lire if the painting is genuine. That would be nice, Leonardo says, but it really isn't about the money; he just wants to bring Italy's stolen art treasure back home. Poggi and Geri look at each other, confused.

The gentlemen climb up the steep steps to the Albergo Tripoli-Italia, where Leonardo's shabby single room is situated on the second floor. He fetches a trunk out from under the bed, throwing its entire contents – underwear, work tools and his shaving things – onto the mattress. Then he opens a false bottom inside the trunk and takes out a board wrapped in red silk: 'Before our eyes, the divine Gioconda appeared, unharmed and in magnificent condition. We carried her over to the window for comparison with a photograph we had brought along with us. Poggi inspected her', as Geri later explained. There is no doubt; the inventory number from the Louvre is even on the back. But despite their excitement, Geri and Poggi keep their nerve – they tell Leonardo that the painting may be the one everybody's looking for, but that they have to make further enquiries. Leonardo, exhausted from the long journey and with the 500,000 Lire in his sights, hangs the picture on his bedroom wall and lies down for an afternoon nap.

Poggi immediately informs the police – when the Carabinieri open the door, Leonardo is still asleep, and the entire contents of his trunk are on the floor next to the bed. He does not resist arrest. The *Mona Lisa* is taken to the Uffizi under police protection. Then, aware of the significance of his find, Poggi doesn't just call the Culture Minister, Corrado Ricci, in Rome, and the French Ambassador, Camille Barrère, but even has his calls put through to King Vittorio Emmanuele and Pope Pius X.

In the Italian parliament two representatives are exchanging blows when someone runs into the plenary hall and cries out: '*La Gioconda è trovata.*' The Gioconda is back! The message is immediately understood. The two adversaries embrace and kiss each other through sheer excitement.

From this moment on the whole of Italy is overcome by *Mona Lisa* Fever. And Leonardo? Leonardo's real name was Vincenzo Peruggia, he was thirty-two years old and had been working as a temporary glazier in the Louvre at the time of the theft. It was he who had put the *Mona Lisa* in the controversial glass frame. And because he had put her there, he also knew how to get her out. He hid himself one evening so that he would be locked in, took the painting out, wrapped it in linen and then walked out of the Louvre the next morning in broad daylight. The guards, who knew him well, nodded to him in greeting.

The whole story was absurd. The police had taken fingerprints from everyone, every cleaning woman, every art historian, every archivist in the Louvre in order to catch the thief, because he had left prints on the picture's frame. But they forgot the temporary glazier Vincenzo Peruggia. During their search for the *Mona Lisa* the police had even visited him at home in his shabby little room at 5 Rue de l'Hôpital Saint-Louis, just like they had every other Louvre staff member. But the policemen didn't look under the bed.

There, just a kilometre away from the Louvre as the crow flies, the most-hunted art work in the world lay for two whole years. The story was a shock: for the Louvre and for the Parisian police. But at the same time it is also a wonderful Christmas message filled with joy. Locked up in his cell, Peruggia receives innumerable thank-you letters, sweets and presents from grateful Italians.

Gabriele d'Annunzio wrote the following: 'He who dreamed of fame and honour, he, the avenger of the thefts of Napoleon, brought her over the border back to Florence. Only a poet, a great poet, can dream such a dream.'

By 13 October the French government officials and art historians had arrived in Florence to check the authenticity of the *Mona Lisa*. The Italian Culture Minister, Ricci, said these wonderful words: 'I just wish the French had declared the picture to be a copy, for then *Mona Lisa* would have stayed in Italy.' But even the French declared the painting to be the original.

Alfredo Geri was given a reward by the Louvre and the rosette of the Légion d'Honneur by the French state. Leonardo, otherwise known as Vincenzo Peruggia, was sentenced to seven months' imprisonment.

On 14 December, watched over by a unique international honour guard consisting of Gendarmes and Carabinieri in parade uniform, the *Mona Lisa* was hung in the Uffizi, carried through the walkways in an elaborate gilded walnut frame as if part of a procession. Thirty thousand people saw her; Italian children even got a day off school to go to Florence and admire the national shrine. Then, on 20 December, the painting was taken to King Vittorio Emmanuele in Rome, in a saloon carriage filled with guests of honour. The next day he handed it over in the French Embassy, the Palazzo Farnese, as part of a symbolic act. Over Christmas 1913 the painting was on display in the Villa Borghese once more – the Culture Minister himself sat next to it during the opening hours; he had promised not to let it out of his sight for a second. At night a dozen police officers stood guard. Next, the *Mona Lisa* was taken to Milan in a saloon carriage – under strict security precautions, the painting was then on display in the Brera Museum for two days. *Mona Lisa*'s journey through Italy was an unparalleled victory parade. Whenever the carriage passed a train station, people would cheer and wave. From Milan onwards the *Mona Lisa* was given a private carriage in the express train from Milan to Paris. She was treated like a queen. Late in the evening of 31 December the *Mona Lisa* crossed the French border. She had left the Louvre as a painting but was returning as an enigma.

❧

The December edition of the *Neue Rundschau* prints a short notice from Oscar Bie, who had recently visited Thomas Mann at his home: he reports that Mann is working on a new novel entitled 'The Sorcerer's Apprentice'. Bie's handwriting was so indecipherable that even he sometimes had problems decoding it. So Thomas Mann ends up spending December putting straight all the friends and acquaintances who write to him about it: 'You won't believe it, but (the novel) is finished. And by the way, it's called *The Magic Mountain* (Bie misread his own handwriting).'

❧

On 15 December, Ezra Pound, the great poet and one of London's most important and proactive cultural mediators, sends a letter to James Joyce in Trieste. He asks the poverty-stricken English teacher for some of his newest poems for the magazine *The Egoist*. 'Dear Sir!' this friendly letter begins, and it ends: 'From what Yeats says I imagine we have a hate or two in common.' This letter has the effect of making Joyce feel as if he has been raised from the dead. Soon Pound sends a second letter from his Kensington home, saying that Yeats has sent him the poem 'I Hear an Army', and that he liked it very much. So emboldened is James Joyce that he sits down that very day and corrects his two manuscripts. After two weeks the first chapter of *Portrait of the Artist as a Young Man* and his short stories *Dubliners* are ready, and he sends them by express train to Ezra Pound in London. A star is born.

Dr. Med. Alfred Döblin, the writer and neurologist, and collaborator on Herwath Walden's magazine *Der Sturm*, spends nights on end in Ernst Ludwig Kirchner's new studio in Körnerstrasse. Döblin wrote again and again about men and women and their relationships, about the battle of the sexes. He wrote this, for example, after one of his lovers gave birth to his son: 'Marriage isn't a shop specialising in sexuality. Equally foolish is the insistence on fulfilling all sexual relations within the framework of the marriage, as if one could predict that you would only be hungry at mealtimes and in certain places.' Kirchner liked that a lot. Back in the summer he had done the etchings for Döblin's novella *The Canoness and Death*, which was published in November by A. R. Meyer's small Wilmersdorf publishing house. The very same publishing house which issued Gottfried Benn's *Morgue* in 1912 and his new volume of poetry, *Sons*, in 1913.

In December, Kirchner starts work on illustrations for Döblin's one-act play *Countess Mizi*, a play about the coquettes Kirchner devoured so hungrily with his painter's eye on their forays along Friedrichstrasse and around the outskirts of Potsdamer Platz. Döblin said this of the ladies of the night: 'Their sexual organs are machine parts.' That is the theory behind the practice painted by Kirchner. This December he tries time and again to transfer the fascination and coldness of Potsdamer Platz into art. The coquettes' fur collars, their pink faces against the pale, icy delirium of the collars, the glaring green feather boas – and alongside them the faceless, hunted men. Kirchner sketches and sketches, and once even writes these words in his sketchbook: 'Coquette = the momentary mistress.'

Christmas Eve in Berlin's Klopstockstrasse, at Lovis Corinth's place.

His life's work has become another year richer. It was mainly in the Tyrol that Corinth expanded his palette, finding the tone for the mountains that he would then fully master in his portraits of Lake Walchen. But he isn't on top form yet. Once the Christmas dinner is finally over and the handing out of presents is due to begin, Papa Corinth asks the children for just a moment's patience. He fetches his easel, a stretcher frame and his paints. Charlotte also slips out of the room, telling the children she's keeping an eye out for Father Christmas. But it's really so she can dress up as Father Christmas herself. The children, Thomas and Wilhelmine, wait with eager anticipation. Then Father Christmas – in actual fact Mother Christmas – arrives, and the giving of presents can begin. But Lovis Corinth leaves his untouched; he only has eyes for his canvas – and with just a few energetic brushstrokes he depicts the Christmas tree with its glowing red candles. Next to it in the painting is Thomas, completely immersed in looking at his new red-curtained puppet theatre. Little Wilhelmine, in a white dress, has just unwrapped a puppet and is already moving on to the next present. Charlotte, on the left, still has her Father Christmas costume on. In the foreground of the picture, to the left-hand side, is the still uncut marzipan cake. But once Corinth has painted it in the most beautiful shades of brown, he wipes his fingers on a cloth and cuts himself a piece.

Meanwhile, Josef Stalin is freezing in his Siberian exile.

Ernst Jünger has finally arrived in Africa. A newly recruited legionnaire in the Foreign Legion, he is in a dusty tent with his comrades in North Africa, near Sidi bel Abbès. Instead of endless freedom, all he finds are endless drills. In the blazing heat they are forced to carry out military training exercises, manoeuvres and endurance runs. What on earth made him commit himself to five years straight? So Jünger tries to run away again, this time *from* the Foreign Legion. He hides out in Morocco. But he is caught and sentenced to a week's imprisonment in the garrison prison. Somehow he had imagined Africa would be completely different. On 13 December a messenger brings the following telegram: 'SENT FROM REHBURG CITY, 12:06. THE FRENCH GOVERNMENT HAS GRANTED YOUR RELEASE HAVE PICTURE TAKEN JÜNGER.' After diplomatic intervention Jünger's father has managed to secure his release and transport home. On 20 December he leaves the Foreign Legion's North African barracks with the following grounds for his discharge written on the release form: 'Father's appeal due to soldier being under-age.' Deeply tanned, deeply ashamed and deeply confused, Jünger sets off by train on the long journey from Marseille to Bad Rehburg. He arrives at his parents' home just in time for Christmas. On Christmas Eve, therefore, he is sitting not under a starry African sky but under a Christmas tree that was chopped down a few days earlier in the Rehburg Forest. There is carp for dinner. Jünger promises his father he will now study hard for his *Abitur*. Then he excuses himself and goes to bed. This time, however, he doesn't read *Secrets of the Dark Continent* before going to sleep.

Emil Nolde has reached the destination of his dreams. On 3 December, two months after their departure, he sails past the Palau islands with Ada and the expedition group on the North German Lloyd steamboat *Prinz Waldemar*. On the small island of Jap, in the Western Caroline Islands, they make their first contact with the native inhabitants, who berth their boats next to theirs and come on board. Then they journey on, towards the equator, sailing past the island of German New Guinea, where August Engelhardt founded his empire. The German reformist, incredibly gaunt by now, lives here in his book-filled hut on the beach, gathering the followers of his coconut religion around him. He believes the coconut to be a heavenly fruit (because it grows at such heights) and preaches that people can only be healthy if they nourish themselves exclusively on its milk and flesh. He loves the wonderful, heavenly sound it makes when opened, that moment when the coconut splits.

Even Nolde is eating many coconuts these days, but it isn't enough for him; he needs the regular supplement of a freshly killed chicken. On 13 December the expedition group reaches Rabaul, the capital city of the Neu-Pommern nature reserve. There they are each appointed with a native 'boy'. Tulie and Matam are the names of the two boys who will tend to Emil and Ada Nolde from now on. So they can all acclimatise, the group now spends four weeks on a small mountain above Rabaul, named Narmanula, where they are able to stay in a newly built but as yet unused colonial hospital. After weeks of waiting, Nolde is overcome by an intense urge to create. He takes his watercolour paper, pours a little stream water into a holder and paints from early in the morning until late at night: Matam and Tulie at first, then the natives' huts too, the women, the children, the tranquillity, the palm trees. He also cuts a block of wood and makes a woodcut of the two boys. Their ears and eyes are delicately carved onto the dark heads, and you can even see Tulie's curious nose and Matam's protruding upper lip, with the lush South Pacific vegetation visible in the background.

Emil Nolde is not only fascinated but also disillusioned. Here in Palau he can no longer see the untouched South Pacific that Paul Gauguin once painted, the one the European poets conjured up in their poems. The native inhabitants of the colonies are sadly Europeanised, 'their defiance broken, their hair cut short', he writes. They are all being brought to Rabaul to learn German or English, and after that they return to their native villages to work as interpreters for tourists. Nolde heads across by boat to the Gazelle peninsula, where he hopes to find a more native way of life – realising that he is witnessing a culture at the moment of its demise, he reaches for his watercolours to preserve the evidence. He searches for paradise in the vibrant pink and red blooms of the bougainvillaea and hibiscus, and in the naked bodies of the natives too. But in their faces Nolde finds a frightening apathy. Instead of unspoilt joy for life, his pictures of the South Pacific speak of the seriousness of the modern era. He writes letters back to his distant homeland: 'I'm painting and drawing and trying to capture something of primordial being. I may have succeeded here and there, but I am nonetheless of the opinion that my paintings of the primordial people and some of my watercolours are so genuine and crude that they could not under any circumstances be hung in perfumed salons.'

Dozens and dozens of watercolours are created in Neu-Pommern that December, melancholic studies of the agony of a culture broken by European pressure. Mothers and children huddle up to one another as if on a sinking ship. So this is the paradise he dreamed of for years on end, and which he spent sixty arduous days travelling to.

On 23 December, Nolde sends 215 drawings and watercolours with the Rabaul post steamer to his friend and patron Hans Fehr in Halle. On 24 December, Emil Nolde notes in his diary how much he misses a white Christmas, the crackle of wood in the fireplace and the decorated Christmas tree: 'It was almost impossible for us to get into the Christmas spirit in this heat. Our thoughts wandered over the seas and across the world to the cosy corners of the German homeland, where the lights burned brightly. I put the little wooden figures that I carved during the sea journey with a pocket knife onto our Christmas table.'

On 25 December, issue 52 of *Die Schaubühne* published the poem 'City Christmas', by Kurt Tucholsky, alias Theobald Tiger. It portrays Christmas as a bourgeois drama in which people no longer have feelings, only roles.

City Christmas

The Christ Child comes! We young ones listen
To quiet, holy gramophone.
The Christ Child comes, prepared to swap
New ties, dolls and lexicon.

And if the bourgeois sits with family
In his chair, at half past nine,
At peace with life and with the world
'Yes, Christmas certainly is fine!'

And cheerily he speaks of 'Christmas weather',
Rain today, or snow perhaps.
Smoking as he reads his paper,
Tales of famous girls and chaps.

So does the Christ Child's flight encounter
Purest bliss down here below?
Good God, they're playing Christmas peace out …
'We're all acting. The clever ones are those who know.'

Arthur Schnitzler is not proud. That December he notes in his journal that he has finally given up hope that anyone will ever really
understand him: 'Dr Roseau is sending around a pamphlet about me
– well-meaning, and in essence, the same thing that is written about
me everywhere. I have now given up on expecting the critics of today
to understand me.'

On 1 December 1913 in Lübeck, Ernst Karl Frahm is born. He will
later call himself Willy Brandt.

Oskar Kokoschka spends Christmas with Alma, her mother and her daughter in the newly built house in Breitenstein. The lighting isn't working yet, so after dusk they all sit around the fireplace, the blazing fire and numerous candles bathing everything in a festive glow. Kokoschka gives Alma a fan which he painted for her; on it a man is pictured losing Alma to a large fish. Kokoschka is convinced that 'there has been nothing of its kind since the Middle Ages, for no lovers have ever breathed into one another so passionately.' (Later, once Alma has been breathing into Walter Gropius for a good while, Kokoschka has a life-size puppet modelled on Alma, discussing every wrinkle and every pad of fat around the hip region with the puppet-maker, and he goes on to live longer with the puppet than he lived with Alma herself. But that's just an aside, after all, because we don't really want to know what will happen next, not here in 1913.)

D. H. Lawrence, who is enjoying his greatest success ever in England with *Sons and Lovers*, according to which a man can only be either a son or a lover (which is a parricide of sorts), has already made the conflict between intellect and instinct into a big topic with this book. Back in the autumn, in an attempt to make his beloved Frieda von Richthofen believe him, he walked through the whole of Switzerland, and now the two of them are celebrating a warm Christmas in a dockside bar by the Mediterranean. That Christmas, Lawrence composes his very own confession of faith: 'My great religion is a belief in the blood, the flesh, as being wiser than the intellect. We can go wrong in our minds. But what our blood feels and believes and says, is always true.'

From his lips to Kafka's ears. Felice Bauer is no longer returning his letters. He writes to her by registered post, he writes to her by special delivery, he even sends his friend Ernst Weiss with a message to her office at Lindström AG, but she doesn't answer. Then Kafka receives a telegram announcing the imminent arrival of a letter. But the letter never arrives. They speak briefly on the phone: Felice begs him not to come to Berlin for Christmas and promises she will write to him soon. But she doesn't. When there is still no sign of a letter by midday on 29 November, Franz Kafka sits down in Prague and starts a new letter, his second proposal. He writes and broods, writes and broods. By New Year's Eve he has reached page 22. By the time he finishes, the letter is thirty-five pages long. Kafka writes: 'Felice, I love you with all that is humanly good in me, with everything that makes me worthy of being among the living.' When the bells of Hradčany ring out at midnight, Kafka stands up briefly and goes over to the window. The family moved in November, so Kafka is no longer looking out over the river and the bridge and the parks, but is looking at the Altstadtring. It's snowing softly and unrelentingly, muffling the cannon shots from the castle, and outside in the streets people are celebrating the arrival of a New Year. Kafka sits back down and continues to write: 'Even the fact that there are things in me you find fault with and would like to change, I love that too, I just want you to know that.'

Käthe Kollwitz, weary of life with her husband and uncertain about which direction her art should take, acknowledges: 'At any rate 1913 has passed quite innocuously, not dead and sleepy, quite a lot of inner life.'

Quite a lot of inner life: probably so. In the dark December night Robert Musil takes notes from which his novel *The Man without Qualities* will later grow. Now he writes the lovely sentence: 'Ulrich predicted the future and had no idea.' Not bad. He takes another sip of red wine and lights a cigarette (or at least that is how one imagines it), then, writing as Ulrich, his protagonist, he turns his attention to the heroine, Diotima, the much-desired beauty, the Woman Full of Qualities; and all the time he had that particular sentence on his lips. So he writes: 'And something was open: it was probably the future, but to some extent it was her lips too.'

There are a few happy people this Christmas Day in 1913. Karl Kraus and Sidonie Nádherný von Borutin are two of those for whom everything remains open. The shock waves of the argument with Franz Werfel have not yet reached their idyll. They are still enjoying each other, secretly, but with a great deal of love. Kraus is overwhelmed by the Borutins' charming castle in Janowitz, still lit only by paraffin lamps, and by its dreamlike park, with the wonderful, 500-year-old poplar tree in the courtyard – the park that also cast its eternal spell on Rilke. Even now, in December, the great poplar still has a few ragged leaves up in its crown, which rustle when the wind blows over the hill. Kraus succumbs entirely to the magic of this place. Here, where his beloved Sidonie is mistress of the horses and the dogs and the pigs, this is his paradise. Here everything is what it is, good, and natural, and true. Sidonie and Janowitz, this liberation from Vienna and its intellectual corset, turn Karl Kraus into a different person. Sidonie's brother wishes his sister to have a suitable marriage, but at night, when Karl creeps down the dark, cold corridors of the castle as soon as the brother has gone to sleep and climbs into Sidonie's warm bed, they stop thinking about suitability. Karl Kraus arrived on 23 December; his friend Adolf Loos will follow him on 24 December. They want to celebrate Christmas together. Loos tries, probably so as not to disturb the young couple for long, to visit the castle of the successor to the throne in Konopiště, next door to the Borutins' castle. He writes a letter and asks to be allowed in. But Franz Ferdinand does not want to be disturbed. A shame, it would have been an interesting encounter: the two opposite poles of Austria-Hungary. Loos, the ice-cold adversary of ornament, and Franz Ferdinand, the hot-blooded commander in chief of the army.

Then a letter arrives for Sidi from Paris, sent by Rilke. 'Is Karl Kraus with you?' he asks, because Sidi has confided in him. And then he asks Sidi – who was so repelled by it – to pass on an essay about Franz Werfel to Karl Kraus, entitled 'About the Young Poet'. He couldn't have sent anything more unsuitable to Kraus, who learns soon afterwards that Werfel has been spreading rumours about his beloved, which makes him as angry as a raging bull.

But this time Rilke's letter does not further disturb the loving idyll in Janowitz. Sidonie sets the letter aside – nothing urgent, she thinks – and goes for another walk in the park with Karl and her beloved dog Bobby. They dance among the snowflakes falling gently from the sky.

Kraus, who never stays away from his desk for more than two days at a time, extends his holiday to the New Year and writes elegant nature poems. Sidonie, the tall, proud beauty, later gives him a dreamy photograph of herself, writing on the back in blue ink: 'Karl Kraus/in memory of days shared by Sidi Nádherný/Janowitz 1913–14.' He immediately hangs it over his desk in Vienna, and never takes it down. And at some point, at some point in his life thereafter, he sends her a postcard from St Moritz: 'Please remember Christmas 1913 tonight.' It must have been lovely, that Christmas.

On 27 December the ministry in Vienna extends the sick leave of the neurasthenic librarian second-class Robert Musil by a further three months. He immediately travels to Germany to negotiate with Samuel Fischer, becoming editor of his magazine *Neue Rundschau* shortly afterwards. On his train journey from Vienna to Berlin he notes irritably: 'Conspicuous in Germany; the great darkness.'

New Year's Eve 1913. Oswald Spengler writes in his diary: 'I remember how I felt as a boy when the Christmas tree was plundered and cleared away, and everything was as prosaic as it had been before. I cried all night in bed, and the long, long year to the following Christmas was so long and bleak.' And again: 'Life in this century oppresses me today. Everything redolent of comfort, of beauty, of colour, is being plundered.'

At the end of 1913 a surprising book is published. Its name is *The Year 1913* – in it is the attempt to give an account of the present, which is 'rich in cultural values' but which at the same time sees an 'increased blunting and superficiality in the masses'. The chief highlight is the last essay by Ernst Troeltsch about the religious phenomena of the present: 'It is the old story that we all know, which for a while we called progress, and then decadence, and in which people now like to see the preparation of a new idealism. Social reformers, philosophers, theologians, businessmen, psychologists, historians signal it. But it is not there.' The old story that was once called progress –how wisely people spoke in December 1913. But who understood those words in the hubbub of that year?

In Babylon the temple site of Etemenanki is discovered. It is the legendary Tower of Babel.

What are women wearing for New Year's Eve? In issue 52, *Welt der Frau*, a supplement of *Gartenlaube*, provides tips for 'fashion at the turn of the year'. 'The delight in colour that distinguishes this season is also apparent in outfits for small festivities. With their loose cut, most fashions suit the slender form. But even for the fuller-figured woman, today's fashions can be charming, blurring lines as they do, if one knows how to choose.' On the following page there is a poem by Marie Möller, which bears the harmless-sounding title 'New Year's Eve'. It includes these disturbing lines:

> So let us work from dawn till dusk
> That a fine year may us befall!
> Bringing after strife and toil
> Victory and peace to all.
> And that the tune of global war
> May cease its gloomy, threatening knell.
> That it may soon in harmony
> Ring out like joyful chiming bells!

Rainer Maria Rilke is in a bad way during those last December days in Paris. He writes: 'I see nobody, it has been freezing, there was black ice, it's raining, it's dripping – this is winter, always three days of each. I have truly had my fill of Paris, it is a place of damnation.' And then: 'Here is the incarnation of my desires for 1914, 1915, 1916, 1917 etc. Which is: peace, and to be in the country with a sisterly person.' He then writes to one of those sisterly people, although her thoughts are elsewhere right now: Sidonie Nádherný: 'Now I would like to be as if without a face, a rolled-up hedgehog that only opens up in the ditch in the evening and cautiously comes up and holds its grey snout up at the stars.'

The complete constellation of Sagitta is observed in the sky for the first time in 1913. South of the Fox and north of the Eagle, Sagitta is a clear, bright arrow flying towards the Swan. Enthralled eyes gaze heavenwards. Sagitta bears the name of the dangerous arrow fired, according to mythology, at Hercules. But the Swan is lucky once again: the arrow just misses it.

It is 31 December 1913. Arthur Schnitzler records a few words in his diary: 'In the morning, dictated my madness novella to the end for the time being.' In the afternoon he reads Ricarda Huch's book *The Great War in Germany*. Otherwise: 'Very nervous during the day.' Then a soirée. 'Roulette was played.' At midnight they clink glasses to the year 1914.

SELECTED BIBLIOGRAPHY

This book is based on a large number of biographies and cultural historical sources. What follows is a selection of the works quoted from which the author drew important information.

Altenberg, Peter: *Extrakte des Lebens. Gesammelte Skizzen 1898–1919*. Vienna and Frankfurt 1987.

Bauschinger, Sigrid: *Else Lasker-Schüler. Eine Biographie*. Göttingen 2004.

Berenth-Corinth, Charlotte: *Lovis Corinth, Die Gemälde. Werkverzeichnis*. Munich 1992.

Berger, Hilde: *Ob es Hass ist, solche Liebe? Oskar Kokoschka und Alma Mahler*. Vienna 2008.

Bernauer, Hermann: *Zeitungslektüre im »Mann ohne Eigenschaften« (Musil Studien)*. Munich 2007.

Bourgoing, Jean de (ed.): *Briefe Kaiser Franz Josephs an Frau Katharina Schratt*. Vienna 1964.

Brandstätter, Christian (ed.): *Wien 1900. Kunst und Kultur. Fokus der europäischen Moderne*. Vienna 2005.

Bülow, Ulrich von (ed.): *»Sicherheit ist nirgends«. Das Tagebuch des Arthur Schnitzler*, *Marbacher Magazin 93*. Marbach 2001.

Decker, Kerstin: *Lou Andreas-Salomé. Der bittersüße Funke Ich*. Berlin 2010.

Dorrmann, Michael: *Eduard Arnhold (1849–1925)*. Berlin 2002.

Dyck, Joachim: *Benn in Berlin*. Berlin 2010.

Ellmann, Richard: *James Joyce.* New York and London 1959; rev. edn 1982.

Feininger, Lyonel: *Gelmeroda. Ein Maler und sein Motiv.* Wuppertal and Halle 1995.

Fest, Joachim: *Hitler. Eine Biographie.* Frankfurt/Munich 1973.

Franz, Erich (ed.): *Franz Marc: Kräfte der Natur. Werke 1912–1915. Katalog zur Ausstellung in München und Münster.* Ostfildern 1993.

Freedman, Ralph: *Rainer Maria Rilke. Der Meister 1906–1926.* Frankfurt 2002.

Freud, Martin: *Glory Reflected: Sigmund Freud – Man and Father.* London 1957.

Freud, Sigmund/Jung, C. G.: *Briefwechsel,* ed. William McGuire. Frankfurt 1974.

Fühmann, Franz: *Vor Feuerschlünden – Erfahrung mit Georg Trakls Gedicht.* Rostock 2000.

Gay, Peter: *Freud: A Life for Our Time.* London 2006.

Gay, Peter: *Schnitzler's Century: The Making of Middle-Class Culture.* London 2002.

Grochowiak, Thomas: *Ludwig Meidner.* Recklinghausen 1966.

Grosz, George: *Ein kleines Ja und ein großes Nein.* Frankfurt 2009.

Güse, Ernst-Gerhard (ed.): *August Macke. Gemälde, Aquarelle, Zeichnungen.* Munich 1986.

Henkel, Katharina/ März, Roland (ed.): *Der Potsdamer Platz. Ernst Ludwig Kirchner und der Untergang Preußens.* Berlin 2001.

Hilmes, Oliver: *Witwe im Wahn. Das Leben der Alma Mahler-Werfel.* Munich 2004.

Hof, Holger: *Gottfried Benn: Der Mann ohne Gedächtnis. Eine Biographie.* Stuttgart 2011.

Hoffmeister, Barbara: *S. Fischer. Der Verleger. Eine Lebensbeschreibung.* Frankfurt 2009.

Husslein-Arco, Anges/ Kalli, Jane (ed.): *Egon Schiele. Selbstportraits und Portraits.* Munich 2011.

Jasper, Willi: *Der Bruder: Heinrich Mann.* Munich 1992.

Jasper, Willi: *Zauberberg Riva.* Berlin 2011.

Jauss, Hans Robert: *Die Epochenschwelle von 1912.* Heidelberg 1986.

Joachimsthaler, Anton: *Hitlers Weg begann in München 1913–1923.* Munich 2000.

Jünger, Ernst: *Kriegstagebuch 1914–1918.* Ed. Helmuth Kiesel. Stuttgart 2010.

Jünger, Ernst: *Afrikanische Spiele.* Stuttgart 1936.

Kafka, Franz: *Briefe an Felice und andere Korrespondenzen aus der Verlobungszeit.* Ed. Erich Heller und Jürgen Born. Frankfurt 1967.

Kafka, Franz: *Tagebücher.* Ed. Hans-Gerd Koch, Michael Müller and Malcolm Pasley. Frankfurt 1990.

Karlauf, Thomas: *Stefan George. Die Entdeckung des Charismas.* Munich 2007.

Kerr, Alfred: *Mit Schleuder und Harfe. Theaterkritiken aus drei Jahrzehnten.* Ed. Hugo Fetting. (East) Berlin 1981.

Kerr, Alfred: *»Ich sage, was zu sagen ist«. Theaterkritiken 1893–1919.* Ed. Günther Rühle. vol. VII.1, Frankfurt 1998.

Kessler, Harry Graf: *Das Tagebuch 1880–1938,* vol. 4: *1906–1914.* Ed. Jörg Schuster, Roland S. Kamzelak and Ulrich Ott. Stuttgart 2005.

Klingsöhr-Leroy, Cathrin/ Schneider Katja (Ed.): *Franz Marc – Paul Klee. Dialog in Bildern.* Wädenswil 2010.

Kokoschka, Oskar: »Briefe 1905–1919«, in: Kokoschka: *Briefe in 4 Bänden: 1905–1976,* vol. 1, Ed. Olda and Heinz Spielmann. Düsseldorf 1984.

Kraus, Karl: *Briefe an Sidonie Nádherný von Borutin 1913–1936.* Ed. Friedrich Pfäfflin. Frankfurt 1973.

Küchmeister, Kornelia/ Nicolaisen, Dörte et al. (ed.): *»Alles möchte ich immer«: Franziska von Reventlow (1871–1918).* Lübeck 2010.

Kühn, Heinrich: *Die vollkommene Fotografie.* Ostfildern 2010.

Kussmaul, Ingrid/ Pfäfflin, Friedrich: *S. Fischer Verlag. Von der Gründung bis zur Rückkehr aus dem Exil. Eine Ausstellung des deutschen Literaturarchivs im Schiller-Nationalmuseum, Marbacher Kataloge Nr. 40.* Marbach 1985.

Kutscher, Arthur: *Wedekind. Leben und Werk,* Munich 1964.

Mächler, Robert: *Robert Walser. Biographie.* Frankfurt 1992.

Mann, Golo: *Erinnerungen und Gedanken. Eine Jugend in Deutschland*. Frankfurt 1986.

Mann, Thomas: *Briefe 1889–1913*. Ed. Thomas Sprecher, Hans R. Vaget and Cornelia Bernini. Grosse Kommentierte Frankfurter Ausgabe: Briefe und Tagebücher, Tl. 1. Frankfurt 2002.

Matisse, Henri: *Radical Invention 1913–1917*. Chicago 2010.

Matuschek, Oliver: *Stefan Zweig. Drei Leben. Eine Biographie*. Frankfurt 2006.

Mehring, Reinhard: *Carl Schmitt. Aufstieg und Fall. Eine Biographie*. Munich 2009.

Mendelssohn, Peter de: *Der Zauberer. Das Leben des deutschen Schriftstellers Thomas Mann. Erster Teil, 1875–1918*. Frankfurt 1975.

Möller, Magdalena M. (ed.): *Karl Schmidt-Rottluff. Ostseebilder: Katalog zur Ausstellung in Lübeck, Kunsthalle St. Annen und Museum Behnhaus Drägerhaus – Galerie des 19. Jahrhunderts. Brücke-Museum Berlin, 11.02.2011–17.07.2011*. Munich 2010.

Möller, Magdalena M. (Ed.): *Emil Nolde in der Südsee*. Munich 2002.

Möller, Magdalena M. (Ed.): *Emil Nolde. Expedition in die Südsee. Brücke-Archiv 20/2002*. Munich 2002.

Möller, Magdalena (Ed.): *Ernst Ludwig Kirchner in Berlin. Katalog zur Ausstellung im Brücke-Museum, Berlin 2008/2009*. Munich 2009.

Montefiore, Simon Sebag: *Der junge Stalin*. Frankfurt 2007.

Morton, Frederic: *Wetterleuchten 1913/1914*. Vienna 1990.

Musil, Robert: *Tagebücher*. Ed. Adolf Frisé, 2 vols. Reinbek bei Hamburg 1976.

Nebehay, Christian M.: *Egon Schiele. Leben und Werk*. Vienna 1980.

Ott, Ulrich/ Pfäfflin, Friedrich (ed.): *Karl Kraus. Eine Ausstellung des Deutschen Literaturarchivs im Schiller Nationalmuseum Marbach 8. Mai–31. Oktober 1999. Marbacher Kataloge Nr. 52*. Marbach 1999.

Rabaté, Jean-Michel: *1913. The Cradle of Modernism*. Oxford 2007.

Richardson, John: *A Life of Picasso*, vol. 2. *1907–1917*. London 1997.

Rilke, Rainer Maria: *Briefe aus den Jahren 1907–1914*. Leipzig 1939.

Rilke, Rainer Maria/ Cassirer, Eva: *Briefwechsel*. Ed. and annotated by Sigrid Bauschinger. Göttingen 2009.

Röhl, John C.G: *Wilhelm II. Der Weg in den Abgrund 1900–1941*. Munich 2008.

Roters, Eberhard/ Schulz, Bernhard (Ed.): *Stationen der Moderne. Die bedeutendsten Kunstausstellungen des 20. Jahrhunderts in Deutschland*. Berlin 1988.

Rubin, William (Ed.): *Picasso and Braque: Pioneering Cubism*. Exhibition catalogue, Museum of Modern Art. New York 1989–90.

Sarason, David: *Das Jahr 1913. Ein Gesamtbild der Kulturentwicklung*. Leipzig and Berlin 1913.

Savoy, Benedicte: *Nofretete. Eine deutsch-französische Affäre 1912–1931*. Cologne 2011.

Schmitt, Carl: *Tagebücher. Oktober 1912 bis Februar 1915*. Ed. Ernst Hüsmert. Berlin 2005.

Schwilk, Heimo (ed.): *Jünger, Ernst: Leben und Werk in Bildern und Texten*. Stuttgart 1998/2010.

Schnitzler, Arthur: *Tagebuch 1913–1916*. Vienna 1983.

Schnitzler, Arthur: *Briefe 1913–1931*, Ed. Peter Michael Braunwarth, Richard Miklin und Susanne Pertlik. Frankfurt 1984.

Schuster, Peter-Klaus/ Vitali, Christoph et al.: *Lovis Corinth*. Munich 1996.

Scotti, Rita: *Der Raub der Mona Lisa. Die wahre Geschichte des größten Kunstdiebstahls*. Cologne 2009.

Simplicissimus, 1913, Munich.

Sinkovicz, Wilhelm: *Mehr als zwölf Töne. Arnold Schönberg*. Vienna 1998.

Spengler, Oswald: *Ich beneide jeden, der lebt: Die Aufzeichnungen »Eis heauton« aus dem Nachlass*. Düsseldorf 2007.

Stach, Rainer: *Kafka. Die Jahre der Entscheidungen*. Frankfurt 2002.

Tomkins, Calvin: *Marcel Duchamp: A Biography*. London 1997.

Tucholsky, Kurt: *Briefe. Auswahl 1913 bis 1935*. East Berlin 1983.

Wagenbach, Klaus: *Franz Kafka. Bilder aus seinem Leben*. Berlin 2008.

Wagenknecht, Christian/ Willms, Eva (ed.): *Karl Kraus – Franz Werfel. Eine Dokumentation*. Göttingen 2001.

Weidinger, Alfred: *Kokoschka und Alma Mahler. Dokumente einer leidenschaftlichen Begegnung*. Munich 1996.

Weinzierl, Ulrich: *Hofmannsthal. Skizzen zu einem Bild*. Vienna 2005.

Welt der Frau, 1913, Munich.

Wolff, Kurt: *Briefwechsel eines Verlegers 1911–1963*. Ed. Bernhard Zeller and Ellen Otten. Frankfurt 1966.

www.wikipedia.de

Wright, G. H. von: *A Portrait of Wittgenstein as a Young Man: From the Diary of David Hume Pinsent, 1912–1914*. Oxford 1990.

Zweig, Stefan: *Die Welt von gestern*. Stockholm 1944.

ACKNOWLEDGEMENTS

The author would like to thank Holger Hof for the important information about Gottfried Benn, Leonhard Horowski about the Prussian Court, Reiner Stach about Franz Kafka and Willi Jasper about Heinrich Mann. My special thanks to the book's polymathic and critical first reader Erhard Schütz.

ILLUSTRATION CREDITS